ALSO BY LAURENCE LEAMER

NONFICTION

Capote's Women: A True Story of Love, Betrayal, and a Swan Song for an Era

Mar-a-Lago: Inside the Gates of Power at Donald Trump's Presidential Palace

The Lynching: The Epic Courtroom Battle That Brought Down the Klan

The Price of Justice: A True Story of Greed and Corruption

Madness Under the Royal Palms:
Love and Death Behind the Gates of Palm Beach

Fantastic: The Life of Arnold Schwarzenegger

Sons of Camelot: The Fate of an American Dynasty

The Kennedy Men, 1901-1963: The Laws of the Father

Three Chords and the Truth:
Hope and Heartbreak and the Changing Fortunes of Nashville

The Kennedy Women: The Saga of an American Family

King of the Night: The Life of Johnny Carson

As Time Goes By: The Life of Ingrid Bergman

Make-Believe: The Story of Nancy and Ronald Reagan

Ascent: The Spiritual and Physical Quest of Willi Unsoeld

Playing for Keeps in Washington

The Paper Revolutionaries: The Rise of the Underground Press

FICTION

Assignment

The President's Butler

HITCHCOCK'S
Blondes

THE UNFORGETTABLE WOMEN
BEHIND THE LEGENDARY
DIRECTOR'S DARK OBSESSION

LAURENCE LEAMER

G. P. PUTNAM'S SONS
NEW YORK

PUTNAM
— EST. 1838 —

G. P. Putnam's Sons
Publishers Since 1838
An imprint of Penguin Random House LLC
penguinrandomhouse.com

Photo credits appear on page 317.

Library of Congress Cataloging-in-Publication Data has been applied for.

Hardcover ISBN 9780593542972
Ebook ISBN 9780593542989
LCCN 2023943235

Printed in the United States of America
1st Printing

Book design by Laura K. Corless

To Marty Bell, an artist in all things

CONTENTS

City of stars, there's so much that I can't see.

CHAPTER 1

A Fairy Tale

Tippi Hedren was not afraid of birds. In her dressing room, the thirty-two-year-old actress had a raven named Buddy. Hedren was costarring in *The Birds*, Alfred Hitchcock's film set in the Northern California seaside town of Bodega Bay, whose avian population was slowly, strangely turning on the residents and attacking them.

Buddy was not like those birds. He pranced around, messing with Hedren's makeup, amusing her endlessly. Buddy was her one true friend on the set, so much so that she put a sign on her dressing room door saying "Buddy and Tippi."

As far as Hedren was concerned, her Hollywood story had begun as a fairy tale. One morning Hitchcock saw the blond model in an ad for a diet drink on television; the renowned director was so enraptured that he signed her to play the female lead in his next film. At her age, Hedren's days as a top model were over. She knew how lucky she was that Hitchcock had come forward. Hedren knew almost nothing about acting, but Hitchcock took her and molded her into the image he desired.

That was all wonderful, but strange things started happening once *The Birds* began shooting. Hitchcock warned the other men involved in the production to stay away from Hedren. She was often alone on set and increasingly isolated. A single mother, Hedren was lonely and missing her child during the long shooting days. One day, she said Hitchcock tried to embrace her in the chauffeur-driven car in which they were traveling.

As Hedren waited to be called to the set, the assistant director, James H. Brown, entered her dressing room. He appeared worried.

"What's the matter with you?" Hedren asked.

"We can't use the mechanical birds," he said, the words barely audible.

"Uh, well, what are we going to use?" Hedren asked, though the answer should have been obvious.

"The mechanical birds don't work, and we have to use real ones."

This startled Hedren, and it took her a while to compose herself.

Hedren had already suffered through the birds attacking her and various schoolchildren as they ran down the street in Bodega Bay. But that was nothing like the scores of birds set to go after Hedren this morning as she opened the attic door.

In Hitchcock's four decades of filmmaking, there had never been a scene like this—two minutes so dangerous and, in the director's mind, so *pleasurable* to an audience seeking vicarious thrills. Hedren knew the scene had to be shot. As apprehensive as she was, what choice did she have but to leave her dressing room and walk out on the set?

Hedren saw that the crew had built a cage attached to the attic door. The trainers inside wore long, thick leather gloves to protect themselves. Beside them sat four good-sized boxes full of ravens and gulls.

As Hedren stood before the closed door, Hitchcock yelled, "Action!" She opened the door, and the handlers started hurling live birds at her. The flapping of feathers, the screams, the squawks—it was terrifying for everyone on set. If this had gone on for a few takes, that would have been one thing. But Hitchcock insisted on continuing until he got every shot he believed he needed.

Days passed.

On the fifth straight day of shooting this scene, to get the most intimate perspectives of the attacking birds, the crew attached elastic bands to Hedren and tied the feet of several birds to the bands.

"Action," Hitchcock shouted. The birds had been trained to claw at a person, and they did their job well. Hedren already had bruises over much of her body from days of working with the creatures, but this was a whole new level of hurt. The assault continued until the middle of the afternoon, when one of the birds pecked near Hedren's eyes. An inch or two closer, and she might have lost her sight.

Hedren could take no more. "I'm finished," she said. The handlers untied the birds and put them in the cartons. Hedren lay on the floor of the set, crying. Silence fell. When she finally looked up, everyone was gone, and she was alone on the vast soundstage. She did not know whether her colleagues were ashamed or just glad the business was over.

When she managed to pull herself together enough to get up and retreat to her dressing room, her raven, Buddy, was there to greet her.

CHAPTER 2

A Naughty Boy

When twenty-five-year-old Alfred Hitchcock arrived in Berlin in the fall of 1924, he was shocked. Not by one thing; by *everything*.

Nothing, it seemed, was verboten in Berlin. Hundreds of nightclubs and bars featured every kind of sexuality, including heterosexual sex, homosexuality, lesbianism, transsexuality, and nudity. In certain corners of this world, it was possible to see the most intimate act between two humans (or maybe more) performed in public like a piece of theater. It was like nothing the cloistered young art director had ever seen back home in England.

Hitchcock was a voyeur, and he had come to the right place at the right time. In Weimar-era Berlin, anything went as bourgeois German society expired. Hitchcock liked to stand outside the circle of life, watching everything that happened within its boundaries. It made sense that his preferred position was behind a camera—observing everything, but at a safe distance.

The young filmmaker had a plain, abrupt face obscured by jowls. At his peak, in later years, he would weigh over three hundred pounds. His size was a burden he could not shirk. But as a young man he was merely portly, and he cared deeply about how he looked and the way he came across to others.

Hitchcock was a natty dresser; he wore carefully selected clothes that shrouded his size and drew attention away from his weight. To an outside observer he appeared a worldly sort but, by his admission, he was at that time a complete rube. In fact, he did not even know how the sex act was performed until he was twenty-three. If he had been less shy at his Jesuit school, some of the boys might have taught him the facts of life in the schoolyard, but he had been friendless.

Berlin was a revelation.

One evening in the German capital, Hitchcock went with two of his associates to a nightclub where men were dancing with each other, a scene straight out of Christopher Isherwood's quasi-autobiographical *The Berlin Stories*, the basis for the musical *Cabaret*. It must have been confusing, disturbing, and possibly alluring for a man of Hitchcock's secret proclivities. He said later that if he had not married his fiancée, Alma Reville, he might have become a "poof." But to a fearful Catholic like Hitchcock, the idea that he would act on his temptation was unthinkable. He boarded up these closeted feelings and walked ahead, never veering from the narrow and straight.

The adventure was not over. The group later met two German women at the nightclub, one in her late teens, the other around thirty. Hitchcock said the women offered to drive them home, but took the group to a hotel room instead. A savvier man would have recognized the situation for what it was, but Hitchcock's naivete again seems to have prevailed.

Once in the hotel, the women attempted to woo Hitchcock into having sex. He was shocked—titillated, yes, but also frightened. No way was he going to lose his virginity to a woman of dubious repute as his acquaintances watched, gauging his performance. As Hitchcock knew too well, fear—real fear—was not only apprehension that some evil menace would come out of the fog to bludgeon one to death. It was something like this evening's event. It was being asked to perform an act he had never performed before, that he did not know if he could do or even *wanted* to do—with an audience no less! But one that he must do if he wanted to be called a man.

Hitchcock kept saying, "*Nein, nein*," his words so definitive that the women gave up, got into bed, and made love to each other. It was a spectacle worth observing, and one of the young women in the group pulled out her glasses so she could watch in detail.

Hitchcock did not need glasses.

Hitchcock never said whether the German women were blondes; if they were, he would have enjoyed the sexual spectacle even more. To Hitchcock, blond women were the epitome of female beauty, and he fixated on them. Blondes, to his eye, were not just some quirk of genetic nature; they were superior beings, Valkyries with coolness as pure as the Arctic snows encasing fiery inner beings that, to the right man, opened up in lusty wantonness.

Blondes' natural home was Scandinavia and other nations around the Baltic Sea, a region where intense sunlight came with a short, bright summer—a sun-drenched season that was gone scarcely as soon as it arrived. The blondes seen in his native London, however, were almost always the product of chemistry and artifice.

Hitchcock looked at the world of women with geographic absolutism. "I more or less base my idea of sexuality on northern European women," he said. "I think the northern Germans, the Scandinavians, and the English are much sexier, although they don't look it, than those farther south—the Spanish, the Italians."

Hitchcock knew that an inordinate amount of his success lay with the women he chose to play in his films. As a young director in London, he often watched films at newly built movie palaces as large as cathedrals. To achieve success, he would have to fill those seats again and again. As he looked across the theaters, he saw that "women form three-quarters of the average cinema audience." Since they often convinced their husbands and lovers which movies they should attend, Hitchcock cannily realized that his heroines "must be fashioned to please women rather than men. . . . Therefore, no actress can be a good commercial proposition as a film heroine unless she pleases her own sex."

Hitchcock was brutally realistic about actresses. Unlike the stage, where a middle-aged actress could masquerade as an ingenue, the camera did not flinch from the harshest truths. Even the loveliest of young women likely lasted no more than a dozen years before the shadows of age arrived and she was shuttled off the set. If the women in the audience did not like her, she was probably gone in three or four years.

Even if the young woman had everything—beauty, amiability, charm—it might not be enough for Hitchcock. "I have to consider whether my potential heroine is sensitive to direction," Hitchcock wrote in 1931. "In other words, whether she is the kind of girl I can mold into the heroine of my imagination." Hitchcock spent his career doing just that.

Creating a Pygmalion appears a glorious thing when it is Professor Henry Higgins transforming the street waif Eliza Doolittle into a beauty who can masquerade as a princess in *My Fair Lady*. But when that journey is about sexual power—a gentleman not lusting after his ideal in his book-lined study, but actually creating her in the flesh—the dark side of such a pursuit is revealed. And Hitchcock did it again and again in his films, getting off on it every time. And his audiences got off on it too.

Hitchcock took what in real life would likely have been considered a sick fixation on the icy, unattainable blond woman and turned it into a central part of his artistic dream. In time, Hitchcock's fantasies about the actresses who starred in his films consumed much of his creative energy—and ultimately defined a large part of his legacy.

Hitchcock made films in a Hollywood in which the sexual exploitation of women was a fundamental part of the culture. Actresses learned if they wanted to succeed, they first must give an Academy Award–level performance on the casting couch. Women were shuttled in and out of back rooms and hotel suites as if their only purpose in life was the pleasuring of men.

In this world, Hitchcock was an anomaly. As egregious as his conduct sometimes was—he gawped, he cajoled, he suggested—he apparently never consummated a relationship with any of the actresses in his films. That did not mean Hitchcock was disinterested in sex. He was obsessed with it. Like a street urchin standing at the window of a candy store, his nose pressed against the plate glass, he could not taste any of the sweet delights that lay within.

"It is clear to me Hitchcock had Asperger's syndrome, now included in autism spectrum disorder," says Dr. Heath King, a psychoanalyst who taught a course on masterpieces of American film at Yale. "He was a loner, an ogler, who sublimated his lack of sex into a voyeuristic cinema technique. The anxiety and fear he evoked in his films were a projection of his own inner anxiety and fear of an actual personal encounter when he was not in control.

"Aspergers are some of the most intelligent and accomplished people anywhere, but in their profound need to speak the truth, they can be curt and unfeeling, totally unaware or dismissive of the effects their actions have on people. This lack of empathy was integral to Hitchcock's enormous gifts."

As Hitchcock became one of the most famous and celebrated directors of the twentieth century, he was fixated on the blond actresses who starred in many of his classic films. The director did not care if these women wore wigs, got their hair coloring out of a bottle, or were the rarest human species—natural blondes—as long as they shone with golden veneers on camera.

The director had no interest in squandering his films on saintlike women, no *The Bells of St. Mary's* for him. *His* blond actresses played soiled women: thieves, adulteresses, murderers, murderers' accomplices, sluts, and vapid socialites. He purified these women in his films by making them suffer until he redeemed them.

June Howard-Tripp was the first blond actress to experience the Hitchcock touch. Known simply as "June" by the London West End theatrical audiences that adored the diminutive musical comedienne, June had never had a significant role in a film when approached to costar in Hitchcock's 1927 silent film *The Lodger.* The director so overworked her in one scene that she almost died.

Madeleine Carroll was an emerging British star when Hitchcock signed her to costar in *The 39 Steps* (1935). In the film, Carroll is handcuffed to her costar, Robert Donat, and chased through the bogs of Scotland, leaving bruises all over her body.

The Swedish-born Ingrid Bergman was the biggest star in America when she starred in *Notorious* (1946). Playing the wildly promiscuous daughter of a convicted Nazi spy, she seeks to redeem herself by marrying a prominent Nazi and spying on him.

Grace Kelly would one day be the number one star too. She was near the beginning of a career that lasted only five years when she costarred in *Dial M for Murder* (1954). In it, Kelly is an adulteress whose husband seeks to murder her.

In *North by Northwest* (1959), Eva Marie Saint is an undercover American agent sleeping with one of her country's enemies in an attempt to learn his secrets. She ends up being chased onto the face of Mount Rushmore, where she and her costar, Cary Grant, almost fall to their deaths.

None of Hitchcock's blond actresses suffered as much as Tippi Hedren. She was attacked by swarms of enraged birds in *The Birds* (1963). In the director's next film, *Marnie* (1964), Hedren is raped on her honeymoon.

Most of these characters made it through to make themselves whole again, but two did not. Hitchcock cast Kim Novak in dual roles in *Vertigo* (1958). An accomplice in a murder in love with a man who spurns her, she falls to her death from a tower.

Janet Leigh's character in *Psycho* (1960) suffers an equally ugly fate. Having stolen from her employer, she decides to face up to her crime. Before she can do so, she is knifed to death in the shower in film's most memorable murder scene.

These eight actresses who starred in fourteen of Hitchcock's most notable films knew the truths of his art as well as anyone. Whether their characters lived or died, they went through intense experiences with Hitchcock, sometimes joyous and playful, other times ugly and demeaning, but all in creating classic films.

As much as Hitchcock sought to control these actresses, critic Camille Paglia writes, "misogyny is a hopelessly simplistic and reductive term for the passionately conflicted attitude of major male artists toward women." As these actresses made memorable films with Hitchcock, he projected his complicated, tortured attitude toward women onto the screen. He recorded what Paglia calls "the agonized complexity of men's relationship to women—a roiling mass of admiration, longing, neediness and desperation."

Many men fear the siren call of the female, leading them to a dark jungle from which there is no escape. That fundamental fear of women is an omnipresent reality across cultures, nations, and eras, no less true because it is so often denied.

Many women in the film audience had relationships with men full of their own "agonized complexity." As much as some of them had been hurt by men, they repeatedly returned to the movies to see members of their sex abused in Hitchcock's films. Some of these women had inchoate anger about themselves and their lives that they saw played out on the screen. Others took pleasure in watching women being put through savage tests. Hitchcock used the fears and complexes of women and men as the basis of much of his art.

Hitchcock did not film traditional tragedies or celebrations of human character. Mostly, he told shadowy tales laced with irony and wit. He directed more than fifty films in six decades. His films received forty-six Academy Award nominations, including six victories. Although Hitchcock never won the coveted Best Director award, despite five nominations, he made more classic films over a longer period than any of his contemporaries.

When the French director François Truffaut did a series of interviews with Hitchcock in 1962, Hitchcock was generally dismissed by serious critics as a calculating commercial hack. That assessment changed as Hitchcock became increasingly recognized as one of the greatest directors in history, thanks in part to Truffaut.

In his book *Hitchcock*, Truffaut led Hitchcock to talk about the detailed attention he showed to every element of his films, from the music to the costumes and the camera shots to the editing and the devotion he showed to the whole process. "He [Hitchcock] works exactly like an orchestra conductor who directs his instrumentalists and advances the symphony whose every note, chord, sigh and silence has been foreseen in the score," Truffaut wrote in 1979, a decade after the American publication of his weeklong series of interviews with Hitchcock. "The young directors [understand this] and have more or less succeeded in adopting it; the new American cineastes are almost all Hitchcock's children."

The American director Martin Scorsese is one of Hitchcock's children. As a young man, he sat in movie theaters watching the director's films. The audience was so absorbed in the moment that the world outside became an illusion. The moviegoers shouted out in disbelief when Anthony Perkins knifed Janet Leigh to death in a motel shower in *Psycho*, gasped in horror as Kim Novak fell to her death in *Vertigo*, and tittered with amusement as Cary Grant and Eva Marie Saint exchanged bon mots in *North by Northwest*.

Scorsese experienced all that too, but as he did so, he took the films apart, appreciating the originality and daring of many of Hitchcock's shots, and analyzing the way the director manipulated and controlled the audience. He consciously used much of what he saw in his own films. "The shower scene in *Psycho* I actually used as a template for one of the scenes in *Raging Bull*," Scorsese said. "But I'm finding that, over the years, the scenes that stay with me are the seemingly quieter scenes, the scenes where it appears not much is happening with the Hitchcock film, and it's all happening."

As Scorsese directed his own films, it was not just the scenes that the young director took away from Hitchcock, but a way of working, a love of pure cinema, and an obsession with detail that only a fellow filmmaker could fully appreciate.

* * *

Hitchcock was born in London on August 13, 1899, the youngest of three children. His father, William, was a grocer who, through disciplined work, built his East London business into several stores and a wholesale business. He was a heavy drinker, and his son recalled him as "a rather nervous man." Hitchcock's mother, Emma Jane Whelan, was Irish Catholic.

The British thought of the Irish as a race full of drunks and loudmouths. As the Hitchcocks rose to middle-class success, they kept their Catholic faith but jettisoned most of what marked them as members of that tribe. In the intensely class-conscious Britain of the early 1900s, Hitchcock never lost that sense of not being one of the anointed.

The Hitchcocks did not coddle their children or embrace them with affection. That sort of fawning, they believed, was for lower-class Irish families. Instead, the Hitchcocks did everything to show they were better than their humble origins. The couple took their children to theater and musical performances, making public entertainment part of their lives.

As a child, Hitchcock was so small and vulnerable that his father called him his "little lamb," but even lambs get in trouble. On one occasion, his father found him guilty of an infraction severe enough to be punished in a way his son would not forget. Mr. Hitchcock sent Alfred to the police station, saying the boy had been bad. The coppers locked him in a cell, saying, "This is what we do to naughty boys."

The cops knew it would not take long to send the fear of God into their young charge. After five minutes, they opened the door and let him go home. That incident created an anxiety within Hitchcock that grew and grew. Many years later, the director could still hear "the clang of the door which was the potent thing—the sound and the solidity of that closing cell door and the bolt." His fear of prison, police, and authority became one of the central realities of his psychological life and a crucial component of his art.

Hitchcock's obsession with bloody crime was more than a mechanistic legacy of his childhood. It was a philosophy, a way of seeing the world around him, a metaphor. Life could turn around in a moment. There was no hiding from the imponderable uncertainties of human existence. Innocence was often nothing but a disguise.

Hitchcock's mother, Emma, was a perfect counterpart to his austere, serious father. Just as proud of her family's ascendency as her husband, this proper woman was as plump as a baker's wife. Always impeccably dressed, she had an imperious demeanor more appropriate to a duchess than a grocer's wife. Every evening she obligated her son to stand at the foot of her bed, telling her of his day. Her silence was the judgment of the gods. With her thick jowls, close-set small eyes, and a nose that projected off her face like a ski jump, she was a female version of her son. He had every reason to believe that his weight problems and features were his mother's dubious gift.

Emma doled out love to her son like a tonic in which a tablespoon a day was plenty. He hungered for an all-encompassing love, a limitless treasure to draw on whenever he needed it. His obsession with actresses was not so much about sex as about love, wanting to touch and to feel. He sought love all his life and never found it, not in the way he wanted it, and it all began at the foot of his mother's bed.

The Jesuits who educated Hitchcock taught their young charge that motherhood was sacred. To criticize the woman who gave birth to him was to bring the wrath of God down on his tousled head. Standing there every evening was the beginning of his tortured relationship with women and love mixed with fear, no less important because he could not talk openly about it. "She [his mother] was always a slightly menacing presence," said Hitchcock's authorized biographer, John Russell Taylor, "which possibly has something to do with his later attitudes to women."

The young Hitchcock was introverted, unathletic, and the son of a greengrocer and an Irish mother, hardly qualities to make him popular at St. Ignatius, the Jesuit school he attended. His life at home was no better. "I would sit quietly in a corner, saying nothing," he recalled. "I looked and observed a great deal. I've always been that way and still am. I was anything but expansive. I was a loner—can't even remember having had a playmate. I played by myself, inventing my own games."

While his contemporaries joshed and jostled among themselves, Hitchcock stood apart watching, an astute student of the foibles of the human race. Wherever he went, whatever he saw, he was picking up these little bits and pieces of life, no bigger than cigarette butts, and remembering what he saw.

Leaving St. Ignatius when he was thirteen years old, Hitchcock fancied he would achieve success in some kind of technical work. At the London County Council School of Engineering and Navigation, chemistry proved to be his curse. That led him to seek a different profession. In November 1914, Hitchcock took a job measuring cables at W. T. Henley's Telegraph Works. It hardly seemed an auspicious beginning, but he soon worked his way up to sales and advertising.

Hitchcock had been there for less than a year when Henley's began a fine in-house magazine. The *Henley Telegraph* had room not just for company news but short stories, poetry, cartoons, and essays. It was here Hitchcock published his first story, "Gas."

What could it be about but a damsel in distress who Hitchcock marches through hell until the sweet denouement. A young woman is walking through the night streets of Montmartre when she is assailed by a group of savage miscreants who intend to kill her. "And then— then, swinging her bound body to and fro, dropped her with a splash into the dark, swirling waters. Down, she went, down, down; conscious only of a choking sensation, this was death."

That was it until the coda: "It's out Madam," said the dentist. "Half a crown please."

Hitchcock got his real education by attending plays and movies, mesmerized by the characters and the themes. He could spend hours at the cinema, watching the flickering screen, completely wrapped up in the stories. Motion pictures, he realized, was where he wanted to be—not tallying lengths of cable in a clerking office across town.

So Hitchcock determined to make it happen. Not content just to observe others, he believed he could create the title cards so crucial to silent films. The ambitious young man presented a portfolio of sample title cards to a local film company—the British subsidiary of Paramount's Famous Players-Lasky, the most important film company in the world. Whatever he wrote has been lost to time, but it was good enough to get him an entry-level job.

It was the most important break in his life.

* * *

One day at his new position, Hitchcock saw a young woman breezing by him in the studio. Her name was Alma Reville. A wee bit short of five feet tall and weighing less than a hundred pounds, she looked like she would be blown away in a heavy wind, but her feet were anchored to the ground. Alma's reddish-blond hair matched her temperament, and she walked through the studio with a confident air. Hitchcock thought her "a trifle snooty to me. I couldn't notice Alma without resenting her, and I couldn't help noticing her."

The young woman was very aware of the impact she had on those around her. "I regarded myself as a very attractive girl, prettier perhaps than I really was," Alma reflected years later. "I was outgoing and social. . . . I loved movies and loved what I was doing." She wasn't beautiful, exactly, but she gave off an aura of confidence and excitement that made her especially attractive to a man of Hitchcock's temperament.

Reville had entered the film business in 1915, when she was only sixteen. She began cutting raw footage at the Twickenham Studios outside London, but she moved on to edit films and write them. The young woman had practically been born into the nascent film industry. As a young teenager, Reville lived down the street from Twickenham, where her father worked in the costume department.

Only one thing pleased Reville more than bicycling down to the studio to watch the actors create this new magic, and that was going to the silent movies with her mother. Some relatives felt Mrs. Reville should not have taken her vulnerable daughter to these dark converted shops that passed as theaters, risking picking up fleas sitting shoulder to shoulder with riffraff.

Mrs. Reville was especially solicitous of her daughter because of her tender condition. Alma suffered a severe case of St. Vitus' dance, a convulsion that affected children. The disease was so bad that Alma's mother kept her out of school for two years. That meant that wherever Alma advanced, she was generally surrounded by better-educated people. As the youthful Alma pranced through the studio with what Hitchcock deemed overweening self-confidence, she was in reality full of insecurities that would remain with her all her life.

Hitchcock was entranced by Alma, but he faced two problems. First, Alma was doing serious work at the film company, while Hitchcock, although the same age, was primarily an errand boy. He was not about to approach a woman in such an elevated position. The second problem was that Alma was a woman, and despite having an older sister, Hitchcock knew nothing about the female sex.

As Hitchcock rose through the ranks at the company with stunning rapidity to become a director, he reached the point where he could introduce himself to Alma with confidence. They soon became inseparable. When he directed *The Lodger: A Story of the London Fog*, she was the assistant director, choosing her a mark of Hitchcock's acumen.

CHAPTER 3

A Passion for Blondes

I t's a February night in 1926, and a woman's body lies on the Embankment that runs along the north side of the Thames. As two police officers methodically take notes, several older women look down at the victim with horror. The London night is foggy, the natural habitat of evil, and one of the women says, "Tall he was—and his face all wrapped up."

No filmmaker had ever been allowed to shoot on the Embankment, but Hitchcock received special permission to proceed. Although the director shot the scene in the middle of the night, crowds drawn to the macabre drama formed of far greater numbers than the extras who stood around the body.

The Lodger begins with a close-up of a blond woman screaming in terror. The scene is the signature for the whole film, and Hitchcock shot it with precision. He placed the woman's head on glass, spread her hair out, and lit her from behind so her hair lit up the screen. Her mouth is wide open. She is captured in her moment of death, making her last mortal gasp. Although this is a silent film, we can almost hear her desperate shout.

One of the officers opens a piece of paper lying beside the victim with the words "The Avenger" written within a triangle. Whenever the killer strikes, he leaves this calling card, suggesting these deaths are revenge for something terrible that has befallen him. By those simple words, the idea of good and evil as absolutes is torn away.

Marie Belloc Lowndes, the author of *The Lodger*, based her serial killer loosely on Jack the Ripper, the psychopath who, starting in 1888, went around the foggy streets of East London murdering five poor women, some of whom may have been prostitutes. He slashed, mutilated, and disemboweled his victims, disappearing one day in the London mist from which he never reemerged.

Hitchcock chose Ivor Novello to play the title character, a mysterious man suspected of being the serial killer. The staggeringly talented composer and actor had come to prominence in 1914 when he wrote the music to "Keep the Home Fires Burning," a popular song during World War I. Not only did Novello write musicals, but he became an early movie star. Given to dramatic eye makeup, thirty-three-year-old Novello was a gay man who played heterosexual characters irresistible to the ladies. Although he claimed to hate the constant attention, Novello was by 1926 a matinee idol swooned over by legions of women.

Casting the male main actor was one thing, but Hitchcock still needed a female lead. Novello convinced the young director that he should choose his friend June Howard-Tripp, a musical star beloved by London audiences. In February 1926, Novello cabled her in southern France, where she was recuperating from a serious illness.

The previous month, June had collapsed onstage during a performance of the musical *Mercenary Mary* at London's 1,340-seat Hippodrome. She tried to will herself up to finish the play, but her acute appendicitis was so severe that she lay there clutching her stomach.

The pixie-like actress was so ill that she could not possibly return to the long-running show. June's illness was front-page news. Almost everyone in London's artistic community knew about her misfortune. She came from a well-known theatrical family. Her father, Walter Howard-Tripp, had been a leading Shakespearean actor. She would have done well carrying his name, but her agent convinced her to put simply "June" on the marquee.

June was trying to recuperate from her operation, but it was not easy with all the pressure she felt to get back to work. June's father spent much of his time playing cards while living off his daughter's largesse. One of her brothers was blind, and she took care of him. Another brother, a painter, was dying of tuberculosis, and June supported him and his family as well.

June knew it would be a good while before she could attempt the rigors of dancing and singing onstage. So the prospect of a movie production—in front of a camera rather than a live audience—was appealing. Novello wanted her to know this job would be a romp; she'd be playing the "curly blond" model Daisy Bunting opposite him. "No dancing required," he cabled. "You will act beautifully, and we shall have fun."

Hitchcock considered *The Lodger* "the first true 'Hitchcock movie.'" It was *his* film, not the actors', not the producer's, but *his*. For a movie to be Hitchcock's, he had to control every aspect. No other director of his time had such concern over details. Hitchcock worked so domineeringly with screenwriters that sometimes he deserved a writer's credit.

Hitchcock sketched out every scene in detail before the actors even arrived (sometimes, before they were even cast). He watched over the construction of the sets, the wardrobe, and even the kind of film stock. Beyond that, Hitchcock oversaw the cinematography, developing inspired, innovative camera shots and partnering closely with the film editor.

In Berlin, the young director had been paying attention to more than just the nightlife. German filmmaking was breaking new ground, and Hitchcock took much of what he learned during his months in Berlin and applied it to *The Lodger*. Much of the German film and theater world had cast aside the shibboleths of bourgeois respectability and created daring, experimental work.

German Expressionism reached its most profound articulation in movies full of shadow and nuance that did not pander to the audience but instead led them down dark alleys. Hitchcock swallowed this whole and made it an essential part of his creative being. "Those were the great days of the German pictures," Hitchcock recalled. "Germany was beginning to fall into chaos. Yet the movies thrived."

Hitchcock was a visual being. From his beginning making films in the silent era, the look of a thing was everything. Sound films were called "talkies," but as he saw it, words were mere commentary on the visual images that told the story. Actors moved back and forth across the screen. If they were good and right, and if the pictures were good and right, the film likely worked.

The young director had found the one thing he could do in which he would not only survive but triumph. As long as he stayed on the set, he controlled the world. *The Lodger* was also the first true Hitchcock film for another reason. In it, for the first time, he revealed his passion for blondes and his pleasure in making them suffer.

Twenty-six-year-old Hitchcock was unlike any director twenty-four-year-old June had worked with previously. To her, he was "a short, corpulent young man who spoke in a curious mixture of Cockney and North Country accents with a laboured stress on elusive aitches. His humour was salty or subtle, according to his mercurial moods, and his brilliance was patent."

June was used to the collegial atmosphere of the theater world. She was taken aback by the formal, distanced ambience on Hitchcock's sets and the way he called actors to attention. One day early in the shooting, Hitchcock was filming Novello walking down the stairs in stealthy silence and creeping out the front door. After rehearsing the scene a half dozen times, Hitchcock shot it twice and was done with it. In the meantime, June came out of her dressing room to discuss the golden wig she was to wear in her scenes.

In most productions, June's hair would have been a matter handled by the wardrobe person or makeup artist, not a major concern for the director. Hitchcock was different. Although in the novel June's character is a brunette, Hitchcock turned her into a glorious blonde, a svelte, classy woman of the very sort the killer would love to choose as his victim.

In June's entrance into the film, a group of models in their dressing room jump up and down, looking at a newspaper story about the Avenger's seventh Tuesday night murder of a young blond woman. Many of these girls are blondes themselves. One of the models, Daisy Bunting (June), has Clara Bow lips like little valentines and teardrop eyes. Daisy appears a class above most of the others. Named after a simple flower that blooms and dies in its own finite time, she is a far more complicated character than that moniker might suggest.

Daisy returns to the house where she lives with her parents, Mr. and Mrs. Bunting (Arthur Chesney and Marie Ault). The couple are in the downstairs kitchen, the center of family life. Daisy's beau, police detective Joe Chandler (Malcolm Keen), is there to visit Daisy. His bow tie is slightly askance, his suit poorly pressed.

"I'm keen on golden hair myself, same as the Avenger is," Joe says, looking at Daisy, his eyes shining with lustful attention. Better than her surroundings and this working stiff, Daisy has such a buoyant, vivacious manner that it is as if she wandered into the wrong film.

Growing up in the early years of the twentieth century, Hitchcock adhered to the British obsession with class. One knew by how a man spoke where he was born, where he belonged, and by all odds where he would stay.

Hitchcock had the Bunting family labeled. Daisy's parents may have owned a house, but they could not hide their lower-class origins. Her mother gets down on her knees to clean the floor. When Mr. Bunting dresses in black tie, it is not to go to a formal event but because he has a gig as a waiter. In Hitchcock's way of seeing the world, most working-class girls in the dance halls and bars flaunted their sexuality, while those of noble birth in their privileged environs kept theirs restrained. In his eyes, the delicate Daisy is different than her rough surroundings would indicate . . . a flower growing out of a dung heap.

Most of *The Lodger* takes place at the Buntings' house. A knock on the door. There stands a tall man in a black hat, wearing a long cape, a scarf wrapped around his neck covering half his face, and carrying what appears to be a doctor's black bag. He looks like the description of the Avenger in the papers, and Mrs. Bunting is frightened.

Whatever Mrs. Bunting thinks, this strange man is a gentleman and must be treated with the natural deference of a class society. His face of such sensitive refinement may mask a murderer, but he has descended from the heights into their modest midst and must be admitted. There is a sign, "Room to Let," in the window, and this wounded-looking man is responding. Before he goes upstairs to see his room, the Lodger looks for an instant at Daisy.

The audience has been here before. By all rights and precedents, they know this mysterious gentleman is the Avenger, and Daisy may be his next victim. It is only a matter of time before he is arrested and hanged for multiple crimes. But this is not some ordinary actor up there on the screen. This is their beloved Ivor Novello.

"Is the lodger really a vile murderer who creeps out at night and foully murders golden-haired girls?" asked the *Daily Mail*, whose reporter Hitchcock invited onto the set one day. "There is an ominous stain on a ceiling and Mr. Novello had a hang-dog way of creeping about. Yet his face is not the face of a criminal." No way can Novello be the author of such dastardly deeds. The moviegoers must only sit for an hour or so more to see him proven innocent and the actual killer exposed.

The chandelier on the downstairs ceiling shakes as if an earthquake has struck London. The ceiling seems to disappear, and we see the Lodger pacing back and forth. Novello is standing on plate glass, but to the audience, it appears we see through the floor. It is only for an instant, but a spectacular effect, symbolic of Hitchcock's inventiveness and daring.

The Lodger, the only name by which we know him, stands with his long hands clasping his head in despair, when a bright, exuberant Daisy enters, untouched by the inchoate fears that consume much of London. He looks at Daisy with eyes full of unknowable complexity, unlike her boorish beau, Joe, whose every lascivious thought and feeling is obvious.

The following day, Daisy enters the Lodger's room wearing a white half apron over her dress, carrying a breakfast tray, and sets it down before him. It is only a tiny scene, but Hitchcock filmed it in his typical manner without any regard for June's condition. The director may not have read the newspaper stories about June's illness. Still, Novello had undoubtedly told him that the convalescing young actress was in a vulnerable state and had to be treated carefully. Nonetheless, Hitchcock filmed the scene endless times, making June run up and down the stairs again and again. It was perhaps a lesson to June that weakness was not tolerated on his set. Or Hitchcock may have done it heedless of her condition because he was a perfectionist, especially when it came to women.

June was a trouper, and she did not ask for special concern. "All I had to do was carry an iron tray of breakfast dishes up a long flight of stairs," the actress recalled in her memoir, "but by the time Hitch was satisfied with the expression of fear on my face . . . I must have made the trek 20 times, the tray seeming to grow heavier every passing minute. During that exhausting hour and a half, I felt a strange, sickening pain somewhere in the region of my appendix scar, but forbore to complain or ask for a rest, because delicate actresses are a bore and a nuisance."

The Lodger had an ending immensely satisfying to the British public. Their beloved Novello was not the murderer. Not only was he innocent, but the Lodger's sister was the Avenger's first victim. That's why the Lodger was furtively sneaking around, trying to find the serial killer. Mistaking him for the Avenger, vigilantes almost kill him. Police detective Joe saves the Lodger from the enraged mob just before they learn the police have captured the real killer.

In the final scene, the Lodger, impeccably dressed in black tie, descends the grand staircase in his home, where an equally well-dressed Daisy stands waiting for him. Her parents are there too, doing their best to be spiffily turned out in such grand surroundings. Daisy and the Lodger glide off into the next room, where they embrace.

The Lodger was an enormous commercial and critical success, raising Hitchcock to the top ranks among British directors. June was the only actual victim in *The Lodger.* The endless repetition of that one shot—carrying a tray upstairs—ended up rupturing June's appendix scar, and she almost died.

* * *

Alma, meanwhile, was making her own successes in the film world. She moved from assisting Hitchcock on *The Lodger* to cowriting *The First Born* (1928), a drama of sordid goings-on in the British upper class. Sir Hugo Boycott (Miles Mander) is married to Lady Madeleine

Boycott (Madeleine Carroll), a stunning, sensitive woman worthy of his devotion. But Sir Boycott is an unspeakable cad.

Lady Boycott is a sophisticated young woman trapped in an abusive marriage. When she has a hard time becoming pregnant, Sir Boycott sets off having affairs with the same energy as when he goes fox hunting. He sleeps with his wife's closest friend and gets Lady Boycott's manicurist pregnant. Lady Boycott throws a shoe at her philandering husband; he throws it straight back at her face, knocking her down. She calls out in love to her husband in a pathetic plea, but he does not listen. In the end, he falls down an empty elevator shaft to his death, and Lady Boycott takes a lover.

Mander played the same role off-screen as on-screen. Not only acting in but directing *The First Born*, he insisted on filming his costar in a naked bath scene, doing it in a way that exposed Carroll to the eyes of the crew. In other matters, he was so disdainful of Carroll's feelings that he pushed her to the point of tears.

Mander was a man who took what he wanted, and on the set of *The First Born*, he wanted his costar and lead actress. His wife, Kathleen, found this as unacceptable as Lady Boycott did her husband's dalliances. Finding Carroll and Mander together in a restaurant, Kathleen bombarded them with plates.

Alma's screenplay reinforced Lady Boycott's position as a hapless victim, brutalized by an unfeeling husband. Where did she get the inspiration? According to many sources (and Alma herself), Hitchcock never struck her or spoke words of abuse. He was no Sir Boycott. But he was embarking on a career in films in which he ran women through gauntlets of pain. Hitchcock considered Alma, like most women, a lesser being. And she, in some measure, accepted that appellation.

Hitchcock married Alma in December 1926. She became his closest collaborator throughout his entire career, working as a screenwriter, an editor, a critic of superb judgment, and the manager of her husband's life. Although Alma was multitalented, she believed she did not have her husband's cinematic genius. Without a moment's qualm or hesitation, she subordinated herself and her desires to her new husband and his career.

Alma was the anchor that held the mercurial Hitchcock in place in the stormiest of seas, the voice that shouted out its truth when no one else dared to speak, and the hand behind him, pushing him forever ahead. The couple had one child, Patricia "Pat" Alma Hitchcock, born in 1928.

Like most men of Hitchcock's generation, he thought women had their place, but it was not out in the world doing the things men do. "Would you expect a girls' school to be built by girls?" he asked in 1929. And members of the female sex did not make directors. "I think women are less versatile in observation than men, who have more 'angles on life,'" he added. "Of course, I am thinking of a woman, as a woman, and not of the type who should have been a man."

As much as Hitchcock loved his wife, he could not help putting Alma down professionally. "My wife has assisted me in certain films," he said. "I found that although she was of the utmost value so far as the story, and even the action went, some of the more unwieldy departments of film producing were difficult for her to control: the art department, for instance."

As Alma understood better than anyone, Hitchcock had an empathetic understanding of human character that he brilliantly translated to the screen. But he was not so good at that understanding in his personal life. She began as a lover and a friend and became, in part, a mother figure, watching over him like he was her needy child.

CHAPTER 4

Goodbye to All That

I n 1935, when Hitchcock was casting *The 39 Steps*, he knew that
the movie based on a famous book by the Scottish novelist John
Buchan would likely attract more attention than any of the director's previous films. The theme would become familiar in Hitchcock's movies: a man (Robert Donat) falsely accused of murder fleeing
his pursuers as he attempts to uncover the nefarious plot. As the victim
runs from the police, he stumbles upon a woman whose help he seeks.

For this role, the director needed an actress loved by female audiences. Alma knew where to find her in Madeleine Carroll, the actress
with whom she had worked on *The First Born*. Carroll was the first
blond actress who truly captivated Hitchcock. Though her hair color
was not natural, her locks shown luminously on the screen and set off
the director's fixation with his female stars that lasted his entire career.

Carroll's resonant voice allowed her to transition easily from the
silent films of the 1920s to the "talkie" pictures of the 1930s and beyond, and she had become a star in Great Britain, the United States,

and Canada. Unlike most of her fellow actors, Carroll was highly educated. Her manner of speaking and refined bearing were not just a fancy cloak she wore to show off in public; they were the essence of her being.

The actress owed much of that to her Irish father. John Carroll was a professor who taught his daughter that ideas mattered. Her French mother showed her there was a world beyond the British Isles, so much so that Madeleine thought of herself as much French as British. She was precocious enough to receive her bachelor of arts degree (Honors French and German) from the University of Birmingham when she was twenty. Six months of teaching in the industrial city convinced her that her father's profession was not for her, and she headed off to London with twenty pounds in savings to make her way as an actress.

Carroll's father disowned her for giving up an honorable calling for a quixotic quest that would likely end in disaster. He may have turned his back on his daughter, but she knew how much she owed him. It did not take her long to get roles onstage and in silent films and for her to be declared "the newest British film 'star.'" By then, her father had reconsidered his daughter's career choice and embraced her.

Carroll had an astute sense of her image and how that was crucial to her success. It was not just how she spoke on camera that mattered, but how she looked, the perfect visage she showed to the world. "Makeup is a serious business," she said, "too bright a lipstick tends to look black when on film. If applied too lightly, it becomes white when seen in a cinema." Whereas some actresses considered sitting for makeup a tedious ritual, Carroll considered it a crucial part of her job. When she endorsed such products as Amami hair and beauty aids and Pond's cold cream facial cleanser, women went to buy them to look like Madeleine Carroll.

Taking little pleasure in the overwhelming attention that came with stardom, Carroll tried to live as private a life as possible. In 1931 she married Captain Philip Astley of the Life Guards, who had won the Military Cross during the Great War. Handsome enough to be on a recruiting poster, the dashing and charismatic Captain Astley had a thing for actresses—including a long-term affair with the English star Gertrude Lawrence. The aristocratic officer had a country house, a villa in Italy, and a house in Cavendish Square, the most stylish of London addresses.

By rights and tradition, the couple should have had a major wedding in London with a church full of impeccably dressed attendees and, outside, a score of photojournalists memorializing the moment for the papers. But no, they traveled to Lake Como, Italy, where they stood before the altar in a small village church as an Italian-speaking priest married them. The only witnesses were a few villagers and a single unwanted photographer.

As Britain's leading female star, Carroll received endless entreaties to come to Hollywood. It was not until 1934 that she agreed, and she and her husband made the seven-thousand-mile trek to Los Angeles, where the actress starred in *The World Moves On*. The script for the multigenerational saga was so tediously uninviting that even the great director John Ford could not save the film. "The truth is that Hollywood brought me in on a tidal wave of publicity," Carroll reflected. "The press screamed. The heavens shook—and I—I flopped. It wasn't anybody's fault. It was just a case of too much publicity and too little story."

Carroll returned to London chastened by her experience in the world capital of film, ready to accept any suitable roles in British films. Despite her prominence, Carroll was not Hitchcock's first choice to play Pamela in *The 39 Steps*, a drama of international political intrigue. But as Hitchcock sought an actress, Alma talked endlessly about Carroll and her role in *The First Born*. Hitchcock signed Carroll to play the female lead in the espionage thriller only two days before production began on January 11, 1935.

"I suppose the first blonde who was a real Hitchcock type was Madeleine Carroll," Hitchcock later said. Before production began, he called her into his office, gave her the script, and asked her to read a few lines. When he met her before, she had been gay and natural, but speaking the part, she retreated back into her skills as an actress and spoke in what he considered "a kind of mesmeric trance."

"I thought I had to act," Carroll said, the worst possible thing to tell Hitchcock.

"For God's sake, be yourself," he admonished.

Hitchcock loved female beauty with unmitigated passion, and it was there before him in Carroll. He flirted with her, tossing his witty ripostes at her. She was, he thought, perfection. But such perfection needed to be taken down a peg. Before long, Hitchcock would turn on the actress in measures both deliberately cruel and casually thoughtless.

Audiences loved Carroll as much for her seeming moral virtue as her looks. Hitchcock was going to end that. Out of her hearing, he referred to her as "the Birmingham tart," shaming the actress. The director's goal as filming began was to topple Carroll off her throne of goodness and bring her down in the muck with everyone else.

It began with the script. "We deliberately wrote the script to include her undignified handcuff scene and being led out from under the waterfall looking like a drowned rat," said Ivor Montagu, a consultant on several of the director's films. Hitchcock wanted her to look beautiful, but made it clear that he also had the power to humiliate her, if he so chose.

In the film, Richard Hannay (Robert Donat) has been arrested for a murder he did not commit by men pretending to be police. So that Richard will not even think of fleeing, the men handcuff him to Pamela (Carroll), who is beside him in the car because she can identify him. It was all perfectly respectable, but Hitchcock understood that the linking together "relates more to sex than anything else." Richard escapes, dragging a reluctant Pamela along beside him. That was the way it was, men and women inexplicably tied together with the woman pulled along to places she knows not unless she finds a way to extricate herself.

The morning the shooting on *The 39 Steps* began, Hitchcock introduced himself to Carroll and Donat, saying, "Call me Hitch without the cock." They had not shot a scene, and Hitchcock had already evoked sexual imagery at its most crass. But he had spoken the words in such a seemingly offhand way that Carroll could not possibly condemn him.

Carroll and Donat would be handcuffed together during much of *The 39 Steps*. As soon as the two young stars arrived on the set, he locked them together.

"That way, you'll get used to the situation and make it look real," Hitchcock said. There could be no argument to that.

"Oh, and I also want you soaking wet," the director went on. In one of their later scenes, they would hide behind a waterfall. There was, however, no reason to drench Carroll and Donat that morning. . . . But neither actor was going to challenge Hitchcock.

For Hitchcock, handcuffs were used not just for work but as a crucial instrument in one of the director's misbegotten practical jokes. He once bet a friend that he would not be able to spend the whole night in handcuffs. Before he locked the device onto his friend's wrists, Hitchcock gave him a cup of coffee laced with a laxative.

Hitchcock had begun playing crude practical jokes when he was a child. That was one of the few ways he stood out. At St. Ignatius, he took eggs from the priests' henhouse and threw them against the windows of their residence. When a priest came out running, outraged at the attack, Hitchcock denied he had anything to do with it.

That was where he got the nickname "Cocky," and cocky he appeared to be. Hitchcock performed acts like this for most of his life. He was asserting his superiority to the fools who did not realize the games he was playing on them. If these actions were attempts to show his power over a race of suckers, only a person of immense insecurity and psychological isolation would need to do such things as often as he did.

Anyone who has felt the steel of handcuffs around her wrists even for a few minutes knows what a terrifying sense of imprisonment it is. Hitchcock left his stars encased in handcuffs for hours, separated from everyone else on the set.

Carroll later said that while she and Donat sat locked together, Hitchcock rehearsed the two wet actors relentlessly, making them repeat the scene again and again. The director knew Carroll and Donat had human needs, but Hitchcock enjoyed pushing them beyond endurance. After two hours, both actors needed to go to the bathroom, but neither dared to admit to such a necessity.

"Please, Mr. Hitchcock," Carroll practically begged, "could I go to my dressing room for a moment!"

"Why, my dear?" Hitchcock asked, his words streaked with a veneer of innocence.

Carroll did not dare to speak the truth. "I need to— I need a book," she said.

"Oh! That's easily solved," Hitchcock said, calling Carroll's bluff. "Your dresser will get it for you."

The actress bore up as best she could but, after a few more minutes, could not go on any longer. "Oh God," she yelled out. "Mr. Hitchcock, I've got to go to the bathroom."

It had been a difficult morning, but through their adversity, Carroll and Donat bonded in ways they could never have in the stylized pattern of the set, and their attraction and mutual concern played out on the screen.

* * *

As in most of his movies, the script to *The 39 Steps* contains what Hitchcock called a "MacGuffin," a device that sets the action off on its wild chase. In this instance, Britain's enemies are trying to steal the secret plans for a military plane and are willing to kill almost arbitrarily to protect themselves.

Despite how irrational his plots might seem, Hitchcock made his audiences believe in them, at least until they walked out of the theater wondering why they had been so mesmerized. It was the same with the way he played a cameo in his films, distracting the audience from the drama on the screen. But it did not matter. He whiplashed them back into the drama in an instant.

In *The 39 Steps*, as Richard attempts to evade his pursuers, the couple ends up in a hotel for the evening. On the day the director shot that scene at Shepherd's Bush studios, a group of gawking tourists stood watching. Hitchcock gave no sign he was perturbed, but within minutes a crew arrived with a velvet curtain to wall off the onlookers.

Then Hitchcock shot the scene where the shackled couple walk upstairs to their room. Carroll and Donat had to climb the stairs while not displaying the handcuffs. That was not easy to do, and all kinds of things went wrong. Hitchcock insisted on shooting the scene fifteen times. Hitchcock appeared imperturbable as the two stars sat in their canvas chairs, waiting for another take.

In a British movie in the thirties, it was unthinkable for an unmarried couple to spend the night together. Hitchcock was a monumental trickster. He did not merely skirt around the censors' rules, but transcended them, playing jokes on these narrow men and their arcane rules. What could the censors do but allow moviegoers to see the beauteous Carroll and the handsome Donat in bed as long as they were handcuffed together?

Before Richard and Pamela get in bed, she takes off her wet stockings. This is the kind of film moment for which Hitch lived, a tantalizing scene, torturing the audience with its sexual possibilities. Carroll could have managed to remove her stockings demurely. Instead, Hitch has her raise her skirt to unhook her stocking from her exposed thigh and roll it down the course of her leg in a gesture and pace worthy of Gypsy Rose Lee. Then she does the same thing with her other stocking. As riveting and revealing as any scene in the movie, the moment suggests that beneath Pamela's decorous image lies sexuality ready to explode.

Donat was appalled by the way Hitchcock treated Carroll. "It would be hard to estimate the number of hours we were handcuffed together in the studio," he recalled. "Shackled to me, she was dragged along roads, through ravines, and across moors; humiliations were heaped upon her. Naturally, we had to play these scenes with realism: the weals and bruises which the handcuffs made on her delicate wrists were ample proof of that—but I never heard her utter one word of complaint."

In filming *The 39 Steps*, Hitchcock attempted to break Carroll down, but he was not quite as successful as he thought. There are many ways to fight, and a frontal attack is often the worse. Carroll flicked off his attempts to rattle her and put in a memorable performance in which her dignity and glamour remained intact. Although she is on screen for only twenty-six minutes of the eighty-six-minute film, during those moments she is almost always the resonant center of the film.

The 39 Steps was an enormous popular and critical success in England and the United States, elevating thirty-six-year-old Hitchcock to a unique position among British filmmakers. The movie made so much money that it was inevitable that he would be asked to follow up with another spy thriller.

Hitchcock was a royally paid commercial filmmaker and had no aesthetic qualms about repeating himself. Not only did the director set out to make a new film, *Secret Agent*, plundering some of the themes of *The 39 Steps*, but he sought the same two stars. Carroll was available, but Donat was busy, so Hitchcock filled his slot with a stage actor, John Gielgud.

For the lead villain, Hitchcock brought in Peter Lorre, who played the serial child killer in the classic German film *M*. Evil characters are often more intriguing than those who exude nothing but goodness, and Lorre commanded attention by projecting creepy malevolence, but much of the time he was off in a corner feeding his morphine habit.

Hitchcock had found it so pleasurable mistreating Carroll in *The 39 Steps* that he went at it again in *Secret Agent*. Gielgud watched with dismay at the way the director abused his female star. "Hitchcock was beastly to her," he recalled. "He was a very coarse man, fond of making dirty jokes all the time."

On most sets the director might go off with a bunch of actors and the crew, exchanging dirty jokes in an act of male bonding. Hitchcock preferred to tell his raunchy stories to his leading actress. Hitchcock boasted of demeaning Carroll. "Nothing gives me more pleasure than to knock the lady-likeness out—that is why I deliberately deprived Madeleine Carroll of her dignity and glamour in *The 39 Steps*," he said. "I have done exactly the same with her in *Secret Agent*—in which the first shot of her you see is with her face covered with cold cream!"

What had Carroll done to raise Hitchcock's ire except put in stellar performances in two of his films? It was hardly her fault that in slavishly copying the themes in its predecessor, *Secret Agent* was a failure at both the box office and with critics. But even when these roles were well in the past, Hitchcock could not pass up opportunities to denigrate her. In 1938, when he was negotiating unsuccessfully to direct a movie about the sinking of the *Titanic*, he said, "Oh, yes, I've had experience with icebergs. Don't forget I directed Madeleine Carroll."

The conduct Hitchcock condemned as coldness was proper for a lady of Carroll's time and class. She stepped demurely over the foulness he placed in her path and, whenever she was asked, had nothing but words of fulsome praise for the director.

Carroll tried to keep quiet, not just about the difficulties she had with Hitchcock, but with the problems in her marriage. As handsome as any of Carroll's costars, Captain Astley was irresistible to many of the women he encountered, and he partook in as much pleasure as he could. When twenty-nine-year-old Carroll sailed for New York on her second visit to America on the steamship *Majestic* in January 1936 to spend at least a half year in Hollywood, Captain Astley did not accompany his wife.

As Carroll approached thirty, her looks had never been more compelling. Able to play almost any role, she was embraced by Hollywood and became one of the great stars of the late thirties. When Paramount was casting *The General Died at Dawn*, the studio chose her to play the only female role alongside Gary Cooper and several other male actors. She had another hit in *The Prisoner of Zenda* (1937), opposite the debonair Ronald Colman. *Blockade* (1938) was set during the Spanish Civil War. It may have been tepid and uninformed in parts, but it was Hollywood's first anti-fascist film. Carroll's concern for the world was such that she was willing to risk her reputation by starring in the controversial movie alongside Henry Fonda.

Carroll's husband was half a world away from her physically and even further away emotionally. She knew Astley had another life in London, and their 1939 divorce over his infidelity was a formality. The other woman, Dorothy Everard, was named in the legal papers, and Carroll was embarrassed to see the whole sordid business played out in the newspapers.

For the first time in many years, Carroll was not so alone. She had fallen in love with a lean, studiously charming Parisian broker, Richard de la Rozière. As she walked the Paris boulevards chatting with her lover in fluent French, she seemed as Parisian as the Eiffel Tower. With some of her Hollywood earnings, the half-French Carroll purchased a château fifty miles outside of Paris, a fabulous place to raise the family she and her French lover intended to have. But when the Germans marched on Poland and her beloved France was threatened, she arranged that two hundred Parisian orphans and refugees and four Sisters of the Poor to watch over them could live in her house, with Carroll paying for their care.

In early June of 1940, as Hitler's juggernaut closed around Paris, Carroll decided she must go to France to rescue the children and see how de la Rozière was faring. It was intrepid, perhaps even foolish, heading out on her own, hardly the thing most celebrities would have considered. On June 8, she flew on the Pan Am Clipper to Lisbon with hopes of reaching Paris. On the fourteenth of the month, German soldiers marched under the Arc de Triomphe, and it proved too late for Carroll's visit to the French capital.

Using her movie star fame as her trump card, Carroll talked her way past the Spanish border guards and visited her aunt in the Pyrenees town of Hendaye. There she learned her cousin had been killed. She kept thinking about her lover, who was flying against the Germans.

Carroll also worried about her family in England. Her parents were living outside London, but the German bombs fell everywhere. She wanted them to come to the States, away from danger, and she implored her younger sister, Marguerite, to come too. Despite her entreaties, they chose to stay in England. As Carroll flew the Clipper back to the States, she knew there was nothing left she could do to help the war effort from Europe and much she might be able to do in America.

First, Carroll had a film to do. Set in the faux Old South of plantations and gracious manners, *Virginia* was a romance in the tradition of *Gone with the Wind*. Filmed in the old plantation country of Charlottesville, Virginia, the one thing authentic about the film was the location. Carroll's role gave her ample opportunity to wear antebellum gowns, twirl parasols, and flirt in an ersatz southern accent.

The unique thing about the project was Carroll's twenty-four-year-old costar, the six-feet-five-inch-tall Sterling Hayden, acting in his first film. Hayden had been a mate on a schooner traversing the globe and had captained another boat sailing to Tahiti. The seas had been his education, and he had learned well. There was a raw directness to the blond actor, who could have come walking out of a Jack London novel.

The first time Hayden met Carroll stayed forever embedded in his memory: "She wears no make-up. Her hair is soft and has the same hue as salt grass in the wintertime. It is swept back and secured with a small blue ribbon." The thirty-four-year-old actress was flawless. He did not meet such women in the ports of the world, and he was stunned by her. They thought alike too, concerned with the world around them. And they shared a disdain for Hollywood. It was "a place to be used, a means to an end, no more."

Carroll's interest was complicated. Hayden was handsome, but so were almost all of Carroll's costars, and he was ten years younger, practically the next generation. She was attracted to highly educated, sophisticated men and had never even considered letting someone like Hayden get near her. Maybe she might indulge in a few nights in the hotel, touching Hayden's rippling muscles, but nothing more than that. And yet she fell in love with the fledging actor.

It wasn't fair to be so happy when others faced endless perils. Carroll's thirty-three-year-old sister, Marguerite, worked at Harrods and shared a house in Lexham Gardens. On October 7, 1941, the German raids went on for seven hours. One of the bombs fell on Marguerite's house, killing her and three others, including two children.

Carroll and Hayden secretly married on Valentine's Day 1942. They knew they could not avoid the world and its miseries, dangers, and pain. To raise money for the war effort, she could give talks commemorating her sister, but she felt that was not enough. Hayden had told Carroll about the bad treatment American Merchant Marines received. Not only were they poorly paid, but their ships were often sent out as unprotected prey to German submarines. Taking off from Hollywood and working full-time, Carroll played an instrumental role in creating the not-for-profit United Seamen's Service, fighting for the betterment of the Merchant Marines.

It took Carroll until the end of 1943 to get the organization well established. Then she joined the Red Cross and sailed first to North Africa and then to Italy, working in hospitals just behind the front lines until the end of the European war.

As for Hayden, he was not about to go to war with his newly famous movie star moniker tied to him. So he changed his name to Hamilton and joined the marines. After officer training, he transferred to the OSS. Swashbuckling adventure for a righteous cause was his thing. From outside Bari in east-central Italy, he ran boats with his steady hand on the tiller, taking weapons and supplies to Yugoslav partisans. When that ran its course, he parachuted into Croatia to work directly with Tito's partisans against the Nazis.

After V-E Day in May 1945, Carroll came to Paris to broadcast in French for the United States Information Service. One day in September, Hayden showed up at her door. It had been a long time since they'd spent much time together. Nobody had to say anything. They knew it was over. They said a few words, but only a few, and then they said goodbye.

CHAPTER 5

A Golden Glow

Although he was Britain's leading director, Hitchcock stood in the shadow of Hollywood. If he was to reach the peak of his profession, that was the mountain he would have to climb. In August 1937, he traveled to California to discuss future projects. On the Hitchcocks' trip across the Atlantic on the luxurious ocean liner the *Queen Mary*, Alfred and Alma had their cabin, while his associate, Joan Harrison, shared another with their nine-year-old daughter, Pat. Harrison was so close to the family that the ship's manifest listed her as "Joan Hitchcock."

Hitchcock had hired Harrison in November 1933. At least forty other young women sat waiting to be interviewed for the much-desired secretarial position. Harrison looked at those odds and asked to go to the head of the line, saying her sister was about to give birth. (It was a revelation that would have surprised her relative, who as far as she knew was not pregnant.)

The first thing Hitchcock noticed: Harrison had the blond hair that he considered a woman's ultimate blessing. It was not just that Harrison's looks equaled those of any of the actresses the director starred in his films. She also had a sophisticated demeanor beyond her twenty-six years. After a short discussion, Hitchcock had an associate tell the other candidates to go home. Harrison so much wanted to work for Hitchcock in the film industry that she accepted the minuscule salary of a pound a week when, in her former position, she made three times that amount.

One might assume that Hitchcock had a leering interest in Harrison or at least bombarded her with the sexual asides and crude jokes that were often his preferred mode of social intercourse. But he did not dare, or perhaps he was too smart to risk offending her. Hitchcock found he had an unusual commonality with Harrison. As a teenager, she had haunted the Old Bailey, sitting in on murder trials, the bloodier and the more bizarre the better, and read all kinds of books about murder, mayhem, and lesser crimes. What better entrée to Hitchcock's soul?

Harrison's upper-middle-class family owned a weekly newspaper, the *Surrey Advertiser.* She began writing film reviews for the paper when she was only about fifteen. After studying for a year at the Sorbonne, she was one of the first women to achieve an Oxford degree. Harrison had always wanted to stand out. When she made her debut, the other young women wore pastel gowns and looked like professional virgins. Harrison arrived in shocking red.

Hitchcock's newest hire turned out to be a miserable secretary, hopelessly inept at mundane tasks. Harrison had disdain for traditional women's work, and her failure may have been partially on purpose. Alma could have been jealous of this woman who had weaseled her way into a position she was incapable of fulfilling properly to get near Hitchcock. An astute judge of her husband's needs, Alma realized Harrison was not a threat but a blessing.

The daringly chic Harrison was soon employing her fine hands in matters beyond taking dictation and became Hitchcock's and Alma's trusted associate. She exuded a glamorous, showy persona, beside which Alfred and Alma appeared dowdy.

* * *

Hitchcock was almost as well known in America as in Great Britain. When the director arrived in New York, he had to deal for the first time with American journalists. He learned immediately that he was not in London any longer.

One evening, Hitchcock had dinner at the renowned 21 Club with H. Allen Smith, a newspaper columnist noted for his irreverent style. Smith might not have mentioned Hitchcock's mountainous bulk, then approaching three hundred pounds. But the director made that story irresistible by supposedly eating three of the restaurant's celebrated steaks, topped off by three ice cream desserts. America was the land of such excess that one earned a measure of fame devouring more hot dogs than anyone in the annual contest. . . . But 21 was far from Coney Island. It did not matter if the story of Hitchcock's monumental meal was literally true or not. It traveled wide and became part of the director's image.

If Hitchcock had been enthusiastically embraced in Hollywood, he might have forgotten the column, but to Hollywood, Hitchcock was untried merchandise. As he arrived back in Britain, the *Hollywood Reporter* noted that Hitchcock was "rather disconcerted" that "the American press boosted him as an expert on food instead of Britain's ace director."

Hitchcock had a perfect understanding of his worth, and it took him many months to negotiate an American deal commensurate with what he had already accomplished and all that he believed he could achieve. In the end, the celebrated American producer David O. Selznick signed him to a four-year contract, later amended to seven years. Selznick was the most significant independent producer of the era, who had mastered the difficult task of combining quality with commerce. Directing for such a man was starting halfway up the mountain.

The Hitchcocks returned to America in March 1939 on the *Queen Mary*, accompanied by Harrison. It all sounded perfectly seamless, moving from making A-list films in London to making them in Hollywood. But from the moment Hitchcock arrived in the gilded capital of filmdom, he knew it was not the same.

Selznick was a large chunk of the problem. As obsessive and detail-oriented as Hitchcock, his conduct hyped up on amphetamines, the producer intruded into what Hitchcock considered his rightful precinct and squatted there. This was so true that when *Rebecca*, the first American film Hitchcock directed, won the Academy Award for Best Picture, Hitchcock did not appreciate the honor as he might have. Selznick had such an overwhelming role in the production that the director did not consider it a true Hitchcock film.

Rebecca was as much Harrison's film as it was Hitchcock's. Over the years she had evolved into a creative force in her own right, getting her first screenwriting credit for *Jamaica Inn* in 1939. Harrison played a crucial role in getting the rights to the Daphne du Maurier bestselling novel *Rebecca* and wrote the screenplay along with the Pulitzer Prize–winning dramatist and biographer Robert E. Sherwood.

Selznick shot Harrison down when she wanted to make the main character less simpering and give her an almost feminist edge. As painful as it was to be so thwarted, it showed that Harrison was going to push to see women portrayed with far more empathy and understanding.

Although Sherwood wrote only the last 10 percent of the script, the playwright got top billing. After all, he was famous and a man.

Harrison was a woman and obscure. It was not fair, but she could take considerable solace that as a first-time American screenwriter she was nominated alongside Sherwood for an Academy Award for Best Adapted Screenplay.

Alma was on the set of *Rebecca* as much as Harrison. Joan Fontaine, who played the lead role, remembered Hitchcock and the two women as "a triumvirate, always conferring." As necessary as Alma was to Hitchcock, she had in some measure a diminished role. Gone was the bold, ambitious young woman who walked through the studio in London with authority and purpose, replaced by a wife and mother who preferred the shadows to the spotlight's glare. When the threesome went out to Chasen's for Thursday evening dinners, the sleek, stunningly dressed Harrison usually sat next to Hitchcock, with Alma on Harrison's other side, so tiny that she looked almost childlike.

Besides that weekly dinner, the Hitchcocks generally stayed home unless the social event was a professional obligation or a major Hollywood party. Then Hitchcock sought out a chair in a strategic part of the event, where he plopped down, never rising until the evening was over. "Hitch had this monumental immobility from which he would deliver his proclamations," says his biographer, John Russell Taylor. "I think this gradually became the real him." As he remained in one place, Alma played the hummingbird, moving from person to person, conversation to conversation.

Harrison was out all the time, partaking in the vibrant social life of young Hollywood. One of those she met was Clark Gable. After the tragic death of his wife, Carole Lombard, Gable took solace in Harrison's arms. The writer Irwin Shaw was another one of her lovers.

After sharing a writer's credit on Hitchcock's film *Saboteur,* Harrison figured she had gone as far up the road with the director as she possibly could. As good as Alfred and Alma had been to Harrison, it was time to move on. She stayed friendly with the Hitchcocks and continued to be a guest at their dinner parties. In the meantime, she made her ascent in Hollywood.

In 1943, Harrison became what the *New York Times* headlined as "Hollywood's Only Full-Fledged Woman Producer." For her first film, *Phantom Lady*, Harrison constructed a female heroine, Carol Richman, that was unique in Hollywood films of the era. Richman is a secretary in New York City. Her boss has been falsely accused of murder, and she sets out to find the actual murderer. She wears smart, provocative clothes and uses her sexual allure to get men to help her find the actual murderer. The young woman is honest, bold, and truthful. Although she secretly loves her boss, she wants him on her terms once she has proven his innocence.

Carol is an idealized version of Harrison herself. The fledgling producer wore the most feminine, alluring clothes wherever she went, believing that it did not diminish her professional position—just the opposite. Like the heroine of her movie, Harrison was not the least bit embarrassed in using her feminine appeal to help her get what she wanted. When a reporter asked Robert Siodmak, the director of *Phantom Lady*, if he liked working for Harrison, he replied, "I love it. She has such beautiful legs." Rather than viewing the director's remarks as demeaning, Harrison said they were "one of the most complimentary things I ever had happen."

In Carol, Harrison created a character emblematic of the women out in the wartime workforce and their newly independent lives. "Carol could have easily stepped off the screen and into the seat next to any of the millions of women who were the intended audience for *Phantom Lady*," writes Christina Lane in her biography of Harrison, *Phantom Lady*. "They were reimagining themselves as resourceful, resilient, and self-consciously modern. They were Carol in the flesh."

* * *

Another part of Hitchcock's problem with Selznick was that the director was essentially an indentured servant whom the producer loaned out to his neighbors in exchange for a full measure of gold. The director needed a place that was his, but Selznick sent him out all over town making movies at most major studios, including Twentieth Century–Fox, RKO, United Artists, and Universal. Hitchcock was well paid, but Selznick made enormous profits from these loan-outs.

Hitchcock knew that if he were to reach the summit on his terms, he would have to get control of the whole artistic process. That meant choosing the film and the actors who would play in it, and directing his way from scripts he had overseen in intimate detail.

A man of great curiosity, no matter what he was doing, Hitchcock was always looking, turning some momentary aside into a possible movie idea, learning about people and their ways, figuring out things that would help him work better. Even when he visited his boss's offices at Selznick International Pictures, he did that. The headquarters was in a colonial-style building that could have been Hollywood's misguided idea of what an antebellum southern mansion looked like, not unfitting since Selznick was producing *Gone with the Wind*.

One day in the Selznick offices, Hitchcock saw a young actress. The director did not have to say a word to the woman to know he had to have her in *his* film. Many stars looked washed-out and ordinary in the bright, unforgiving light of a Southern California day, or they appeared overglamorized, showing themselves off with made-up presences. This woman was different. She gave off the magical luminosity of a star, but not in a showy way. She had impossibly long eyebrows like no one in Hollywood. Her beauty appeared natural, untouched by artifice, and she projected what seemed to be goodness and a certain understated sensuality.

The young woman's name was Ingrid Bergman. Hitchcock had never seen anyone quite like her. The five-feet-nine-inch-tall Swedish woman was one of those Valkyries Hitchcock considered the ideal woman. Not a pure blonde, her auburn hair was touched by a golden glow.

Like Hitchcock, the Swedish star had been brought to America by Selznick with a long-term contract. She too was being loaned out all over Hollywood. It was natural for them to work together on a Selznick production, and Hitchcock quickly came up with an idea.

The director was more interested in Bergman's sexuality than her aura of virtue. "Hitch told me what sounded like a very interesting, if rather erotic story, that he thought would be wonderful for Bergman, and that I think he would like to direct," Selznick wrote to his West Coast editor.

The film idea was based on the true story of a young married woman and a male friend kidnapped by a band of Chinese brigands. The bandits chained the unmarried couple together for six months, the sort of kinky business that attracted Hitchcock. It wasn't handcuffing, but it was good enough. The director worked on the project with a team of writers for several months, but they could not make it work. So Hitchcock moved on for the next two years, trying to develop an idea for Bergman.

The director and his wife invited eclectic groups of movie people they found intriguing to their Bellagio Road home for dinner parties. The Bel Air home was modest by Hollywood standards, but there was plenty of room for dinners at a long table and dancing in the living room, with walls large enough to display Hitchcock's growing art collection.

Hitchcock was an oenophile, who boasted about the bottles stored in his wine cellar. Over dinner, he brought out one rare vintage after another, proclaiming its virtues before decanting the bottle and soon bringing on the next. It was like a scene in Hemingway's *The Sun Also Rises.*

Bergman and her husband, Petter Lindstrom, were frequent guests. Ingrid had hearty appetites for almost everything in life. She drank as much as anyone, and not just Hitchcock's wines. Upon arriving in New York, she discovered that American invention the cocktail. In Sweden, gin, whiskey, and brandy were mainly taken straight. But in America, one could sit on a barstool and the bartender would bring one exotic mixture after another, and there was always something deliciously new. "When I came to America and saw all the names—stingers, daiquiris—I just started with 'A' and went down the list!" she said.

Although Lindstrom did not drink like his wife, he dominated the Hitchcock dinner parties. The tall, sinewy dental surgeon with a body as hard as marble had ideas about everything and boldly proclaimed them. That was nothing compared to what happened when the dancing began. He worked up such perspiration, leading the women guests in the most intricate steps, that he often changed into a second shirt. Bergman did not have Lindstrom's sense of rhythm and love of the dance and usually just sat there, watching her mate doing his thing.

Bergman had arrived in Hollywood already a major star. She was the most popular actress in her native country when she starred in the 1939 Swedish film *Only One Night.* It is the story of a handsome, seductive carnival roustabout, Valdemar Moreaux, played by the Swedish star Edvin Adolphson. Living in a caravan with the widow who owns the carnival, Moreaux is as wild and free as the beasts of the forest.

When Moreaux learns he was born due to his mother's one-night stand with a wealthy landowner, he goes to live on his father's estate, exchanging his carnival garb for black tie. Moreaux then falls in love with the landowner's gorgeous charge, Eva Beckman (Bergman).

This was the kind of role Bergman played so much that she became known as the *herrgårdsflicka*, the manor house girl, a beautiful upper-class young woman as untouchable and distant as if imprisoned in a tower.

Spurning Adolphson in the love scene did not take much acting skill. Bergman had been doing it in real life for years, starting when she was an eighteen-year-old extra in a play the forty-one-year-old had directed. Adolphson's reputation as a lecher was well known, and he was the kind of sexual predator who navigated largely unchallenged in the theater and film worlds both in Sweden and the United States, his serial misconduct justified by his charm and fame.

It is possible the teenage Bergman had once succumbed to him, but by the time she costarred with him, three years later, in the comedy *Dollar*, she had nothing but disdain for his advances. "I almost took the life away from him tonight," she wrote her fiancé, Petter. "Surely he never had experienced something like that in his love-seeking life."

Adolphson still wanted a bite out of that sweet apple. "Adolphson put his two arms around her to protect her," said another actor in the film, "but I knew his motives. I thought it was awful. He was well known as just taking the girls."

One evening during the shooting, Bergman's close friend Elsa Holm visited the Lindstroms in their Stockholm apartment. "Ingrid was upset because Edvin Adolphson was trying to flirt with her," though "flirt" was not the operative word. "She told Petter that he should say that if they were going to continue with the film, he should act properly. She was very upset. And she told Petter to take care of things."

That was Lindstrom's role in life: to take care of things. He adored his young bride, who was eight and a half years his junior, and he wanted to do everything for her. In his way, he had risen as spectacularly as his wife. Scarcely thirty years old, he was not only a dentist but a professor of dentistry and a student of medicine at Stockholm's Karolinska Institute. As handsome and charismatic as the actors who made love to his wife on the screen, he was a *sportif*, a great skier, and an athlete, full of life.

Lindstrom had arrived from the small village of Stöde in northeast Sweden. Looking askance at what he considered the moral compromise and corruption of the city, he was full of immense pride about the values he had taken from his village and its Lutheran faith, his work as a dentist, and especially his wife.

Bergman was a complex mixture of cultures, values, ambitions, and desires. Her German-born mother, Friedel Adler Bergman, died when Bergman was not yet three years old. Bergman's relatives tried to impose on the motherless child the German values they represented. The bourgeois family believed in order and discipline and keeping around your own class and kind. They had been upset when their German kin married a Swede whose lifestyle mocked their values. A man with a bohemian soul living an itinerant life, Justus Bergman had aspirations of becoming a painter until he met his future wife. To win her, he gave up his artistic ambitions and opened a successful photographic store in downtown Stockholm.

Enough of that bohemian soul remained that the fifty-three-year-old widower began an affair with Greta Danielsson, Bergman's eighteen-year-old governess. The young woman was like an older sister to Bergman, and she was almost as happy with the relationship as her father. But Justus's spinster sister, Aunt Elsa, who had replaced Friedel as a mother figure, was appalled at Bergman living in the midst of sin and succeeded in pushing Greta out of the house. Soon after that, Ingrid's beloved father died of cancer, leaving the twelve-year-old an orphan.

Bergman had not been abused or shuttled off to an orphanage, but she had grown up without a mother's nurturing love and yearning for her father's attention. As she struggled to achieve self-reliant adulthood, her new husband assumed control over much of her life, stepping easily into the role of the solid authority figure that Bergman so desired.

Bergman loved to act. Nothing else mattered. Lindstrom set out books she should read and tried to discuss politics or literature with her, but she had no interest unless she saw a potential role. He did what he could to help her advance in her chosen world. Early in her movie career, he got up in the morning and strapped Bergman's bicycle to the back of his car. Then, after Bergman carefully applied light makeup, they drove out of central Stockholm, stopping on the outskirts a few blocks from the Svensk Filmindustri. There he took the bike down so Ingrid could ride into the studio, this windblown innocent without makeup or guile, an actress like no other.

Selznick had become professionally enamored of Bergman when he saw her 1936 film *Intermezzo*, a movie that made her the biggest star in Sweden and was popular even in America. In it, she plays Anita Hoffman, a pianist who falls in love with Holger Brandt (Gösta Ekman), a world-famous violinist. Brandt leaves his loving wife and family and heads off on concert dates with his new accompanist/mistress. In the end, Brandt realizes this is wrong and returns to his family. As his daughter rushes across the street to meet her remorseful father, she is struck by a car.

Bergman's character is an adulteress who plays a major role in breaking up a family, hardly a noble character. But she turns the pianist into an immensely sympathetic being, and from the first reel, *Intermezzo* is filled with poignant melancholy. Bergman could take a flawed character and turn her into someone about whom the audience cares, something she did again and again in her career.

Selznick wanted not just Bergman but also *Intermezzo*. He brought her first to Hollywood in 1939 to star in an American remake of the film, which became such a hit that it established Bergman as an American star. At first, the producer wanted to run his newest acquisition through the Hollywood body shop—plucking her eyebrows into submission, fixing her teeth until they were sheets of ivory, and painting her with enough makeup to meet the requirements of Los Angeles glamour. He soon realized he should not tamper with what worked and decided instead to sell her to the public as a breath of not only fresh Swedish air but of truth.

Bergman was promoted in America as a Swedish star, but her mother was German. As a child, she spent summers with her aunt Elsa Adler and other German relatives in Hamburg, where she developed a near fluency in German. When Hitler came to power, the family embraced Hitler and his fervent anti-Semitism. "The man Frau Adler was living with was a high Nazi who was selling uniforms to the SS," recalls Lindstrom. "Ingrid was brought in with these people who heiled Hitler, and in Hamburg she would heil Hitler herself. Frau Adler had left a mark on her. I wanted her to read a book about Nazism, but she wouldn't."

UFA was the most important film company in Europe. In 1938, Bergman signed a multipicture deal with them. Although Lindstrom says he opposed his wife making films in Nazi Germany, he negotiated her contract. UFA publicized their newest star with a picture of her looking like a Teutonic princess. The caption read "Daughter of Germany."

Bergman thought she could have a career both in Hollywood and Berlin. But others around her soon realized what she did not: if her family ties became common knowledge and her relationship with Hitler's Germany were exposed, it might devastatingly impact Bergman's career.

Selznick knew he had a potential problem he had to squelch. When Bergman was shooting *Intermezzo* in 1939, he vetoed almost any interviews. One of the few she gave was with the prominent Swedish-

American journalist Åke Sandler. Bergman's English was a work in progress, and Sandler interviewed Bergman in her native language.

Sandler was told he must not write about UFA and her German films, but the journalist considered that a legitimate part of the story. "I was banned from the Selznick studios and from interviewing her again," he said. "I didn't say anything that negative, only that she was naïve and didn't understand what was going on politically. But Selznick was very adamant about it. He didn't want any suspicion that she might be a German actress."

Bergman had been scheduled to shoot a film in Berlin in the summer of 1939. If there had not been a problem with the contract, she would have been there when the Germans marched into Poland, setting off World War II, and likely never again would have come to Hollywood.

Bergman was not a notably introspective person. She had little interest in her past and was glad she was free of what she considered the provincial limitations and narrowness of Sweden, free of her melancholy beginnings, and free of some troubling decisions. There was no merit in looking back when she was in America with a bright new life.

In America, people are constantly reinventing themselves, nowhere more so than in Hollywood. Selznick excised Bergman's time in Nazi Germany from her public résumé, painting her as a glorious, ethereal *Swedish* star. That was the actress who radiated on the screen in *Casablanca*, the 1942 film that made Bergman an actress the world would never forget. In it, she once again played a morally dubious character she transformed into an empathetic being loved by the audience.

That was not an easy task. *Casablanca* opened in theaters in the early months of America's entrée into World War II when, in the minds of most Americans, their country was in a straightforward struggle between good and evil. Those who stood back, refusing to take a righteous stand, were cowards unworthy of the attention of decent people.

Most of *Casablanca* takes place in Rick's Café. When Ilsa Lund (Bergman) walks into the Moroccan saloon one evening, she enters a den of thieves, scam artists, Nazis, Vichy French pretenders, desperate refugees, and uncommon crooks, few patriots among them. There she comes upon the owner, Rick Blaine (Humphrey Bogart), with whom she had an affair before the war in Paris and shortly after the assumed death of her heroic husband, Victor Laszlo (Paul Henreid). Either she had discarded her widow's weeds prematurely, or hers was an adulterous affair. Rick appears just the kind of fellow who would take advantage of a vulnerable woman, a proud cynic prepared to stay on the sideline making a buck.

Laszlo could have been Lindstrom's brother. As admirable as the Czech patriot is, his nobility and consistency of purpose make him a little boring. It is no wonder Ilsa still loves the charming, irascible Rick, but how can she even think of betraying her husband again? But she appears to do so.

Bergman and Bogart made the wartime audience accept this as a great romance, not an immoral tryst. In the end, everyone does the right thing. Ilsa flies off with her husband to Lisbon, and Rick goes off to fight, speaking the immortal lines: "I'm no good at being noble, but it doesn't take much to see that the problems of three little people don't amount to a hill of beans in this crazy world. Someday you'll understand that. . . . Here's looking at you, kid."

One of the likely reasons *Casablanca* was such a big success and won the Academy Award for Best Picture is that it resonated with significant, unspoken ideas. America in the late thirties had been like Rick's Café. Citizens across the nation had embraced the isolationist America First movement and thought their country had no business fighting a foreign war. They had no concern for refugees like those huddled in Casablanca except to keep them away from our shores. President Roosevelt had the difficult task of getting Congress to support the Allies. Not until the Japanese attack on Pearl Harbor did most Americans realize that this was their war too. And like Ilsa and Rick, they did the right thing. And so did the filmgoers and critics embracing *Casablanca* as one of the greatest films of all time.

Bergman had a personal life as complicated as Ilsa Lund's, and one day, like *Casablanca*'s heroine, she would fly off to a new life, but that was years away. Her relationship with Lindstrom was full of knotty intricacies almost impossible to unravel. With her acquiescence and desire, he managed much of her professional life. A forceful, uncompromising negotiator, he irritated Selznick, who wanted to be the one controlling the actress.

If managing Ingrid had been Lindstrom's primary role in life, perhaps she would have been more satisfied with her husband. But he was not about to be known simply as Mr. Ingrid Bergman. From the time Lindstrom arrived in America, he set out to learn where he could get a first-rate American medical degree as expeditiously as possible. That turned out to be at the University of Rochester in upstate New York.

The movie magazines thought it a glorious idea, the ethereal star living with her idealistic medical student husband in a provincial city far from the lights of New York or LA. For Bergman it was glorious for a few days, giving her a chance to be with their daughter, Pia, who was living with her father, to eat fresh food reminiscent of Sweden, and to talk to her voluble husband. But she soon became bored. No homemaker, her father's bohemian soul took over, and off she went. A movie, a play, a publicity tour, she did not care that much what it was as long as it kept her active; none of those dreadful moments with nothing to do.

When Lindstrom finally got back to LA, he sought to take charge. Until he finished his residency in 1947, Bergman would be their little family's sole wage earner, which rankled him beyond measure. In part to assuage those feelings, he was overwhelmingly the man of the house.

For Bergman, those endless weekends when she was supposed to do the family thing with Petter and Pia dragged on interminably. She counted the hours until Monday morning back at the studio. But nothing worked to lift Bergman out of her periodic malaises, not a man, not a role, not a drink, nothing. She had to keep busy to avoid the dark shadows that pursued her.

Other men filled holes in her life for a short while, and then she moved on. There was fifty-two-year-old Victor Fleming, who directed the twenty-five-year-old actress in *Dr. Jekyll and Mr. Hyde*. Gary Cooper said that no woman in his life had been as much in love with him as Bergman during the shooting of *For Whom the Bell Tolls*, but "the day after the picture ended, I couldn't get her on the phone."

One of the ways Lindstrom dealt with Bergman's lovers was to challenge them to arm-wrestling contests. He was a strong man. One after another, he defeated them and walked away, trumpeting his masculinity.

Lindstrom was a devoted doctor, a loyal husband, and a caring father. It hurt him beyond measure to have a wife who acted as Bergman did. Yet he knew what an exquisite creature she was. Although Lindstrom could smell the scent of other men on Bergman, this man of moral rectitude could not even think of leaving his wife or confronting her. In a troubled marriage, the words not spoken speak loudest, and so it was with Ingrid and Petter. They did not talk about Bergman's affairs. They rarely talked about anything that mattered.

Most Americans considered Bergman a saintly goddess who lived on an ethereal plane above mere mortals. Moviegoers conflated the enviable characters Bergman played in her films with the actress who inhabited the roles. Nobody challenged that. In those years, there was no TMZ, no Page Six, no internet sleuths trying to pull the stars down from the heavens, exposing their every transgression.

Bergman's fellow Swedes saw through this gauzy veneer and recognized their compatriot as she was. It's not that they disliked her or thought her unworthy of emulation, but they understood her, and that was not something she sought.

"Ingrid was like a character in Swedish folklore," reflected Alf Kjellin, a Swedish actor and director who played beside Bergman in their native country. "There are men who work all night making coke in the forests. They see these visions of a beautiful woman with red hair peeking out of the trees. They seek to go after her, and they find that her other side is only a hollow tree with a fox tail. Bergman had that other side too. She was a smart woman and had a coldness about her. She could fend for herself and still need a man. One side was completely open, and the other completely steel."

For five years, Selznick had been loaning Bergman out to other studios. When the producer came to her early in 1944 with a movie idea, she had not been in one of his films since 1939. The actress was not about to shout hallelujah simply because the film would begin with the credits "Produced by David O. Selznick," "Directed by Alfred Hitchcock," and "Written by Ben Hecht." By this point, Bergman was as big a star as there was in Hollywood, and she would not agree to be in a film that might drive her back into the scheming pack.

In *Spellbound*, Bergman was to play a psychoanalyst, Dr. Constance Petersen, a serious professional woman who has no interest in the tawdry games of romance. Bergman liked to think she was the same, dalliances yes, but impervious to emotional entanglements. Yet the black-and-white film scarcely begins when Dr. Petersen falls uncontrollably in love with Dr. Anthony Edwardes, the new head of the Green Manors mental sanatorium in Vermont.

"I won't do this movie because I don't believe the love story," Bergman told Selznick. "The heroine is an intellectual woman, and an intellectual woman simply can't fall in love so deeply." The audiences in the movie theaters sought love, and in movie after movie, Bergman gave it to them. Even if it did not always work out, love was always out there somewhere, the salve that cured all. That was Hollywood's gospel. Yet Bergman believed such deep love was a vulgar emotion that serious women eschewed.

Selznick and Hitchcock spent two hours talking to their star about the film, trying to convince her that *Spellbound* was right for her. There was another problem: her proposed costar, Gregory Peck. He had been nominated for an Academy Award for playing a Christlike missionary, Father Francis, in *The Keys of the Kingdom*. A halo never left his head. That wasn't what bothered Bergman. She was scheduled to play Sister Benedict in *The Bells of St. Mary's* and was Peck's equal in the saint department.

Bergman's problem was a different one. The twenty-eight-year-old actress was at the peak of her beauty without a line marking her countenance. But when she looked into her mirror each morning, she feared that one day soon she would no longer be the fairest in the land. Peck was twenty-eight years old too, seven months younger than his costar, and had astonishing, youthful good looks. Despite the parity of their ages, Bergman worried that in their love scenes she would look like a worn hustler robbing the nursery school.

Flattery is the cheapest form of currency. Selznick and Hitchcock spent it on Bergman in prodigious quantities, convincing the actress that under their tutelage, she would look breathtaking. Dewy. Youthful. No way would the boyish Peck outshine her.

It made it easier when Bergman learned the cameraman was to be

George Barnes, celebrated for working with female stars. Actresses liked him because Barnes worked to create a soft, forgiving look—a look that Hitchcock in fact despised and considered little better than visual pornography. Hitchcock disdained Barnes as "a woman's cameraman whose whole reputation and living was built on the demand for his services by certain stars."

Another conflict was brewing on the publicity front. *Spellbound* explored concepts of Freudian analysis, then a new and relatively mysterious world to much of America. Freud had died only five years before, and *Spellbound* was one of the first Hollywood films to deal directly with the Vienna sage's ideas. Hitchcock was perfectly willing to use this Freudian business to propel his story along, but no way would he let psychological mumbo jumbo slow up his tale. He did, however, understand how certain concepts—Freudian symbolism, sexual innuendo, suggestive imagery—could titillate an audience and slip through strict Hollywood censors.

As Hitchcock set out to make *Spellbound*, he had his battles with Joseph Breen, the head of the censorship office. In the early thirties, Hollywood had produced any number of films full of sexually provocative material and risqué content loaded with double entendres that filmgoers were perfectly capable of deciphering. The Catholic Legion of Decency and their Protestant counterparts believed godless Hollywood was leading America into a sordid world of decadence, and they threatened a boycott.

Nothing woke up the film moguls faster than Christian leaders suggesting they were less than patriotic or—heaven forbid—godless. To combat such suggestions and to end the talk of a boycott, the producers' organization created the Production Code Administration. The Hollywood mandarins gave the office the mandate to control what moviegoers saw on the screen and were to their era what political correctness is to ours. To head the office, they chose the Irish-

American Catholic Breen, who proceeded with all the moral fervor of Savonarola to make movies as clean as a First Communion gown.

Breen set out to wash *Spellbound* of innuendo. Hitchcock and Selznick would have to scrub their script of such words as "lecherous," "frustrations," "libido," "sex," and "mating." And no way would the filmmakers be able to trick the censors by talking about the sex lives of animals. The book title *The Love Habits of the Borneo Apes* would have to go.

Spellbound opens in Dr. Petersen's office at Green Manors. Bergman is dressed in an exaggerated version of Hitchcock's ideal of a northern European woman before she is sexually awakened: wearing a tentlike white medical gown, her hair in a bun and with thick glasses, the director's metaphor for sexlessness. She is smoking, sublimation pure and simple, and is using a cigarette holder, suggesting just how classy she is. When a fellow doctor who hopes to spur a romance reaches out to touch her, he retreats, saying, "It's rather like embracing a textbook."

From this first scene, Bergman knew how she wanted to be shot, and she told Hitchcock. The director might have summarily put down another actress who confronted him this way, but he was infatuated with Bergman, and he let her rant. Then he shot the scene precisely the way he wanted to shoot it.

Bergman did not let up. She pestered him like a needy ingenue in her first film. "I don't think I can give you that kind of emotion," Bergman said, seeking more advice.

"Ingrid, fake it," he said. That quieted Bergman; years later, she remembered Hitchcock's words as some of the best advice she ever received.

On the set, Hitchcock was a martinet, allowing nothing to challenge his authority. If the actors irritated him, he would treat them dismissively, saying, "Well, all my fun is over now that you actors are here."

Selznick dared to think *Spellbound* was *his* film. To disabuse him of that delusion whenever the producer showed up, Hitchcock made one excuse or another to shut the shooting down until Selznick left.

· For years Hitchcock had been waiting to direct the actress he considered his ultimate woman. He had worshipped Bergman from behind distant pillars. Now she was with him every day.

One evening at a dinner party at his home, Hitchcock said Bergman accosted him in his bedroom and said he must make love to her then and there. Bergman was rarely blatantly sexually aggressive— she did not have to be—and it's hard to imagine her approaching Hitchcock in such a dramatic fashion. More likely, the tale is akin to the extravagant sex stories told by teenage boys that in reality would have terrified them. Even if Hitchcock's story is nothing more than a fantasy, it showed Hitchcock's obsession with Bergman.

In *Spellbound*, Dr. Petersen falls in love the instant she sees the handsome, craggy-faced Dr. Edwardes. If a picture is worth a thousand words, then a look from Bergman is worth a thousand pictures. The psychoanalyst signals her feelings with a look of yearning that suggests she fears she is losing control of herself.

Peck is almost as good as Bergman in projecting longing. In a later scene, they look at each other with desire and start to kiss. The love scene had a special verisimilitude, since Bergman, having gotten over her apprehension at working with Peck, had now embarked on a full-fledged affair with the married actor.

One day the couple came out of their dressing rooms with rumpled clothes, signaling to the uninitiated what was going on. When asked years later if he'd had an affair with Bergman, Peck said, "That's not the kind of thing I talk about," a gentleman's way of saying yes.

"I had a real love for her, and I think that's where I ought to stop," Peck said. "Except to say she was like a lovely Swedish rose. I was young. She was young. We were involved for weeks in close and intense work."

In the film, Dr. Petersen helps Dr. Edwardes reach deep within his psyche to retrieve the truths that save him. On the set, Bergman was not only his lover but was also like an older sister guiding him in the world's ways. When she liked someone, she could be immensely thoughtful, proposing things that might help the person and seeing that they followed through. She helped Peck overcome much of his self-doubt.

Trained as a Method actor, Peck considered himself a serious artist who reached into his character, understanding every gradation. When he arrived on the set, he worried he did not know how to play his role. Working with Hitchcock made his self-doubt worse. "I felt I needed a good deal of direction," Peck said, but that wasn't something Hitchcock gave.

"My dear boy," Hitchcock said dismissively to the anxious young actor, "I couldn't care less what you're thinking. Just let your face drain of all expression."

Hitchcock may not have given Peck much direction on-screen, but off-screen was a different matter. Hitchcock liked formality on his sets, signified by the cast and crew wearing suits. Peck committed a sartorial crime by wearing a brown suit. "One wears brown in the country, you know, but gray or navy in the city," Hitchcock instructed. Despite all Hitchcock's lessons, on another day, Peck showed up wearing a blue suit and *brown* shoes, cause for yet another stern admonition.

Hitchcock was not through instructing Peck in the ways of the world. The director sent the actor a case of wine, including with each bottle a note telling him the foods with which he should drink it. Wine was not yet the drink du jour in many American homes, and Hitchcock fancied himself a gentleman of class instructing a man of lesser taste.

Like Lindstrom challenging his wife's lovers to arm-wrestling contests, Hitchcock was attempting to show his superiority over this actor who possessed the woman he wanted for himself. He distanced himself from the pain as best he could. Sometimes he slept on the set, likely his way of trying to show that none of this mattered, but, of course, it did.

"I had the feeling that something ailed him, and I could never understand what it might be," Peck said. He never seemed to realize that his affair with Bergman was likely the problem.

In the film, it turns out Dr. Edwardes is an impostor. An amnesiac whose real name is Dr. John Ballantyne, he believes he has murdered the real chief of the sanatorium. Like Daisy in *The Lodger*, despite what appears to be overwhelming evidence, Dr. Petersen believes in Dr. Ballantyne's innocence.

As in so many Hitchcock films, the female lead is the strongest character. Dr. Petersen is convinced the only way to save Dr. Ballantyne is to reach deep into his psyche and remove the secrets that imprison him. The person best able to help her do that is the Rochester-based psychoanalyst Dr. Alex Brulov, who mentored her. Prodded by the two psychoanalysts to retrieve his memories, Dr. Ballantyne has an epiphany. He had always thought he killed his little brother when they were children, but he realizes now it was an accident, and he is freed of guilt. He remembers too how he was with Dr. Edwardes the day he plunged off a cliff to his death. To pretend Dr. Edwardes was still alive, Dr. Ballantyne assumed his identity.

Dr. Petersen concludes that the disturbed Dr. Murchison killed Dr. Edwardes so he would be reinstated as head of the sanatorium. When she confronts him, Dr. Murchison kills himself with the same gun he used in the murder.

Dr. Petersen and Dr. Ballantyne go off on their honeymoon—the kind of happy ending Breen would have found immensely satisfying. As did the public, which made *Spellbound* one of the biggest hits of the year. Hitchcock received an Academy Award nomination for Best Director.

When Bergman was not embedded in a film role, she was filled with the restless urge to be off somewhere. Thus, in the summer of 1945, she agreed to join a USO tour to entertain the troops in liberated Europe. One evening in the grand house in Augsburg where the group was billeted, she heard a piano playing in the living room. Not much of a devotee of music, she was nonetheless mesmerized by the poignant chords and the little man playing them. His name was Larry Adler, and he was the most famous harmonica player in the world. Adler could make the instrument sing like a virtual orchestra.

Both Bergman and Adler were married, but they were far from their spouses, and they began an affair. "You felt she'd never read a book," said Adler. "She had no interest in world affairs. She loved working. And I don't think any individual was as important as her work. I think she needed to show her power over men. She wasn't coquettish or a tease. Ingrid wasn't interested in sex all that much. She did it like a polite girl."

When the tour reached Paris, Bergman stayed at the Ritz and she found a note under her door from two Americans offering to take her to dinner. The letter was witty and irreverent. Since she had nothing to do that evening, she said yes. Bergman might have then gotten it on with Irwin Shaw, who would later write *The Young Lions*, but she was more attracted to his darkly handsome, wildly intense friend.

Robert Capa had made his name, and a great name it was, photographing war. Wherever there was a big battle, from the beaches of Normandy to the forests of the Ardennes, he was there capturing images no one else caught. His technique was no great secret. He got closer than anyone else. Born Endre Friedmann in Hungary, he took on an American name when he moved to Paris. Capa lost the love of his life, the photographer Gerda Taro, when a tank ran her over in the Spanish Civil War.

Most of the men with whom Bergman had affairs were actors not half as interesting as their roles. Capa was different, and Ingrid fell in love. The time came soon, too soon, when Bergman flew back to Lindstrom, but that was not the end of Robert Capa.

* * *

While Hitchcock was directing *Spellbound*, he was already working with Ben Hecht on his next film, *Notorious*, which would also star Bergman. Whereas the actress had doubted Dr. Constance Petersen's overwrought love, this time she believed in Alicia Huberman and wanted to play the tortured, morally ambiguous character. Bergman understood Alicia so well. She had sex with many partners because she did not care. So what if she slept with yet another man?

Many movie stars will not consider a role that risks tainting their heroic screen images; they sometimes ruin movies by insisting no dark coloring be allowed anywhere near their role. At a time when Americans were beginning to learn the full horrors of Hitler's Germany, and despite her German blood, Bergman did not flinch at being asked to play a woman of "loose morals" whose father is a convicted Nazi spy.

For the first time in his Hollywood career, Hitchcock was both director and producer, controlling every film element. Beyond that, the film was for RKO, freeing Hitchcock from Selznick's shadow hovering over the project. In *Notorious*, Hitchcock dealt with the psychological complexities of human beings as he rarely had before.

Hitchcock had worked with Hecht on *Spellbound*, and he was the perfect choice to write *Notorious*. No prima donna, Hecht worked together with the director, writing quickly and accepting suggestions until everyone concerned felt the script was right. With a first-rate screenplay in hand, Hitchcock surrounded Bergman and her costar,

Cary Grant, with a superb supporting cast, even the tiniest role chosen with care.

As always, Hitchcock had to work around Joseph Breen at a censors' office put in place not by the government but by the film industry. Once Breen received the original script for *Notorious*, he got out his brush and Bab-O and started trying to clean things up. He found Hecht's script "definitely unacceptable under the provisions of the Production Code."

The central problem with the script, from Breen's perspective, was Bergman's character in the film. After learning her father was a Nazi spy, Alicia Huberman starts sleeping around. To the censors' office, that was beyond the pale. If a man has several lovers, he's a stud. If a woman has the same, she's a slut. Huberman was "a grossly immoral woman, whose immorality is accepted 'in stride' in the development of the story." It simply would not do. That Bergman in her personal life was as promiscuous as Huberman in the film was a distinction that did not concern Breen. He was only cleaning up the script.

Devlin (the Cary Grant character) and his associates are government agents, and that brought up another problem. "I think you know that the industry has had a kind of 'gentleman's agreement' with Mr. J. Edgar Hoover," Breen wrote, "wherein we have practically obligated ourselves to submit to him, for his consideration and approval, stories which importantly involve the activities of the Federal Bureau of Investigation." Hollywood was a virtual advertising campaign for the FBI, with rarely a negative note written about the agency in any script. Thanks in part to Hollywood's rosy lens, Hoover was the most admired public servant in America.

Hitchcock had long ago learned to deal with Breen by fighting a war of attrition. The director gave up on minor points and went back to Breen again and again, prolonging the process. When Breen finally approved the screenplay, he could show a thick file of communications, but from Hitchcock's perspective, the essential elements stood largely unchanged, including Huberman's sexual conduct.

There's an open sensuality in Bergman's character of Alicia Huberman never before seen in a Hitchcock film. The film's opening scene takes place on the day Huberman's father is sentenced to twenty years in federal prison for treason against the United States. She deals with the shame and embarrassment by having a party at her Miami house, where the inebriated woman appears likely to pick up a man for the night. Dressed provocatively in what costume designer Edith Head described as "a zebra-skin print blouse with her midriff exposed," Huberman is talking to a startlingly handsome man (Cary Grant), slurring her words as she does so. The man appears strangely disinterested in being handed such a treasure for his apparent pleasure.

Grant made his name in romantic comedies nailing scenes with a superb sense of timing and studied understatement. He always stood back from the scene with bemused amusement. *Notorious* is different, forcing him to be openly emotional.

When Huberman learns this gentleman is not a potential lover, but a government agent named T. R. Devlin, she is infuriated. Devlin tells her that the German gentry who paid her father are living in Brazil. The American agent asks Huberman to redeem herself by flying to Brazil to spy on her father's Nazi comrades, who are attempting a rebirth of Hitler's world. She agrees to the assignment in South America. Why not? Nothing matters. On the flight south, she learns her father has committed suicide with a poison capsule.

"You've been sober for eight days, and as far as I know, you've made no new conquests," Devlin tells Huberman as they sit in a Rio café. Those were hardly the words of a troubadour of love, but bitchy banter is their preferred idiom. "Once a tramp always a tramp," she replies, displaying her low level of self-regard.

"I've always been scared of women, but I get over it," Devlin says.

"You're afraid you'll fall in love with me," Huberman replies. There, in two sentences, is the whole movie. The fear of women that Devlin articulates is a frequent idiom in Hitchcock's films, as it was in his life. He loved Alma, surely, but he deferred to his wife in ways that masked his fear. She knew too much. She had entered into his psyche in ways he could not control.

Grant tried to wrap himself in the protective shield of his public image, but he was no more comfortable within himself than Hitchcock. The key was his childhood. He doubted if he had been "a happy child." He believed that was why he remembered so little of his early years in Bristol, England. Why would he want to revisit his life with his disturbed mother, who treated him "as her doll" and sought complete control over her son? Was his tortured relationship with his mother one of the reasons his marriages never seemed to work out? Was it a fear of women that was her ultimate legacy to her son?

Whereas thirty-year-old Bergman worried her days as a romantic film star might not last much longer, forty-one-year-old Grant was at the height of his immense attractiveness. Although he eventually married five times, Grant was most likely bisexual, enjoying lovers who were counterimages of himself. During the thirties, he lived for several years with Randolph Scott, another handsome young actor. That relationship did not end simply because they both became stars. During the filming of *Notorious*, Grant was going through a divorce, and it helped to hang out again with Scott.

The screenwriter Arthur Laurents, who knew Grant, said the actor "was at best bisexual," as if homosexuality was a curse to be avoided, but the actor's biographer Scott Eyman is not so sure. "Gays have been eager to claim Grant as one of their own, while straights have been every bit as insistent about his presumed heterosexuality," writes Eyman in *Cary Grant: A Brilliant Disguise*. "So much talent, so many mysteries."

Whatever his proclivities, Grant did not make a pass at Bergman. This was the first time they had been in the same film, and their notable friendship began by working together to make their parts mesh. One morning Bergman had a hard time saying a particular line. It could happen to anyone. Instead of stomping off to his dressing room, upset at the delay, Grant stayed and worked with Bergman for two hours until she got it right.

Hitchcock understood the caliber of his two stars, and he saw them working together not as a threat to his authority but as a bonus. "Hitch never said anything," Grant recalled. "He just sat next to the camera, puffing on his cigar. I took a break, and later, when I was making my way back to the set, I heard her say her lines perfectly. At which point Hitch said, 'Cut!' followed by 'Good morning, Ingrid.'"

In December 1945, Hitchcock hosted a banquet for Bergman amid the filming. This was not the kind of thing he often did, but he loved Bergman, and she was standing at the top of the Hollywood world. In November, *Life* had put her on the cover, calling it "Bergman's Year," and so it was. She had three wildly successful films in the theaters: *Spellbound*, *Saratoga Trunk*, and *The Bells of St. Mary's*. Her popularity was such that she received twenty-five thousand fan letters weekly.

On the set with the cameras rolling, Bergman was magnificently alive, but the cameras did not roll forever, and when the shooting ended, she had to go home. Often, Lindstrom wasn't there. He was as much a workaholic as his wife, and as he rose to become the chief neurosurgical resident at Los Angeles County Hospital, he was as much admired in his world as Bergman was in hers.

When Bergman first went out with Lindstrom in Stockholm, he was her friend, lover, and father figure. To a young fatherless woman, it had been a lovely thing. Most of what remained now in LA was the patriarchal figure. The more she fled from his embrace, the more anxious he became and the more he sought to dominate her.

Growing up a motherless child, Bergman had no model for motherhood. She did not enjoy spending hours alone with her daughter. One evening after returning home late, she sat in front of her mirror taking off her makeup. As she did so, seven-year-old Pia came up to her mother and asked, "Why aren't you home more?" The next morning on the set, Bergman talked about her daughter's poignant plea.

Another day, Bergman told Adler, "All I care about is my work, and anybody who gets in my way, I take it out on them." As ashamed as she was, she could not help the way she behaved.

Bergman continued seeing Capa as well, though given all her obligations and Lindstrom's suspicious eye, it was not as often as she might have liked. This was not the same Capa she had met in Paris at the end of the war. The photographer believed the atomic bombs on Japan had destroyed his profession. There would be no more wars to cover.

All Capa felt he had left of value was his own life. His story was richly deserving of being told, but there was something unseemly about the most important war photographer in modern history peddling his own tale. But he still had Ingrid. To see her, he told RKO he had an assignment from *Life* to photograph the production. He showed up on the set and started spending time in her dressing room.

Hitchcock had a reputation for being focused on nothing but the scene he was shooting that day. Everything else was extraneous. And yet he was so obsessed with Bergman that he missed nothing going on around her. He saw Capa as he was. The photographer was a creature of war. That was life to him. When the guns went dead, so did he. At loose ends, he drank until the bottle was dry, gambled until his money was gone, and partied until the sun came up. At one point, Bergman thought vaguely of marrying Capa, but that would not have worked out for either one of them. Yet she wanted to continue seeing him.

To get away, Bergman lied to Lindstrom with impunity. At the end of December, Hitchcock shut the set down for two days. She did not tell Lindstrom, and when she headed off from their home at 1220 Benedict Canyon Drive in her Oldsmobile, he assumed she was going to the studio. But she drove off to Malibu, where she met up with Capa at Irwin Shaw's beach house.

Then there was Hitchcock. "When they were in the hotel during the making of *Notorious*, he said she threw herself across his bed, and she wept," recalled screenwriter David Freeman, who, during the last year of Hitchcock's professional life, spent much time with the director. "It's not hard to think that Hitchcock had some sort of crush on Bergman. But I don't think he could manage it in a way that would make either of them happy. It was very sad. Each time something like that failed in his life, it made him all the more private. It drove all his emotions inward until they only came out in his films."

Bergman was looking for something more, but she did not know what it was and where she might find it. Opening box after box, they were all empty. So she moved from lover to lover, affair to affair, always returning to Lindstrom in the end.

In *Notorious*, standing on the patio of an apartment overlooking the beach, Huberman and Devlin have one of the longest, most celebrated kisses in film history. They nuzzle. They brush lips. They kibitz. She is the aggressor, both physically and emotionally bemoaning "the fact that you don't love me." The government agent is passive, disregarding her assertiveness.

Devlin speaks cruelly at times to Huberman, a weak man's idiom. He loves her, and the more he cares, the more his vulnerability threatens him. When his superiors want Huberman to begin an involvement with the German Alexander Sebastian (Claude Rains) in order to spy on him and his Nazi friends, he does not dare tell his colleagues of his feelings for Huberman. Instead, he tells her to do whatever she must do, showing not even a perfunctory sign of regret. Soon afterward, Sebastian asks Huberman to marry him. As emotionally disengaged as ever, Devlin calls it a "useful idea."

Devlin asks the newly married Huberman to set up a party and invite him so he can search the wine cellar for whatever may contain the Nazis' secret. With the key she has stolen from her new husband, Huberman and Devlin enter the wine cellar, where he breaks a bottle filled with black sand that turns out to be uranium ore.

After Sebastian discovers Huberman's duplicity, he goes to his mother's bedroom and sits at the end of her bed, the same position Hitchcock assumed as a boy. The director's mother had died in 1942, freeing him of any need to portray mothers as saintly souls. There is nothing sweetly feminine about Madame Sebastian (Leopoldine Konstantin) and nothing good. She is the most perfectly evil figure in the whole film.

From the beginning, Madame Sebastian had been suspicious of Huberman. When her son tells her he has married an American agent, she has an "I told you so" smirk on her face. Treating Huberman with the utmost politeness, Madame Sebastian serves her coffee laced with poison, slowly killing her.

When Huberman does not show up for her regular meetings with Devlin, he guesses something is wrong and goes to pay a social call. Told that Huberman is sick in bed, Devlin stealthily walks upstairs to her bedroom. He half carries his beloved down the stairs and outside, past the suspicious saboteurs, and drives away, leaving the Nazis to their fate.

There is nothing more complicated than making things look simple. No director took that axiom further than Hitchcock. He arrived at the set of *Notorious* each day with storyboards setting out a precise vision of each shot. When he finished shooting, he spent more time editing and performing other postproduction work than on the set with the actors.

Hitchcock described editing a film as undemanding and obvious. "All that has to be done is to cut away irrelevancies and see that the finished film is an accurate rendering of the scenario," he said. But in Hitchcock's hands, the process was complicated and ingenious. In many scenes, he insisted on switching perspectives again and again in what Hitchcock said Selznick condemned as the director's "goddamn jigsaw method of cutting." The moviegoers in the theaters knew nothing about Hitchcock's endless tinkering. They saw only a scene that was seamless and richly evocative.

Hitchcock was great at small things. Enough small things done right lead to greatness in big things. Hitchcock's film—and *Notorious* is his film—is on many lists of the greatest movies. Grant remembered *Notorious* as "the one Hitch threw to Ingrid." He did not so much toss it to her as she took it with Hitchcock's complicity.

Bergman moved from a sensitive portrayal of Alicia Huberman in *Notorious* to a triumph as the martyred *Joan of Lorraine* on Broadway. That was a role she wanted to play beyond any other, and she played her again in a movie directed by Victor Fleming. Bergman had grown tired of Hollywood's commercial compromises. She wanted to do a different kind of film, and *Joan of Arc* was the beginning. This would be true art, a spiritual film that would win critical accolades and massive box office receipts.

During the production of *Joan of Arc*, Bergman renewed her affair with the fifty-eight-year-old Fleming, who was even more in love with her than during the making of *Dr. Jekyll and Mr. Hyde*. Capa had not gone away. The Hungarian-born photographer wrote her love letters when he was not around, sometimes two a day. Adler may not have been so profuse in expressing his feelings, but the harmonica virtuoso was still a lover.

Lindstrom was not some mindless cuckold. He knew what his wife was doing, but this man of overweening pride could not admit it. He refused to see what stood before his tearful eyes. When Ingrid was in New York, he wrote her, "The boy that made sure you had flowers at Oscar's Theater—he is still longing for you." It was an admirable sentiment, but surely done in part to invoke guilt.

Bergman was not just unhappy in her marriage but also dissatisfied in her artistic life, seeking new challenges wherever they might be. In the spring of 1946, in New York City, she saw *Rome Open City*, directed by the Italian Roberto Rossellini. The actress enjoyed the neorealistic masterpiece, but gave it no more thought until two years later when her latest film, *Arch of Triumph*, flopped miserably. For years the taint of failure had never come near her; she was fixated on expelling that stench. When she saw another Rossellini film, *Paisan*, it was a revelation. At a moment of great personal and professional discontent, the movie haunted her with its possibilities.

Rossellini was a fisherman of life who went out into the streets looking for people with stories that became his films. Whether it was the dangerous byways of Rome in the last days of World War II or American soldiers confronting Italy, his movies showed life as it was, or so it seemed, unburdened by the artifices of Hollywood.

Bergman adored the Rossellini films, doubly so since she was monumentally dissatisfied with almost everything in her life. Of course, there was Lindstrom, but that was not the main problem. She was thirty-two years old, late middle age in the life of a female movie star. For years her life had sped along like a Le Mans racer, with no time to slow down to appreciate all that she had, and now she feared it might be over.

Bergman needed something new and daring to get back where she felt she belonged, and she thought it could be Rossellini. She did not ask herself where the Italian director would place an expensive, world-famous actress in one of his modest black-and-white neorealistic films. She simply shot off a letter expressing her desire to work with him. "If you need a Swedish actress . . . who, in Italian, knows only 'ti amo,' I am ready to come and make a film with you," she wrote. Although Bergman did not mean the words literally, writing "I love you" to Rossellini was like waving a beefsteak in front of a Bernese mountain dog.

Although Rossellini's films had the gritty substance of everyday truth, in his personal life he was a mythmaker and exaggerator who treated facts like balloons that had to be blown up to be seen. He pretended he had known and loved Ingrid's work for years and her letter was a miracle. In truth, he knew almost nothing about her and viewed the prospect of working with her as a gigantic publicity stunt. At the same time he was wooing her, he was trying to get Jennifer Jones to star in one of his films. As for Ingrid, the Italian was only one of five prominent directors she was contacting. And thus, Ingrid and Rossellini approached each other not with the scent of romance but primarily with cunning self-interest.

Rossellini replied to Ingrid in a lengthy, richly emotive missive that sketched out the film they could make together. He was a magician laying out what was not even a story but a vague idea. He told her how, driving north of Rome one day, he saw a group of refugee women enclosed behind a barbed-wire fence. Stopping his car, he walked up to the fence, where a Latvian woman reached out to him "just like a shipwrecked person would clutch at a floating board." He was so taken with her that another day he returned to the fence, but she had gone off somewhere with a soldier. That was the woman Ingrid would play. "Shall we go together and look for her?" he asked. "Shall we together visualize her life in the little village near Stromboli, where the soldier took her?"

Hitchcock was still in love with Bergman. He gave the actress the best gift he could give her—a film expressly conceived to allow her to soar. *Under Capricorn* was outside the director's usual fare, but it appeared perfectly made to show Bergman's creative chops. The role was that of Lady Henrietta, an alcoholic, troubled aristocrat who has come to live in the frontier society of early-nineteenth-century Australia. In July 1948, Bergman flew to London to shoot the movie.

Ingrid was lonely for Petter and Pia and her life in America. Although Ingrid thought at times of leaving her husband, there are few things as complicated as a marriage. No one who stands outside its boundaries can ever fully understand. Even the two participants don't always appreciate the emotional parameters that envelop them.

Bergman and Lindstrom had left their native Sweden together to journey to the farthest reaches of America, where they rose to the peaks of their chosen professions. Despite all their squabbles, they remained bonded profoundly to each other.

As Ingrid sat in her London hotel room, she waited for the letters Lindstrom wrote her every day. Sometimes they arrived three or four at a time, and that was a special treat, along with the packages of goodies he sent her. With all the hours on the set, she did not respond as frequently, but when she did, it was a long, chatty conversation with the man who was closer to her than anyone.

On July 19, 1948, Ingrid wrote a four-page letter to Petter. She began it *"Kara lilla Husse,"* Swedish for "Dear little Master." The letter continued in English, written in her fine cursive hand. It was the first day of shooting, and she described "Hitch, like a little rock in the middle of the ocean in turmoil, men and women to visit and stare—all drinking this. So, we have begun!!"

Petter was planning a visit with Pia later in the summer. Ingrid told him they should sail so that their daughter could see the Statue of Liberty and the White Cliffs of Dover. And they should come early enough to attend the London Olympics. But she had learned long ago that there was no telling Lindstrom what to do. "Well, do what you want, because that's what you'll do anyway," she wrote. In the last paragraphs, she changed her tone. It was as if she were speaking to her manager, telling Lindstrom the next role she wanted and how he could help her to get it.

Bergman's previous two Hitchcock films had been on happy sets, with almost everyone working collegially together. This film was different. Bergman could criticize Hollywood, but there everyone was professional. Here the crew was intolerably slow, and Hitchcock insisted on interminably long takes that had to be shot repeatedly.

At one point during rehearsals, Bergman broke down into tears. She reamed out Hitchcock for insisting on these takes that went on for as much as ten minutes, almost impossible to do the first time successfully.

"It's just a movie," Hitchcock said. That was not the thing to say to an actress who cared so much about her performance.

In September 1948, Bergman and Lindstrom traveled to Paris to meet Rossellini at the George V Hotel. When Roberto greeted her, he kissed her hand. "I was looking at those dark eyes of Roberto's," Bergman said. "He was very shy, and he didn't look like a movie man—not the sort I was used to anyway."

Rossellini was as plump as a Strasbourg goose. His hair made a steady retreat from his forehead; he combed the remaining strands back and greased them. He had a sharp nose and tiny eyes, but his most commanding attribute was his voice. That was his instrument of seduction, and it worked to perfection.

Rossellini did not wear tight clothes or walk with the disdainful sneer of the Roman boulevardier, but he was the classic Italian lover. The Italian author Luigi Barzini described the breed as full of "charm, skill, lack of scruples and boldness." None of them had more of it than Rossellini.

The director was married and had a young son. That was hardly an inconvenience to his wanderings. He juggled more balls than a circus performer. Rossellini's volatile relationship with the actress Anna Magnani was punctuated by as many curses and shouts as sweet words of love. He did not limit his dalliances to Italians; when he ventured far and wide, he went high and low. There was Marilyn Buferd, Miss America of 1946, whom he cast in one of his films; Roswita Schmidt, a German nightclub performer; a blond Hungarian who made occasional appearances; and others whose names hardly mattered.

When a delicious dish is set before a man of Rossellini's appetites, he must partake, and Bergman was a succulent main course. After the meeting, the director bragged to his friends about how he would have Bergman. "I'm going to put my horns on Mr. Bergman," he said, as if scoring wasn't enough; Lindstrom must look the betrayed fool.

When Ingrid got back to London, she gushed extravagantly about the genius of the Italian maestro and what it would be like making a film with him. Hitchcock felt that he had given much to the actress. It was almost unthinkable that Bergman would leave him for this Italian fakir. As Hitchcock saw it, Rossellini was not making real films. He was sticking the snout of the camera out into the world, seeing what it picked up.

While Bergman was shooting *Under Capricorn* in London, *Joan of Arc* opened in America in November 1948. Nothing in her career meant more to the actress, but the movie was an artistic and commercial disaster. The film was embarrassing in its overwrought pretensions, the dialogue clunky as the armor. She had given every ounce of her emotions to that role, but as the *New York Times* said, "Miss Bergman, while handsome to look on, has no great spiritual quality."

Fleming died soon afterward, in part perhaps of all the misplaced ardor in directing his failed attempt at a masterpiece. The *Joan of Arc* debacle made the Rossellini project even more exciting. It was not just a role. It was an adventure, a shared artistic journey to places she had never gone.

Rossellini came to Hollywood in January 1949. Soon after he arrived, Bergman and Lindstrom gave the director a party at their home. To greet him, Ingrid set out a thirty-foot-long red runner. As she showed him around Los Angeles, they spoke in a strange mixture of Bergman's rudimentary French and Rossellini's nearly nonexistent English.

Rossellini thought living the high life was his due. He had run through his inheritance years ago and always seemed to be in debt. When he no longer had money to pay for his suite at the Beverly Hills Hotel, Bergman invited him to stay in their guesthouse, where they spent much time alone.

Bergman and Rossellini went to see Howard Hughes, who had recently purchased RKO. He agreed to finance their film, including paying Bergman her high American salary. With that set in place, Rossellini returned to Italy to make plans for Bergman's arrival and to film their movie on the island of Stromboli in southern Italy.

On March 9, 1949, Ingrid said goodbye to Petter and Pia and took the train to New York City on her way to Rome. When Lindstrom returned to the house, he was drawn to Ingrid's bedroom, which still carried her scent. He slowly realized she had taken almost everything that mattered: fur coats, favorite dresses, jewelry, clipping books, letters, photo albums. As he stood there, he knew Bergman would never return.

* * *

As painful as it was for Hitchcock to lose Bergman, he had Alma. She was usually there on the set all day long and at home at night cooking and doing other things for Hitchcock. Wherever they went, he was the center of it all, robustly telling his tales. Alma had heard them before as she sat dutifully, pretending to be fascinated. As she knew better than anyone, her husband was a man with few concerns beyond his career. That was what she shared with Hitchcock more than anything else: his career and a daughter. She asked for no credit, and that was what she received.

When Hitchcock spoke about how he had not had sex since his twenties, was that not a condemnation of his wife? He had this masterful soliloquy where he riffed on the bizarre mechanics of the act. "I was so fat I had to conceive my daughter with a fountain pen!" he said. As for his unrequited infatuations with actresses, Alma shielded her eyes as best she could, but wasn't that another humiliation?

Although Alma would never have thought this, she was as intriguing in her own way as was her husband, but few people got close enough to Alma to see and appreciate her attributes. Many of those who did their best to charm her were looking for an entrée to her husband.

The Hitchcocks had some friends who were close to both of them, none more than Whitfield Cook. They met the playwright in 1944 when Cook directed his comedy *Violet* on Broadway, starring fifteen-year-old Patricia Hitchcock. Called by the producer "the most promising juvenile star in this country," the Hitchcocks' daughter got stellar reviews, but the play failed and so did her career. A sensible, grounded young woman, she was in some ways the best collaboration between Alfred and Alma, a stellar sign that theirs was a strong family.

In the late 1940s Cook became virtually a member of the Hitchcock family. A Yale graduate and a debonair gentleman, he could talk about almost anything with wit and discernment. No wonder they both enjoyed his company. His looks were somewhat androgynous, and when he wasn't with the Hitchcocks, he often hung out with Hollywood's gay set. By notes in his diary, he appears to have had a number of male lovers.

Alma and Cook began working on a screenplay, spending hours

together. Here was a man who listened to her and cared about what she felt. She poured herself out to him, opening her emotional veins. It was all terribly exciting. In June 1949, when Hitchcock was directing in London, Cook visited the British capital, where he wrote in his diary that he had "Alma to my room for breakfast." Three days later, he had a "wonderful drive with Alma to Oxford + Stratford-on-Avon [*sic*]."

In August, when Alma arrived back in Los Angeles, Cook met her at the airport and had dinner with her at the Bellagio Road residence. Their screenplay gave them ample excuses to spend time together. And when they were apart, she missed him terribly.

"I've been very lonely this week, and recovered my equilibrium— or I thought I had until the days mail arrived," she wrote him on August 23, 1949, presumably about his letter.

In all the times and places that Alma and Cook were alone together, it is just speculation that they had an affair. There are all kinds of betrayals in a marriage, and sex is only one of them, and often not the worst. Alma still loved Hitchcock, but she hungered for something beyond what her husband gave her, some abiding warmth and emotional kinship. For Cook, Alma's feelings must have been overwhelming. No way was he going to let himself become known for having a relationship with the great director's wife. He backed away and a few years later married another woman.

CHAPTER 6

Swan Song

When Bergman flew to Rome to the embrace of her Italian lover, as far as Hitchcock was concerned she was betraying not only her husband but him. And when she became pregnant with Rossellini's child, the American public felt she had betrayed *them* and everything they thought she represented.

Hitchcock watched Bergman's vivisection with dismay and apprehension. The public was a fickle beast that turned on Bergman with a vengeance. Moviegoers had seen her play nuns and saints, and they believed in that image of her. As Americans saw it, Bergman and Lindstrom had invited this Roman Lothario into their home. The married Rossellini had repaid the couple's hospitality by seducing Ingrid, taking her back to his troubled land, where he impregnated her, leaving her loyal husband and daughter to their cruel fate.

Not only movie fans were outraged. On March 14, 1950, Senator Edwin C. Johnson of Colorado got up on the Senate floor and condemned "the vile and unspeakable Rossellini who sets an all-time low in shameless exploitation and disregard for good public morals" and then went on to call Bergman "one of the most powerful women on this earth today—I regret to say, a powerful influence for evil."

The early fifties was a time of immense insecurity in Hollywood and not just because the brightest star in the firmament had been shot down for an indiscretion. With the inexorable rise of television, the longtime studio system that controlled every part of the business had begun to crumble.

Wisconsin senator Joseph McCarthy smelled Communists everywhere. If you had signed a certain petition or attended a certain meeting, you feared the FBI might come knocking on your door. And then there was *Confidential*, the celebrity scandal magazine that printed stories that previously rose no further than gossip among the Hollywood knowledgeable. For all these reasons, it was best to be careful about what you said politically, to be discreet in your private affairs, and careful about whom you cast in your films.

Hitchcock had contemplated starring Bergman in *Dial M for Murder*, to be shot in 1953. It would not have been much of a stretch for her to play the wily adulterous Margot Wendice, but even if Bergman was willing to return to Hollywood, it was unthinkable that moviegoers would come to see her. That left Hitchcock with the unenviable task of trying to find an actress to replace her.

The director was a man of artistic decisiveness. When Hitchcock saw a screen test for twenty-three-year-old Grace Kelly, he believed he had found Bergman's replacement. The blond actress was the essence of coolness, and on the screen had an irresistibly appealing aura.

In June, Hitchcock invited Kelly to his office to discuss her playing Wendice. Kelly was so in awe of the celebrated director that she could scarcely utter a word. "In a horrible way, it was funny to have my brain turn to stone," she recalled. "I was very nervous and self-conscious, but he was very dear and put me at my ease."

Hitchcock was nervous and self-conscious in these situations too, and he did what he almost always did. He paraded out a list of cultural artifacts that showed he was a man of taste and refinement. Wine was at the top of the list, discussing vintages of such rarity that mere mention of them impressed even teetotalers. Then there was talk of travel. Most Americans had never traveled to Europe, and that was another winner, along with food and fashion. He talked about everything but Kelly's possible role in his film.

Seeing Kelly in person confirmed everything Hitchcock suspected about Grace, though her high, thin voice was a problem. Hitchcock felt she appeared "mousy" in the Fred Zinnemann directed *High Noon* (1952), but that was the point of her role as a pacifist Quaker.

Hitchcock would never have made a film like *High Noon*, where the heroine is a noble character from beginning to end. He would star Kelly in *his* kind of film. No Quakers need apply. She would begin as a character flawed to her very roots. He would take her on a journey through a world of pain until she suffered enough to be free of her sins.

* * *

A young child does not know if she is rich or poor. It took Grace Patricia Kelly, born on November 12, 1929, a number of years to realize most families did not live in seventeen-room brick mansions with a tennis court, maids, and a gardener on a hill in the East Falls neighborhood of Philadelphia.

The Kellys arrived in the United States during the mid-nineteenth century, when many Americans viewed the Irish as invaders polluting the very land. Grace's father, John B. "Jack" Kelly, may have been president of the biggest brick-masonry firm in the country but no proper Philadelphian wanted anything to do with Kelly's kind. These unwanted hordes bred like rats. With his nine siblings, Kelly was a perfect example. As the elite saw it, these Irish immigrants were a peasant race of maids, nannies, road builders, weavers, and barrel makers. Even if they achieved wealth, Irish Americans were unwanted in the clubs and institutions of the Protestant establishment.

Jack Kelly told everyone he had started from nothing, when he was a successful man's son. The teenage Kelly had worked as a brick-layer in his older brother's building company. He did not do that job long, but in America, if you were not born rich, there was nothing better than rising from nothing, and Kelly bragged how he had started life laying bricks.

The six-feet-two-inches-tall Kelly was a vibrantly healthy young man with such handsome, sharp, bold features that one newspaper called him "the most perfectly formed American male." His sport of choice was the one-man scull. Like polo and squash, rowing was fa-vored by upper-class gentlemen, not some upstart Irish kid with an eighth-grade education. You did not win by bragging over a pint of beer. You won by rowing on the Schuylkill River until your arms ached and you almost collapsed. You did that day after day, year after year.

Kelly won six national championships before he planned to sail to England in June 1920 to compete in the World Cup of the sport, the Diamond Challenge Sculls, at the Henley Royal Regatta. The Henley officials knew Kelly had done a stint as a bricklayer. Thus, he was not a gentleman and had no business competing against those who were. His Irish background did not help. The British elite despised the Irish even more than the American nativists, another reason not to allow him to pollute the race with his presence.

Later that summer, Kelly won a gold medal at the Summer Olym-pics in the single sculls and a second one rowing with his cousin in the double sculls. That was not the Henley Royal Regatta, but it was enough that one hundred thousand Philadelphians welcomed their hero home. That was glorious, but it was not enough. Kelly would get even. It might take decades, but one day he would best the narrow men who controlled the British competition and the dying world they represented.

Kelly had been a heavyweight boxing champion in the army in the Great War, and he wanted to beat everyone at everything. Athletics was the venue to take on others as equals. His children must share in his quest for greatness on the athletic field. Life was one long competition. Second place was no place at all.

On the weekends, the Kellys devoted themselves to all kinds of athletic endeavors. The estate was full of training equipment. In the summer, workers from John B. Kelly, Inc., brought onto the lawns a giant cement-mixing container to be used as a makeshift swimming pool. The family also traipsed down to the Penn Athletics Club to work out in the gym and swim in the pool.

Grace's sisters, Margaret "Peggy" and Elizabeth Anne "Lizanne," became competitive swimmers. It was to Kelly's only son, John Jr. ("Kell"), to whom he gave the crucial challenge. Kell was the vehicle of his father's revenge. He must one day give him the one gift he wanted beyond all others: to win the Diamond Challenge Sculls at the Henley Royal Regatta in the Kelly name.

Her father set no such task for Grace. This inward-looking, preternaturally sensitive little girl did not have the fire of athletic competition in her, and Jack did not have the interest in her that he had in her more athletic siblings. It was painful to love a father whom you believed did not love you as much as you loved him. "We were always competing," Grace reflected, "competing for everything—competing for love." She lost that battle. The only way Grace dealt with that was to withdraw a little further.

Jack Kelly had married a woman who was herself a champion swimmer. He met Margaret Majer at the Philadelphia Turngemeinde, a traditional German-American athletic club, where he had ample opportunity to admire the German-American's blond hair, light features, and robust presence. Glimmering with vitality, she could have been the model of Teutonic womanhood. Although the Lutheran Margaret converted to Catholicism in 1924, before marrying Kelly, and tried in other ways to emulate her Irish-American husband, she remained in many respects German, the only language she spoke until she was six years old.

"I was always on my mother's knee, the clinging type," Grace recalled. "But I was pushed away." Margaret was not a mother to embrace her children or to express the love that she felt should have been simply understood. She was the parent who brought out the hairbrush when she felt it needed to be applied. Disciplined, orderly, and frugal, she wasted neither money, time, nor emotion.

Margaret often dressed Grace in clothes handed down from Grace's older sister, when she could have marched her down to John Wanamaker's to purchase the finest dresses in the city. That did not mean Margaret was cheap. She was trying to teach her daughter to respect her possessions and value them. Idle hands drew the devil's attention, and when the nanny was not directing the Kelly girls to one worthy activity or another, Margaret had them crocheting or knitting.

In an era when it was rare for a woman to have a college education, Margaret not only had a degree from Temple University in physical education, but she became the first woman to teach the subject at the University of Pennsylvania. She also taught at the Woman's Medical College of Pennsylvania, a groundbreaking institution whose graduates included the second Black woman physician in America and the first female to earn a pharmacy degree.

Margaret wanted to pay back a small measure of all the good

that had come to her family. "The good fortune of the entire Kelly family—their good health, their good luck in everything they've ever undertaken—has always been astonishing to me," she wrote in 1956 in a widely syndicated newspaper series whose royalties went to the Woman's Medical College. "I've often had the feeling that the Kellys have been on the receiving end for so long that I'm sure we haven't given enough in return."

Jack was such a philanderer that it was no wonder his wife spent much of her time on charitable pursuits. He likely would have been diagnosed as a sex addict. One Christmas, he ordered twenty-seven identical gift-wrapped makeup cases and had them mailed to twenty-seven different women. Jack traveled so wide in his sexual sojourns that he doubtlessly thought none of these women would get together to discuss their mutual experiences or betray him to Margaret.

It is not until women have their own children that many of them begin to appreciate the sacrifices their own mothers made for them. It took years before the Kelly siblings understood the dynamics of their family and how their mother, at a great psychic cost, maintained the veneer of a perfect family.

The Kellys had no thespians among their ancestors, but the Irish are a race of storytellers with an inbred love of language, and that was heritage enough. One of Jack's brothers, George, became an actor and a Pulitzer Prize–winning playwright. Another brother, Walter, made a career performing funny skits onstage. And his sister, Grace, who died so young that her namesake never knew her, was a comedienne who performed wearing a tartan and speaking with a Scottish accent.

Jack was an actor too. His stage was his home, where he acted out the part of a loving husband and father. It was a great performance, and Grace and her siblings did not know about his other lives until they were adults. But a child with Grace's sensitivity surely knew all was not as it seemed. She always seemed to be sick, constantly sniffling.

In this family of such vibrant health, Grace was, in her mother's words, "a frail little girl," and by that measure, an outlier.

When Margaret kept her sick daughter home from school, Grace set her dolls out and wrote plays for them, each one speaking a different part. Her dolls were as alive to her as her parents, and it was there that her acting began creating a world apart from them.

Margaret wanted to impart one thing above all others to her three daughters. They must live orderly lives and finish whatever they began. Peggy and Lizanne followed their mother's mandate, but Grace did not. That bewildered her mother. Grace would start knitting a scarf, but soon grew bored and dumped it in her bureau drawer. Then she would start another one, and before long, it too would be cast away. As for the clothes she wore, when she took the garments off, the floor was as likely a repository for them as the closet. Although Grace never spoke out against Margaret, the child's conduct was a passive attack on her mother's values.

What was indulgent behavior for a child was unacceptable in a proper young woman, and Margaret kept thinking that one day Grace would wake up to how she must behave. "I was always picking up after her and hoping she would grow out of it," she said. "She did to some extent, but not entirely."

Margaret had become a Catholic more as a condition of her marriage than as a deeply felt conversion. As for her husband, he saw no reason to commune with God when he enjoyed a good eighteen holes of golf on Sunday. Despite the Kellys' lack of true fidelity, in the fall of 1934, they sent the soon-to-be five-year-old Grace to the Academy of the Assumption in Ravenhill, Philadelphia.

In those years, Catholics, especially women, knew the Church more through the nuns in the schools, hospitals, and other institutions than through the priests standing before them saying mass. The Sisters of the Assumption were a French order who made the Pennsylvania academy their first establishment in America. The nuns prided themselves on their joyous love of God. When they walked down the corridors in their long habits, the sisters had a mysterious aura about them. At school, Grace was known more for her impish behavior than her devotion, tossing food out the window when the nuns weren't looking. Despite her seeming disregard for the rituals of faith, when she left the academy, approaching her thirteenth birthday, she had become Catholic as an essential part of her being.

Her father insisted Grace transfer to the all-girl Stevens School in Germantown, not because the Academy of the Assumption was academically weak or religiously excessive, but because the school did not have sufficient athletic programs for a Kelly. Grace carried a few extra pounds on her five-feet-six-and-a-half-inch-tall frame, and her glasses looked as if they had been chosen to make her look unappealing.

As Grace struggled through the awkward years of early adolescence, acting was her salvation. Being onstage pulled her out of her timid self, set her up beyond her peers, and gave her recognition. She starred not in school productions before audiences largely of her classmates but for the Old Academy Players, a well-regarded amateur group in East Falls.

As Grace won accolades for her performances as Peter Pan and Kate in *The Taming of the Shrew*, she began molting her old being to emerge as a stunning young woman. If the world had considered her beautiful from the time she was an infant, she might well have concluded her looks were enough to get her whatever she wanted. But among the Kellys, she was viewed as rather ordinary in everything, including her appearance. Beauty descended upon her as if out of nowhere, and she did not consider it enough by itself to advance her in the world.

The boys, and these were definitely in the plural, thought Grace's prettiness was quite enough. They were a generation brought up to treat young women with equal measures of affection and deception.

When they were around them, they were all attention and concern, but later, when they met with their buddies, they described just how far they had gotten. Had they copped a feel, unhooked a bra, got their finger far below, or stripped to accomplish anything short of sexual intercourse? They knew just how far the girls at Stevens would go, and few went as far and as often as Grace, who enjoyed it as much as the boys. She flitted from one relationship to the next as quickly as a soap opera heroine, and as she moved from youth to youth, she took her pleasures in the back seat of more than one car, always stopping before giving out her ultimate treasure.

If the boys came to the Kelly residence in hordes because of Grace's attractiveness, she sought after males who were themselves handsome, tall, and manly. Harper Davis met all three categories, plus he had the blessing of being three years older, a man in the teenage parlance. Her father insisted that she break off the romance. When Davis left to go into the navy in 1944, she was momentarily heart-broken. When he returned and came down with multiple sclerosis, Grace's love was long gone, but she was there for him as he suffered through a long, painful death.

Grace's best inheritance from her Kelly blood was her overwhelm-ingly positive attitude. She was not some mindless Pollyanna. It took moral discipline to face life's blows straight on, rarely shirking from them, and then to get up and look up at the sky with fulsome anticipa-tion at the new day. Despite her upbeat attitude, Grace was a more complex person than most around her imagined, and far more ma-nipulative and shrewd than her angelic face might suggest. People huddled around her, seeking her attention, and she knew how to use them. "She always had a way of getting people to do things for her," her sister Lizanne reflected. "You really thought she needed help but she did not need help at all."

No one gets far without luck. Grace had scads of that precious quality without ever kissing the Blarney Stone. Sometimes it was bad luck turned upside down. The year 1947 would forever be known in the Kelly family as the time Kell won the Diamond Challenge Sculls at the Henley Royal Regatta and served his father a frigidly cold dish of revenge.

Everything in the Kelly family focused on Kell's triumph. Grace's parents had no time or interest in taking Grace on a tour of women's colleges until August, when it turned out the schools were all full. That was when Grace decided to apply to study acting in New York City at the American Academy of Dramatic Arts. That was as difficult to get into as any of those colleges, and only by invoking her uncle George's name did she win admittance.

Shortly before Grace left for Manhattan, she went over to pick up a married friend and go off somewhere for a few hours, but when she got there only the husband was present. That should have been signal enough for her to leave, but she made another choice. "I stayed, talking to him, and before I knew it, we were in bed together." Thus, seventeen-year-old Grace lost her virginity.

When Grace arrived in Manhattan for the first time in her life, she was out of hearing of her mother's admonitions and her father's studied disregard. "I rebelled against my family and went to New York to find out who I was—and who I wasn't," Grace said.

Grace was not heading off to college with her girlfriends, excited about sororities and football games. Instead, she was entering a narrowly focused two-year program that created professional actors. Housed in a number of modest rooms above Carnegie Hall, the American Academy was a serious institution skilled in teaching the craft of acting. She was not used to such threadbare quarters, but no matter. The students were an intriguing, richly varied lot, unlike any group with which she has ever been associated.

The academy turned out ladies and gentlemen of the stage and screen who dressed and spoke well. Speaking well meant a strange, crypto, upper-class British accent unlike anything ever heard in England. Appalled at Grace's Philadelphia twang, her teachers did everything but tear out half her tongue to get rid of it. When she went home, her parents thought she would stop fooling around and speak once again like a normal person, but she never did.

Among the promising young actors in her class, Grace did not stand out as likely to join the ranks of such luminary graduates as Lauren Bacall, Kirk Douglas, and Spencer Tracy and become a Hollywood star. She stood out in another way that brought as much jealousy as appreciation. To pay for her thousand-dollar tuition and her room at the Barbizon Hotel for Women, she took modeling gigs. Her face graced the covers of *Redbook* and other magazines and was within their pages selling such sundry products as Old Gold cigarettes and insecticides.

As a candidate for Miss Rheingold, Grace looked down on the city from the tops of buildings. Rheingold was the workingman's beer, and candidates for the honor smiled out of placards in subway cars, where men going to work compared the merits of the various young women and fantasized about what they would like to do with them. It was all far from the Main Line of Philadelphia.

* * *

On her first day at the American Academy, when the new students eyed one another, Grace and Mark "Herbie" Miller stood out by their sheer physical attractiveness. Beautiful people are drawn to beautiful people, and they began a playful love affair. For Grace, it was not enough. She made no pledge of fidelity to Miller. Sex was her great adventure, and she was just beginning that journey.

One of the men Grace met in New York while seeing Miller was Alex D'Arcy. The darkly complexioned, Egyptian-born actor was as handsome as Miller in his way, but he was about forty years old. Most of Grace's peers would have considered it disgusting to have a middle-aged lover, but she was drawn to far older men.

D'Arcy could not have imagined this would be an easy conquest. Beyond the dramatic age difference, Grace seemed shy and reserved, giving off vibes that said, "Do Not Touch." After they had known each other for a few days, D'Arcy reached out to touch Grace's leg in a taxi-cab. "She jumped into my arms," he recalled. "She was a very, very, very sexual girl. You would touch her once, and she would go through the ceiling." D'Arcy learned what many men who followed in his wake would experience. Although dressed in a conservative, pristine manner that was the opposite of provocative, Grace exploded in sexual pleasure if approached properly by the right man.

Grace was the fully realized model of Hitchcock's fantasy woman. As the director envisioned it, a woman dressed as primly as a school-marm could, in an instant, change to a being of unrelieved sexuality. "Anything could happen to you with a woman like that in the back of a taxi," Hitchcock said.

In Hitchcock's scenario, the man was always the aggressor and the woman his conquest. He could hardly imagine a woman manipulating a man into bed, but that was how it often was with Grace. Her looks drew men to her, and she chose men for her pleasure, even if they did not always realize what was happening.

At the beginning of her second year at the academy, the teenage Grace began an affair with another older man, thirty-year-old Don Richardson. The swarthy Richardson had the looks of a leading man, but he had become a Broadway director and was also one of Grace's teachers. When they started talking one evening, he invited her to dinner. Needing some cash, he asked her to come to his walk-up apartment so he could grab some dollars. Richardson was separated from his first wife, and his quarters were furnished so modestly that, he said, "compared to her wealth, this looked like Raskolnikov's lair in *Crime and Punishment*." Fully aware Grace was his student, he had not brought her to his quarters to seduce her.

The unheated apartment was so cold that the first thing Richardson did was to make some coffee. As he returned with the cups in his hands, he found Grace nude on his cot. He knew that what he was about to do was wildly inappropriate, but he was overwhelmed by Grace's body. "I never saw anything more splendid," Richardson said. "She was like something sculptured by Rodin. She had the most beautiful, delicate figure—small breasts, small hips—and her skin was almost translucent." As much as Richardson enjoyed this night of lovemaking, he realized he had done something wrong. But he was in love with Grace, and she was so alluring that he continued the furtive affair.

Richardson was astutely observant. He found it strange the way Grace could hardly talk about her father. It became clear to him she did not have a father in the way she desperately wanted one. "She was always looking for somebody with a father image, somebody who could replace Papa," Richardson said. It wasn't just an emotional alternative she was seeking, but a man who would watch over her and advance her in life. Thus, Richardson was valued in part because he got her an agent at MCA, the powerful Hollywood agency. That was doubly important because, as Grace's time at the academy drew to an end, she had proven herself and could look ahead to an acting career.

Grace was serious about Richardson and had no intention of ending their relationship just because he was no longer her teacher. It was time to take him home for the weekend to Philadelphia to meet her family. Richardson believed Grace was attracted to him in part because he was Jewish, so different from anyone she had known before.

When Grace's family learned about his religion, they had a different reaction. In those years, anti-Semitism was common among Irish-Americans, and the Kellys were appalled Grace would be with such a man.

Jack turned to his son, Kell, to put this interloper in his place. It is often a curse to be the son of a famous man, a double curse if he is seen as a hero, and a triple curse if he is so incomparably strong that a son could never equal him.

Kell did whatever Jack asked him to do. In this instance, Jack had him invite three of his biggest athlete friends, young men whose mere presence was intimidating, to greet Richardson when he arrived. Mrs. Kelly described her daughter's teacher in such a manner that Kell concluded he was "a bit of a creep," and he knew what he and his friends must do.

When Richardson entered the grand living room in East Falls, he expected a convivial greeting. Instead, Kell and his friends told Jewish jokes. They did the stereotypical accent and told stories that would have been offensive enough if passed among their fellow Irish-American Catholics, but unthinkable when spoken to someone Jewish. Demonstrating both his abilities as an actor and how much he cared for Grace, Richardson showed no sign of how insulted and disgusted he felt. As he looked at Grace, he saw her retreating back into this ignored, frightened child in the shadow of the rest of the Kellys.

The next morning, when Grace and Richardson returned to the house after a ride in the countryside and a visit with her playwright uncle, Mrs. Kelly stood in the doorway in a blustering rage. While they were out, she had gone up to Richardson's room and rifled through his belongings. There she found a package of condoms and a letter from his lawyers talking about his divorce.

"Gracie, go to your room," Mrs. Kelly commanded, and her nineteen-year-old daughter meekly obeyed.

"As for *you*," Mrs. Kelly said, not even mentioning Richardson's name, "I want you to leave this house immediately."

Grace and Richardson continued their relationship in an often furtive way, afraid they were being followed by Jack's hirelings. One evening in the middle of the night, Jack showed up at Richardson's apartment to see if the offer of a Jaguar would get him to leave his daughter alone. Richardson could not be purchased for coins of the realm, but as Grace's budding career took her other places, the romance cooled down to room temperature.

In the summers, the Bucks County Playhouse was a favorite venue for New Yorkers and Philadelphians to spend a pleasant evening enjoying theatrical performances. Each year, the academy chose two graduating students to become part of the highly regarded residential company. In the summer of 1949, it was a double honor for Grace to be chosen, since her first role was the ingenue in Uncle George's play *The Torch-Bearers*.

As Grace continued to see Richardson sporadically, she took up with an even older lover, forty-year-old Claudius Charles Philippe. The banquet manager of the Waldorf Astoria Hotel, Philippe projected a worldly image, unlike Richardson's bohemian persona. In an era when, to most Americans, foreign food meant Chinese chop suey in a take-out cardboard box or Italian spaghetti and meatballs, Philippe purveyed to the hotel's clients the most sophisticated of French dining and wines their equal. Speaking English with an accent that was a mixture of French and upper-class British intonations, he persuasively sold events.

On Philippe's arm, Grace no longer appeared the young actress doomed to play the ingenue, but a lady in designer frocks and artful makeup. She walked into the elite venues he took her to with a confident air, as if she had always been there. When the debonair young shah of Iran stayed at the Waldorf, Grace made him one of her conquests. The divorced monarch was satisfied enough to give her jewelry and talk about marriage.

One evening, Grace invited Richardson over to the apartment the Kellys rented for their daughter. As always, they made love. Afterward, she pirouetted before him in one gorgeous gown after another. He had no idea where she'd acquired such outfits. Then she paraded before him nude, except for a gold bracelet laden with emeralds.

As Richardson looked at the bracelet, he remembered he had seen it before on a woman who had slept with Aly Khan. The short, olive-skinned playboy prince had an endless number of affairs. He employed a method he called "*imsak*," which allowed him to make love endlessly, a technique much appreciated by his lovers. At the age of thirty-eight, his stamina was not diminished. Famed for his generosity as much as for his sexual prowess, the bracelets were tokens of appreciation. With so many lovers, it made sense that, as often as not, he passed out the same gift.

Richardson also had other lovers, and he had no reason to feel betrayed, but he did. Grabbing the bracelet, he tossed it into the fish tank, saying he wanted no more to do with her.

"Does the bracelet have anything to do with it?" Grace asked.

"It has everything to do with it," Richardson said.

Richardson got dressed and hurried out the door. As he did so, he turned for one last sentimental glance. Maybe Grace would be crying or wringing her hands in despair. But it was nothing like that. Still nude, she was reaching down into the water to fish out the bracelet.

* * *

Sometimes Grace practiced her signature so that she would be ready to sign autographs when fans deluged her. Her dream was to star on Broadway, and in November 1949, she made her debut playing the distraught daughter in August Strindberg's tragedy *The Father.* She got good reviews, but the production did not and closed after a few weeks. From then on, although Grace continued to perform in summer stock, she largely made her living playing in all kinds of dramas in the early years of television.

Then, in the summer of 1951, came the telegram from movie producer Stanley Kramer that changed Grace's life: "Can you report August 28, lead opposite Gary Cooper. Tentative title *High Noon.*" It was not quite the honor it must have seemed. As an independent producer, Kramer had spent a fortune to sign Gary Cooper, one of the top stars of the day. The producer's wallet was empty, and he could not possibly pay for a second star. "I wanted somebody unknown opposite Gary Cooper," Kramer recalled. "I couldn't afford anybody else. So I signed her."

Cooper played Marshal Will Kane, standing alone against evil. Grace played his bride, Amy Fowler Kane, an uptight, nervous Quaker from the east dropped unceremoniously into a rude frontier town where merciless men come stalking her husband.

Grace's role in the film was subordinate to Cooper's in every way. Despite all the pressure she felt costarring in the film, she had an affair with the fifty-year-old Cooper. The character she played in *High Noon* had a pristine, standoffish quality with not a hint of Grace's volatile sexuality, and the affair had nothing to do with enhancing her performance. Estranged from his wife and ending a relationship with Patricia Neal, Cooper had no place for a public relationship. But Grace loved the surreptitious nature.

Grace's sister Lizanne saw her falling in and out of love with manic speed. She was like the teenager she had been in East Falls, with hordes of boys pursuing her as she flitted from one to another, never settling down for more than a millisecond. These relationships were not just indulgences, affairs out of boredom. She was madly in love for each moment. "Grace was infatuated with Gary Cooper," her sister said. "She was in awe of him, very star-struck." And love or not, when the shooting was over, the dalliance was over.

Cooper won an Academy Award for his performance in the classic Western. Kelly felt she had been too intimidated and insecure to do a good job playing the wife, but her performance worked brilliantly, set off against the stern, uncompromising marshal.

For her next role, Grace flew to Nairobi, Kenya, in November 1952 to play opposite Clark Gable and Ava Gardner in *Mogambo*. Gable is big-game hunter Victor Marswell. One day, the weekly boat delivers the sensuous Eloise "Honey Bear" Kelly (Gardner) to the remote jungle camp. Disappointed to find her maharaja lover has stiffed her and not shown up, Honey Bear quickly turns her attention to Marswell.

Their affair ends almost the moment the next boat arrives, carrying anthropologist Donald Nordley (Donald Sinden) and his wife, Linda (Kelly). She is sporting a pith helmet and a British accent. The repressed Linda looks as if she could have been Amy Kane's sister in *High Noon*, but the unhappily married woman does not stay repressed for very long. When the group goes off on a safari, Linda kisses Marswell, her lips quivering, beside a waterfall, a censor-tolerated metaphor for sex.

The scene was not a difficult one to shoot. Twenty-three-year-old Grace had begun an affair with fifty-one-year-old Gable. The oldest lover Grace had ever had, she called him "Baba," preferring the Swahili word to calling him "Daddy" in English.

Shot at the right angle, Gable still gave off the masculine charisma that made Rhett Butler in *Gone with the Wind* one of the grandest romantic figures in film history. But the shadow of age was descending on the actor. Twenty-eight years older than Grace, he wore false teeth.

Wanting a little macho beefcake, director John Ford had Gable strip to the waist and show off his legs in shorts. But Gable had no hair on his chest. That bothered him so much that he insisted Sinden shave his chest hair and no other cast member expose a hairy chest. For a Christmas spent 9,000 miles from Hollywood, Grace decided to knit Gable a pair of socks. As far as that craft goes, she continued to be full of good intentions rarely fulfilled. When Christmas Eve 1952 approached in the jungle of Tanganyika, the socks were nowhere near completion. So she took one of the actor's own socks, filled them with his belongings, and hung it up as Santa's gift.

If a woman can pilfer a man's socks, it is reasonable to think their intimacy does not end there. Gossip about an affair reached London, where a columnist cabled Gable: "Rumors sweeping England about your romance with Grace Kelly. Please cable confirmation or denial."

"This is the greatest compliment I've ever had," Gable told Grace. "I'm old enough to be your father." Thus spoke the angel of truth.

Mogambo is about as authentic as the Jungle Cruise at Disneyland. Filmed at the beginning of the Mau Mau uprising against the British colonial rule in Kenya, the movie is an apolitical pipe dream full of happy dancing natives and no hint of bloody rebellion. The African actors have no speaking roles. When they are not carrying the sahibs' belongings or paddling them down the river, they stand in a line, raising their spears up and down, chanting in Swahili.

The American film audiences loved *Mogambo*. They knew no more about Africa than did Ava Gardner's character, who thought kangaroos were native to the continent. And the film had an ending that satisfied the moral sensibilities of the time. Linda goes back with her husband, and Marswell takes up again with Honey Bear, intending to marry her. Hollywood loved the movie too. Gardner and Kelly were both nominated for Academy Awards, Ava for her starring role and Grace for Best Actress in a Supporting Role.

* * *

Grace moved on from the African melodrama to playing the female lead in Hitchcock's *Dial M for Murder*. Set in London, where Grace and most of the other actors speak with ersatz British accents, Grace's character, Margot Wendice, had an affair with an American crime writer, Mark Halliday (Robert Cummings). Having discovered his wealthy wife's betrayal, her husband, retired tennis pro Tony Wendice (Ray Milland), decides to have her killed. To do so, Wendice creates an intricately designed murder.

Dial M for Murder is based on a one-set play by the British playwright Frederick Knott that was still playing to full houses on Broadway. Hitchcock left Knott's work largely intact, but made several changes important in creating what proved to be an immensely popular movie. In the play, Margot has come to terms with her marriage and is through with her lover. Thus she is quasi-innocent when her husband sets out to kill her. Hitchcock was not about to have Margot redeem herself at the beginning of the film. *His* Margot is a duplicitous, lustful woman who might well renew her affair with Mark while she stays married to Tony. She is so soiled that it will take a long, tortuous swim through turbulent seas for her to cleanse herself.

Hitchcock believed his task would be to open Grace up and expose the rich sexuality that he knew lay within. "An actress like Grace, who's also a lady, gives a director certain advantages," he reflected later. "He can afford to be more colorful with a love scene played by a lady than one played by a 'hussy.' With a hussy, such a scene can be vulgar, but if you put a lady in the same circumstances, she's exciting and glamorous."

Hitchcock had another reason why he cast "ladylike women" in his films and had nothing but creative disdain for "a big, bosomy blonde." "I have found that an actress with the quality of elegance can easily go down the scale to portray less exalted roles," the director told the *Hollywood Reporter* in 1962. "But an actress without elegance, however competent she may be, can hardly go up the scale. She lacks the range as an actress because she lacks the range as a person. A woman of elegance, on the other hand, will never cease to surprise you."

Although Hitchcock stayed true to the *Dial M for Murder* play, he still found plenty of places to apply his ineffable touch, sometimes aided by Kelly. In the scene where Tony's Oxford classmate Charles Swann (Anthony Dawson) attempts to strangle Margot to death, Swann stands hidden behind a curtain in the living room, near the telephone. He is wearing a trench coat and has a scarf in his hand. At the time agreed upon with Swann, Tony calls the house. Margot rises from her bed and walks through the darkened living room to pick up the phone.

Originally, Hitchcock had Margot wearing a velvet gown. Grace thought that might work for Lady Macbeth in her sleepwalking scene, but not for a woman getting up from bed to answer the phone. Grace had the considerable audacity to challenge the wardrobe choice. Hitchcock was not amused. "Well, what would you put on to answer the phone?" he asked. "I wouldn't put on anything at all," she replied. "I would just get up and answer the phone in my nightgown." "Maybe you're right," Hitchcock said, shrugging.

As Margot hurries across the living room, she is wearing a white gown and looks like a virgin sacrifice. That Tony can call his wife on the phone, knowing that when she picks up his paid killer will strangle Margot, takes his wickedness to an even darker place.

This was the most crucial scene in Kelly's young film career as Margot saves herself from certain death by killing her assailant. The actress wanted to fill the moment with unforgettable horror. Working in television, she had received ample instruction on how to project emotion on-screen. As the camera focused on her, she squinched up her face, eyes wet with fear, mouth twisted in disbelief, effectively portraying the terrible instant.

Hitchcock wanted none of it. He showed only Grace's hand on the scissors that she drove into her would-be killer's back. The actress wanted to do so much more. "He flattered me by telling me my hands were good actors, too," she told *Motion Picture* magazine in 1955. "What he meant was that acting was more than a trick of waving your eyelashes and that to be a success, you had to learn to act with your whole body. I worked so hard after that."

That was one of the great lessons Hitchcock taught Grace. Less is often more. *Dial M for Murder* was shot in color. Most other directors would have drenched the death scene in blood. Hitchcock needed not one drop to create a moment that chilled the audience.

Hitchcock took a whole week to shoot this one-minute scene. He filmed it as a ballet of death. Only the two actors could fully grasp the magnitude of what the director was doing, the precision, the choreography, and the endless attention to each moment. Hitchcock insisted that the living room be dark, further complicating the filming. He shot the scene twelve hours a day. Grace went back to her Hollywood hotel in the evenings with bruises all over her body.

In the scene, the would-be killer Swann reaches out from behind the curtain, puts the scarf around Margot's neck, and begins to strangle her. Reacting instantaneously, Margot turns toward her assailant. Swann pushes her down with brutal resolve and pulls on the scarf. Margot's bare legs twitch as if they are in their death throes. She reaches her hand back and grabs a large pair of scissors and plunges them into Swann's back. He writhes in pain and disbelief and falls backward to the floor, driving the scissors deeper into his dying body.

One of Hitchcock's pleasures in making *Dial M for Murder* was his growing infatuation with Grace. After all these years, he had found his ideal woman. She was an ice princess who melted with the most fervid sexuality, and he was a voyeur who enjoyed watching her. He treated her with a deference that he had shown to none of his other actresses. He called her "Miss Kelly," and she called him "Mr. Hitchcock."

Hitchcock often invited the single actress to his home for dinner. Alma had long since learned to accept her husband's peculiar relationships with his actresses, and she enjoyed Grace's company.

On the set, Hitchcock spent what was for him an unusual amount of time working with Kelly. As he did, he subjected her to the same full range of dirty jokes as the other actresses. Some of them were so foul that they would have turned a cloistered nun to stone, but nothing bothered Kelly. She was endlessly amused, or pretended to be.

"Are you shocked, Miss Kelly?" Hitchcock asked her one day after telling a particularly raunchy story. That was the point, after all.

"Oh, no, Mr. Hitchcock," she replied. "I went to a girls' convent school—I heard all these things when I was thirteen." It probably wasn't true, but telling Hitchcock that whatever he said would not offend her was the best way to shut his ribald stories down.

Hitchcock watched as half the men on the set, it seemed, pursued Kelly, sending flowers to her hotel, wooing her in all kinds of ways. The director expected *his* actresses to apply certain standards in their affairs. Thus he was stunned when Kelly took up with Knott, who had written both the play and the script for *Dial M for Murder*. The British man was as short as a fireplug and a mere writer. By Hitchcock's reckoning, that made him doubly uninviting. "That Grace! She fucked everyone!" Hitchcock exclaimed, something of an exaggeration. "Why, she even fucked little Freddie, the writer."

Knott had been in love with another woman, Ann Hillary, but

Kelly's allure was so overwhelming that it could uproot even the strongest of relationships. The couple made no attempt to hide their affair. It did not take fantastic sleuthing for Sidney Skolsky to write in the *New York Post* on September 8, 1953, "Grace Kelly, who stars in it, and Frederick Knott, who wrote it, are hand-holding after Dial Murder hours."

Soon after that, Knott moved back to his former love, whom he married later that year. Kelly moved on to another lover, who fulfilled Hitchcock's standards. That was her costar, the Welsh-born actor Ray Milland. Unlike Gable, Milland had his own teeth, but the forty-seven-year-old actor wore a toupee. The married Milland presumably knew it was a mistake to get involved with Kelly, but lust has its own logic, and he was enraptured with the young actress.

Milland had a wife problem. Muriel "Mal" Milland married her husband in 1932, when the actor was nowhere in the business. They had two children, and theirs was one of the longest marriages in Hollywood. Mal had helped create the secure home life that allowed her husband to rise to the place where, in 1945, he won an Academy Award playing an alcoholic writer in *The Lost Weekend*, and for a while was the best-paid actor at Paramount.

The couple's marriage had long since lost its early ardor. Milland was not beyond sampling the sweets that passed his way. Mal tolerated these dalliances, but this affair was so serious and so provocatively public that *Confidential* picked up on it. "The whole town soon hee-hawed over the news that suave Milland, who had a wife and family at home, was ga-ga over Kelly. Ray pursued her ardently and Hollywood cackled," the scandal sheet wrote.

Mal did more than cackle. She told one of her friends that if Milland did not return to the fold, she would publicize the letters Kelly had written to her husband. It would not have been a scandal as big as

Bergman's affair with Rossellini, but it likely would have been enough to damage their careers severely. Milland returned to home and hearth, and once again Kelly moved on, but with a growing reputation as a seducer of her leading men. The *New York Journal-American* was so bold as to call her "an off-screen jinx domestic-wise to her leading men."

While romancing Kelly, Milland played an unspeakable villain with perfect aplomb. Tony manipulates the death scene, so Margot is convicted of murdering Swann and sentenced to death. Evil is often more complex and fascinating than goodness, and Tony dominates the film, not Margot, who blandly accepts her unspeakable fate. Early in the movie, Margot is dressed in brilliant red and stunning scarlet. In these last scenes, she wears somber brown, and her face is as pale as a death mask.

On the day before Margot is to be hanged, Chief Inspector Hubbard (John Williams) proves Tony had contracted to kill his wife and that Margot is innocent. "What's the matter with me, Mark?" Margot laments to her former lover. "I don't ever seem to feel anything." Kelly may have been speaking not only about the character on the screen.

* * *

During the shooting, Hitchcock was more excited discussing with Kelly his next film, *Rear Window*, than musing about *Dial M for Murder*. "He sat and talked to me about it all the time, even before we had discussed my being in it," Kelly recalled. "He was very enthusiastic as he described all the details of a fabulous set while we were waiting for the camera to be pushed around."

For Hitchcock, making a film meant solving one problem after another. In *Rear Window*, Hitchcock got into the filmmaking process at the earliest point and put his stamp on every element. He did that in the most disciplined, systematic way.

The film is based on a short story by the prolific mystery writer Cornell Woolrich. In Woolrich's tale, a man with a broken leg overseen by a Black helper looks out the window to see that in another apartment a husband has murdered his wife. Out of that threadbare foundation, Hitchcock built an intricate psychological drama full of complexity and nuance.

With the help of screenwriter John Michael Hayes, Hitchcock turned the main character into a photographer based in part on Robert Capa. The director had known Capa as he pursued Bergman on and off the set. Hitchcock appreciated the drama of the photographer's life and transposed elements of it to *Rear Window*.

Capa only came alive at the forefront of war. In peace, he could find nothing to shoot that gave his life meaning. Shortly after the completion of *Rear Window*, forty-year-old Capa died in Vietnam stepping on a land mine while covering the war, the only thing he felt called to do.

Hitchcock was filming a romantic thriller, and he could not fill the lead character, L. B. "Jeff" Jefferies (James Stewart), with as much darkness as Capa, but the dilemma was the same, even if in places he painted in pastel shades. Photojournalism is a young man's profession, and the aging Jeff traveled the world shooting wars and all kinds of compelling stories. His was a tough, competitive business, and by the measure of the images on his apartment walls, he was good at what he did. Jeff can't face up to a different kind of life any more than Capa could.

Jeff's masculinity is based on what he does, not what he is. He hurt himself standing on a race track, taking pictures, when a wheel came off a car. In doing so, he broke not only his leg but his manhood. As he sits alone, mildly disheveled, he is an impotent man unwilling to assume the full mantle of adult manhood.

The director could not make a film without a significant love interest. That became the fashion executive Lisa Fremont. When Kelly signed early on to play the part, there was plenty of time for her to have input. To her face, Hitchcock was always flattering. Out of her sight, he was, at times, not so complimentary. "She has a lot of charm and talent," Hitchcock told Hayes, "but she goes through the motions as if she is in acting school. She does everything properly and pleasantly, but nothing comes out of her."

Kelly had not had roles that allowed her to display her abilities at full force, but that failure was not hers. The director asked the screenwriter to get together with the actress to see if he could open her up. That was a patronizing thing to suggest, and when they met, Kelly had no idea what Hayes was trying to do.

Hayes was a handsome young gentleman and a classy dresser of the sort appreciated by the sartorially concerned Hitchcock. The screenwriter had a gorgeous blond wife and a penchant for quick, witty dialogue, both qualities the director also admired. The screenwriter and the actress spent many hours together during the following week. No man could be near Kelly without being struck by her beauty. There was no longer a touch of the winsome ingenue in her. She was a woman at the height of her allure. That could not help but affect the role he created for her. It was not just her looks that intrigued Hayes. She was droll and whimsical, full of sides he had hardly imagined, a fully realized person in her own right.

Thanks to that week and the screenwriter's empathetic understanding, Hayes produced a character tailored to Kelly. "I combined the best that I saw in Grace Kelly, the best in my wife, and created the character of Lisa, and it went very well," he said. For Kelly, it was the difference between being presented with a store-bought suit to wear or an outfit tailored so perfectly to her frame that she could play the role as a version of herself.

Lisa's beauty opens the world to her, and she travels in the haut monde of the rich, apart from the rest of humanity. She is drawn to Jeff because he is different. The man is dangerous and compelling, and she wants to rein him in and take him into her world properly bridled.

Hitchcock had gotten down to 189 pounds, a little more than half his highest weight of 340 pounds, and he felt good about himself. *Rear Window* proved to be one of the best directing experiences of Hitchcock's career. The director appreciated better than anyone the extraordinary instrument of filmmaking constructed in six weeks on Stage 18. One of the largest sets ever built at Paramount, it rose five and six stories high and was 185 feet long and 98 feet wide.

This realistic rendering of a gritty Greenwich Village apartment complex included a courtyard and thirty-one apartments, twelve of them fully furnished. Lighting the massive set took a thousand or more giant arc lights supplemented by two thousand smaller lamps. There was even audio linking the director and his team to the actors in the various apartments.

As unique as it was, the set was worthless without a strong script. Hayes had delivered that in spades. As for his two stars, Hitchcock had worked with Stewart and Kelly before and would work with them again. They understood what the director wanted and gave it to him in quantities big and small. They were never needy and were always there. Compelling actors surrounded the two stars. Even the smallest part had been cast with consummate concern.

To the director, clothes were a way of exposing character and enriching the story he was telling. That was simpler in *Dial M for Murder*, where Kelly's dresses evolved from scarlet to somber as she changed from a privileged young woman to a convicted murderer. There was no such dramatic evolution in *Rear Window*, and Hitchcock told dress designer Edith Head to create five outfits that made the actress "look like a piece of Dresden china, something slightly untouchable."

There was only one problem with the costumes. That was the scene in which Kelly wore a dressing gown. As she walked onto the set, Hitchcock was disappointed that his young star's breasts appeared small. As close as he had grown to Kelly, that was not a matter he was about to discuss with her. Instead, he called over Head and said Kelly would have to wear falsies.

Head had the unenviable task of going to the star's dressing room and telling her. "I told her I wouldn't wear them," Kelly recalled. "Finally, she said, 'I'll try to take it in here and pull it up there.' So I pulled the peignoir down, and I stood up as straight as I could and walked back to the set without falsies. Hitch took one look and smiled. 'There, now, Grace—that's more like it. See what a difference they make?' We never told him that we changed nothing."

Hitchcock would do almost anything to make the movie he wanted to make. One day they were shooting a scene in which the director wanted to show Jeff and then move across the courtyard to the apartment of the murderous traveling salesman Lars Thorwald (Raymond Burr). Cameraman Robert Burks told Hitchcock that to get that shot with both characters in focus, he would have to cut the lens way down and bathe the scene in brilliant light. There weren't enough lights on the soundstage to do that, so Hitchcock appropriated all the unused lighting at Paramount. When that did not work, he called over to MGM and borrowed all their big lights, and when that still was not enough, he got a few more big lights from Columbia.

At this point, the lighting was so intense that it was as if the tropical sun had risen over the set. Burks was finally satisfied that he could get the shot the director wanted. Just as he was beginning filming, the heat set off the sprinklers, not just a dribbling of water, but a torrent so intense that the actors could hardly see one another across the set.

"Well, see if somebody can turn off the water," Hitchcock told Burks. "And, in the meantime, could somebody bring me an umbrella?"

That day the waters came down without Hitchcock calling for them, but the director controlled every other moment on the set. He wanted even his friend Stewart to know there was only one god on this set: Alfred Hitchcock. One day, he took him aside and showed him a shot of the actor looking at Miss Torso, who is displaying herself half-naked to her neighbors in the courtyard. Naturally enough, Stewart's eyes sparkle with lascivious intent. Then he showed him the same shot, but this time he is watching a mother and her baby, and his eyes appear full of tender sentiment.

The actors could boast all they wanted, but Hitchcock was the puppeteer, making his marionettes dance to whatever music he chose. And dance well they did.

Rear Window was shot in a roughly chronological order, making it easier for the actors to relate emotionally to their parts. As the film begins, a deeply tanned Jefferies sits in his wheelchair with a cast on his leg. The photographer looks out his window to observe the scene in the courtyard apartments day and night. Sitting immobile with a broken leg, he has little else that interests him.

"He's a real Peeping Tom," Hitchcock told François Truffaut in his lengthy series of interviews with the French director. Hitchcock shot the film from Jefferies's perspective. The audience are Peeping Toms too, standing behind Jefferies, looking at everything he sees. Hitchcock is the high prince of voyeurism. Jefferies is his surrogate doing the master's bidding.

New Yorkers know they are living in a city of voyeurs, and they learn to keep their blinds down. But here, most of these apartment dwellers are full partners in Jefferies's obsession, keeping their shades up and their lives open to whoever cares to observe. As Jefferies looks out shamelessly, he witnesses a series of lives in urban America with full measures of joy, hope, determination, uncertainty, pathos, and despair.

Across the way, Miss Torso is performing her dance routine, which looks like a burlesque performance in the photojournalist's honor. A songwriter (Ross Bagdasarian) sits at his piano, the one person at work on this torpid day. Lars Thorwald, a traveling cosmetic jewelry salesman, rolls up his sleeves. At the same time, in an adjoining window, his bedridden wife (Irene Winston), in her negligee, puts a compress on her forehead. Later on, Jefferies observes the aging Miss Lonely Hearts (Judith Evelyn), who has only one thing on her yellowing docket: to find a man.

For a Peeping Tom, the ultimate get is a couple in the act. A newlywed couple (Rand Harper and Havis Davenport) have arrived in their apartment. Surely sooner or later, and probably sooner, they will go into their bedroom, and as likely as not Jefferies will be there watching.

As Jefferies continues shamelessly observing this world, he receives a call from his editor at the *Life*-like magazine that publishes most of his work. The editor says that because of Jefferies's broken leg, he is sending another photojournalist to troubled Kashmir.

Jefferies is distraught. "I'm gonna get married, and then I'll never be able to go anywhere," he tells his editor. If he marries Lisa, he fears he will lose his itinerant, restless, peripatetic lifestyle and end up in the suburbs of the soul in a life dominated by his wife.

Early in his career, the young James Stewart starred in two films directed by Frank Capra that celebrated ordinary Americans behaving in extraordinary ways. In the days of the Great Depression, films such as *You Can't Take It with You* and *Mr. Smith Goes to Washington* were wonderful uplifts for moviegoers. Stewart left that world to enter the armed forces. He never talked much about all he had seen and felt flying B-24s over Germany.

When Stewart got back, he found people had gotten more sophisticated or cynical, call it whichever you want, and Capra's take on life seemed sentimental. The audience had moved on, and so did Stewart, who began taking on roles of moral complexity. "I look for a man whose judgment is not always too good and who makes mistakes," Stewart reflected. "I think human frailty is a very nice thing to portray."

In *Rear Window*, Stewart manages to maintain his immensely likable on-screen image while not shirking from portraying the dark sides of the character he plays. To protect his home life, Stewart almost turned down the part. His wife, Gloria, was friends with Muriel Milland, who told her how the jezebel Grace Kelly seduced her poor husband on the set of *Dial M for Murder* and how the shameless actress might do it again to her husband. During the shooting, Stewart paid inordinate attention to his wife and kept his distance from Kelly, trying to dampen his wife's suspicions.

"I could see why many of her leading men fell in love with her," Stewart reflected. "If I'd been of a mind, I could have been one of those fellas who fell for her when working with her. But I'm too darned sensible for that." It is easy to be sensible when your wife stands behind you, sniffing the air for a scent of betrayal.

Most directors would have filmed Kelly's first scene in *Rear Window* by having Lisa enter Jefferies's apartment as the camera lovingly focuses on her. Then the stunning young woman would walk forward as the audience travels along until she kisses Jefferies.

Hitchcock had a more inspired idea. Jefferies is half-asleep in his wheelchair when a streak of darkness passes across his face. He looks up to see Lisa so close he can smell her perfume. Her lips are a vivid red, matching in intensity the blue of her eyes and the limpid milkiness of her skin. After kissing him intensely yet gently, she steps backward. As she does, she turns on the lights in the shrouded apartment until she is bathed in light, standing in a dazzling gown. It is not only the room Lisa has lit up but Jefferies's life.

During World War II, women wore sexless uniforms, pants, long skirts, and austere outfits to march off to parade grounds, factories, and offices. But now the war's masculine business had ended, and with it the restraints on how women dressed. Femininity returned with a vengeance, asserting its full rights.

Lisa stands before Jefferies dressed in a layered white net skirt, black fitted top, and pearl necklace, a hymn to femininity. The outfit celebrated the female form in the tradition of Christian Dior's 1947 New Look. In this role and others, Kelly portrayed a postwar woman who uses her femininity to get what she wants as aggressively as any man. Because she projects a cool-to-the-core essence and unmatchable gentility, she can do things and say things that would have been vulgar coming from another actress.

There is nothing passive about Lisa's womanliness. She taunts the largely disinterested Jefferies with her sensuous allure. Not just a sexual creature, Lisa is warm and vulnerable. This exquisite creature has descended onto earth and entered Jefferies's modest apartment, seeking to marry him.

"Isn't it time you came home?" she asks him, suggesting he start a studio and become a fashion photographer.

Jefferies is unwilling to face up to any other kind of life than his own. "Let's stop talking nonsense," he says.

Lisa is so angry with Jefferies that she mocks his beloved profession, saying, "It's like being a tourist on an endless vacation." Jefferies tells her to shut up. He fears Lisa will neuter him, turning him into her boy toy.

Lisa is, in some ways, a narcissistic, spoiled woman. Her love for Jefferies is the most generous thing in her life, an overwhelming emotion that takes her out of herself. As she leaves that evening, shutting the door behind her, it appears doubtful she will wait much longer for this man who spurns her.

Sitting in his wheelchair, Jefferies looks out on a courtyard as dark as his mood. It is raining. For the next six minutes, no words are spoken. The moviegoer sees what Jefferies sees, and although there is no dialogue, they understand not only what he sees but what he thinks. It is Hitchcock at his best.

Jefferies watches as Thorwald leaves his apartment wearing a rain slicker and carrying a suitcase. It is 1:55 in the morning per Jefferies's watch. At 2:35, the salesman returns with the same bag. Thorwald leaves again with the suitcase. Jefferies nods off. When he wakes, he sees Thorwald returning yet again carrying the same valise. Jefferies is dozing again, when Thorwald and a woman leave the apartment. Jefferies is growing convinced that Thorwald has murdered his invalid wife.

When Lisa arrives in the evening wearing a svelte black dress, she believes Jefferies is a sick voyeur whose disease is growing out of control. She glances out the window and sees Thorwald putting ropes around a large wardrobe trunk and decides her love is not as loony as she suspected. He is onto something. We have a murder mystery on our hands, and Jefferies and Lisa are equal partners in its unraveling.

The next evening, Lisa arrives and takes a sensuous negligee out of her Mark Cross bag. It is not an outfit worn at a pajama party, and the audience has the right to surmise that it is not only a murder mystery being consummated that night in Jefferies's apartment.

But the mystery trumps the romance, and the next day Lisa daringly enters Thorwald's apartment, looking for evidence. Thorwald returns, and while he wrestles with her, Jefferies calls the police, who arrest Lisa for robbery. She is bailed out and returns to Jefferies's apartment, where it is clear Thorwald is onto them. The salesman enters the apartment and fights with Jefferies, throwing the photographer out the window, where he breaks his other leg. The police arrive to arrest Thorwald.

Hitchcock thought Hollywood happy endings were a fraudulent betrayal of life as it is, but in this instance, in the last few moments of the film, he and screenwriter Hayes threw fairy dust across the courtyard. Jefferies sits in his wheelchair, fully domesticated, both of his legs in casts. As Lisa monitors her charge, she tries to read *Beyond the High Himalayas*, prepping herself on Jefferies's world, but it is tough going, and she puts the book down to read a more inviting matter, *Harper's Bazaar.*

Years later, when Hitchcock was asked if he thought the romance would last, he said he did not think so. Once Jefferies got back on his own two legs, he would be off somewhere exotic, and Lisa would be back among her stylish friends. But even if their romance wasn't fated to last, the movie was. Not only did *Rear Window* prove immensely popular, it won Hitchcock his fourth Academy Award nomination for Best Director and is considered by critics as one of the best thrillers of all time.

* * *

Kelly had such singular success working with Hitchcock on *Rear Window* that she was delighted to fly to France in May 1954 to co-star in *To Catch a Thief,* a frothy romantic thriller as substantive as a dessert soufflé. This elegant travelogue of a film opens with a shot of a travel agency window featuring posters of France ("If you love life you'll love FRANCE!") and the model of a passenger ship. Mass travel had not yet begun, and the moviegoers would vicariously travel to the French Riviera, a land that, to most of them, is as exotic as the steppes of Tibet.

Kelly plays Frances "Francie" Stevens, an American heiress who has come to Cannes with her mother (Jessie Royce Landis) in pursuit of a husband. Francie's coolness hides a startling sexual aggressiveness similar to Lisa's in *Rear Window*.

The man Francie pursues is Cary Grant, who came out of semiretirement to play John "The Cat" Robie, a retired jewel thief and Resistance hero. The fifty-year-old actor is so perfectly tanned that he looks like he had been turned out on a spit. Twenty-four-year-old Kelly may have been half Grant's age, but the actor still was legitimately a matinee idol, and the April–September romance does not appear as improbable as their ages might suggest.

The burglar Robie is the key to the tale. As lithe as a feline, he descended into the homes of the rich, plucked away their jewelry, and disappeared into the night before they realized he had even been there. After serving time in prison in the thirties for his crimes, he redeemed himself by fighting in the French Resistance. His former colleagues had a similar career path. They are angry with him because a jewel thief has gone to work on the Riviera using Robie's signature techniques. They fear the cat burglar has returned to work, putting them all at risk of being locked up again.

One of the retired thieves, Bertani (Charles Vanel), owns a Monte Carlo restaurant, where many of his old associates work. Like Robie's friends, the police are convinced he has returned to his criminal ways, and they will soon be arresting him. The only way for the legendary thief to save himself is to find the actual criminal and find him quickly.

John Michael Hayes scattered sexually charged banter throughout his screenplay, which propelled the story along. Despite his efforts, it remains a wildly improbable tale with holes in the plot as large as those in the soles of a beggar's shoes. The film has little of the tension and popcorn-gorging drama of a typical Hitchcock production. It is done with playful banter and wit, a romp through some of the most beautiful scenery in the world. There is one stunning scene after another along the Mediterranean, filmed with as much concern as the close-ups of Grant and Kelly.

Much of *To Catch a Thief* takes place at the Carlton Hotel in Cannes. Francie and her mother are staying at the luxury hotel when, one evening, they meet Robie. The reformed jewel thief is dressed impeccably in evening clothes that fit him like skin. Francie is wearing a powder-blue Grecian-style gown without jewelry. Robie studiously ignores the young heiress, a patented means to attract a woman who thinks she demands attention. The camera pays no special notice to her either.

At the end of an evening gambling at the casino, Robie escorts the Stevenses to their rooms. As he says good night to Francie, she reaches out and plants a passionate kiss on his surprised lips, before immediately retreating to her suite. Hitchcock viewed the scene like a lustful teenager. To the director, "it was as if though she'd unzipped Cary's fly."

The embrace was such a non sequitur that it might have been faulted as bad writing on Hayes's part, but the scene did precisely what Hitchcock wanted it to do. It defined Francie as ready to explode sexually. From the director's perspective, the momentary embrace was not so unthinkable. He fondly recalled the evening in New York when he walked Kelly back to her hotel room and she kissed him, then turned and shut the door. If that moment was more than the director's wishful memory, it was probably a sisterly peck.

After their first meeting, Francie and Robie go for a swim in the Mediterranean on the beach across from the Carlton. Also in the water is the youthful Danielle Foussard (Brigitte Auber). Danielle is infatuated with Robie and views Francie as over-the-hill competition.

"But what has she got more than me except money?" Danielle asks Robie. "Why do you want to buy an old car if you can get a new one cheaper? It will run better and last longer."

Auber cringed at the dialogue. "Danielle, my character, has terrible manners," the French actress said. "I was ashamed that she would dare talk like that about Grace Kelly."

Auber and Grant had something in common. The actress had grown up in the circus. She had performed everything from the high wire and the trapeze to bareback riding. Grant had done much the same as a young man. Aspects of that remained within him.

A successful cat burglar is an athlete capable of stealthily creeping along roofs in the dead of night and climbing down walls and chimneys. Auber noticed how Grant incorporated that in his portrayal of Robie. "What I loved about his character, The Cat, was that feline way he had of walking," Auber said. "He invented that for this film."

Hitchcock had little time for Auber during the shooting, but the two kept in touch. Her father had died recently, and Hitchcock treated her with what she took as "parental tenderness." His concern so moved her that she did special things for him. Knowing how much he loved vintage burgundy, she had a special bottle delivered to him in London, where he was on a business trip.

Whenever Hitchcock was in Paris, he took Auber to dinner, where the conversation was as memorable as the wine. On one occasion, as they sat talking in Auber's little car after another special evening before saying goodbye, Hitchcock reached over and kissed her on the mouth. "I shied away immediately," the actress told Patrick McGilligan, author of the definitive Hitchcock biography, *Alfred Hitchcock: A Life in Darkness and Light.* "I said, 'It's not possible.' It was an enormous disappointment for me. I had never imagined such a thing."

Auber was not angry but sorrowful. She remembered what Grant had said about the director. He told her Hitchcock "likes me a lot, but at the same time, he detests me. He'd very much like to be in my place because he can imagine himself in my place." Grant was irresistible to women. Hitchcock was the opposite, and it pained him beyond measure.

"It is difficult when someone is so ugly, like him," Auber said. "That turned-out lower lip. When someone is ugly, it isn't their fault. The poor cabbage had a wonderful soul, I know."

Hitchcock wanted to continue the friendship, but Auber said that was impossible.

* * *

Grant and Kelly had romantic rapport on-screen, the equal of Katharine Hepburn and Spencer Tracy, but off-screen, they were nothing more than buddies. Grant's wife, Betsy Drake, was with him in Cannes, as was Kelly's latest flame, the dress designer Oleg Cassini, and there was not even thwarted desire between the two stars. But when the cameras rolled, not only did they play off each other, but they added their own bits to the romantic repartee. Hitchcock generally abhorred improvisation, but the two actors were so attuned to their characters and so adept at tinkering with Hayes's dialogue that Hitchcock let them go at it.

In those years, many Americans thought of the French as an amoral people whose main contribution to postwar society was the bikini. The fact that few of the decriers had ever been to France did not stop them from envisioning beaches full of young women prancing around in what in a decent country would be considered underwear, and skimpy underwear at that. It figured that if one was going to make a mainstream film full of sexual innuendo, the Côte d'Azur was the place to do it.

Hitchcock let the double entendres roll. The director was still a naughty boy, proud he could ignore the stern voices of authority. In *To Catch a Thief,* he scooted past the censors some of the most suggestive dialogue to make it into a popular film of the era. As a master at light comedy, Grant spoke the words with the gentlest of touches, and Kelly replied in kind.

When Robie and Francie sit in a roadster high above the sea, she pulls out a lunch basket and offers him a piece of cold chicken. Knowing that she would be making a pass at Robie in the scene, Kelly conferred with Edith Head about just what she should wear. They chose a sleeveless coral-pink top emblazoned with white patterns, a pink pleated skirt, and white driving gloves. It is perfectly ladylike, but somewhere there lay seductive powers.

"Do you want a leg or a breast?" Francie asks.

"You make the choice," Robie replies, looking at her, not the chicken.

"How long has it been?" Francie asks, not referring to a meal of chicken.

In a later scene, Robie is with Francie in her suite. She is wearing an exquisite strapless evening gown garnished with a sparkling diamond necklace. As Robie kisses Francie, the fireworks explode like a barrage on D-Day, rising to a thunderous climax. Hitchcock wanted to match those images and blistering sounds with equally orgiastic music, but to disarm the censors, he toned that down. Terminally repressed America feasted on even the most rudimentary sign of sexual activity. Given that, the Paramount publicity department proudly noted that Kelly had been "kissed continuously by Grant for two and a half working days—20 hours." It was a wonder the two stars had any lips left.

Kelly's relationship with Oleg Cassini set off their own belated fireworks. He had been introduced to her by the French actor Jean-Pierre Aumont, with whom she'd had an affair in 1953. The dress designer had been wooing her for months, inundating Kelly with flowers almost daily. When the actress was physically attracted to a man, she did not play the reluctant maiden. Thus, it was somewhat inexplicable that when Cassini flew from New York to be with Kelly in Cannes, she had still not slept with him.

Cassini fancied himself a great lover. To him, the physical act was the least intriguing part of the drama. It was the quest, the hunt, the seduction. That he had never spent so many weeks bedding a woman made Kelly even more desirable and, in his mind, his inevitable success a more incredible triumph.

Cassini's father, Count Alexander Loiewski, lost almost everything in the Russian Revolution. Oleg inherited something more valuable than a title and money: tawny good looks, championship skills on the tennis court, and social confidence that could take him anywhere. Although he created no great original styles as a dress designer, he knew what worked in the haute couture salons of Paris, and he gave versions of that to his customers and sold them with boundless acumen. He had been married twice, most notably to the actress Gene Tierney, and in most places would not have been considered premier marriage material.

Kelly was absorbed in making the film and had little time for her would-be lover. He flitted in and out of her daily life at her beck and call, waiting for the opportunity he was sure would come. Although he appeared to be Kelly's devoted servant, Cassini never forgot what he had flown across the Atlantic to obtain.

As much as Cassini sought his ultimate prize, the designer had a business to run in New York, and there was a limit to how long he could play Kelly's lapdog. Deciding to give it one last shot, he concocted a well-thought-out scheme. First of all, he had to get Kelly away from any distractions. He took her on a raft to a secluded cove, just the two of them, a picnic lunch, and bottles of cold duck and Montrachet '49.

Cassini was not as handsome as Grant, nor as masculine as Cooper, but he was the master of romantic soliloquy. He wooed Kelly with words. "My persistence and devotion should give you some indication of the depths of my feelings," he said. "I am tired of chasing about. There is no need for artifice any longer."

When the couple returned to Cannes, Kelly invited Cassini to her suite, where they made love. "I was enraptured, aware only of the transcendence of the moment, the perfection that she was," he said, excessive in everything, including language. Cassini decided the hell with his business; he would stay in Cannes for what he called "the most enchanting days I ever had in my life."

Hitchcock often invited Kelly and Cassini for dinner. Not only did the director choose the restaurant he went to each evening, but he also selected the menu and the wine and dominated the conversation. Anticipating a gourmet repast, the director starved himself all day long, justifying his gluttonous assault on the plates before him. The other guests were often the Grants.

It was apparent from the day Grant and Kelly arrived in Cannes that they treated stardom differently. A master of public image, Cassini told Kelly it was a mistake that she arrived on the set dressed down. "Be glamorous, be *perfect*," he lectured. "It will create a mystique about you." With *Rear Window*'s success, Kelly became one of the most prominent female stars in America, but she was not going to let that consume her life. When the cameras were on, she played the Grace Kelly the public came to see. The rest of the time, she wanted to play herself.

As one of the highest-paid stars in Hollywood, Grant had perks beyond any other actor. His contract stated that work had to stop at 6:00 p.m. The agreement also said he would have an American limousine with a liveried driver. That would have been fine in Los Angeles, but the massive vehicle was absurdly out of place on the narrow roads above the Mediterranean.

Even if the enormous car had not been so miscast, Kelly would have cringed at the idea of riding in a vehicle that brought constant attention wherever it went. After a while, even Grant decided it was not such a great idea. The actor said he preferred a modest roadster. But modesty was not Grant's thing, and he soon decided he wanted his limousine back. As much as that infuriated the producers, they ordered up another limousine, flown in a freight plane to Nice.

In July, after six weeks in southern France, the cast and crew returned to the Paramount studios in Hollywood to do the interior shots. The film ends with a spectacular scene at a fancy-dress masquerade ball in a grand villa full of rooms where diamond-wearing guests are staying, an irresistible venue for a jewel thief. As the elaborately garbed guests parade by, it could have been a ball at Versailles during the reign of Louis XIV, though those ball-goers would not have been quite so excessive in their dress.

Hitchcock had no higher purpose in shooting this elaborate scene over a week than to display Kelly. This exacting creature walks in wearing a gown that looks as if it was made out of spun gold. Robie is wanted by the police. He walks behind Francie wearing a Moor's black mask as his elaborate disguise and holding a grand parasol.

Despite the heavy security, a cat burglar cannot resist the allure of scores of bejeweled ladies, and he strikes in the middle of the night. Robie lights out after him onto the roof of the villa. The police think they have their man and shoot at him. Evading their bullets, Robie pursues the lithe, darting figure of the secretive bandit across the roof. Robie had suspected for some time that it was none other than Danielle, and he is right.

This was a long, difficult shot high above the soundstage. Grant and Auber had plenty of time to talk between takes. As Auber looked down, she saw two priests standing below. It did not occur to her that they were likely extras in the crowd scene at the ball.

"Who are they?" Auber asked.

"Just some friends of mine," Grant replied.

"You know some priests?" the actress queried. She had not known Grant had contacts with minions of the Catholic Church.

"Well, they're there for you," he said, perfectly deadpan. "If you fall, they will give you the last rites."

With Danielle and the gang's leader, Bertani, off to jail, there is nothing to prevent Robie and Francie from living happily ever after. But there is always a footnote. As Francie prepares to ensconce herself in Robie's villa, she says, "Mother will love it up here."

Almost every morning of the shooting in Los Angeles, Cassini drove Kelly to work. She had agreed to marry him, and they were inseparable. As excited as the dress designer was, he was taken aback when his fiancée started talking about the wedding details with all the giddy enthusiasm of a Long Island debutante. Kelly's sisters were getting married, and she wanted what they sought: a loyal husband, a warm home, and healthy children.

Before Kelly and Cassini married, there was one task they both viewed with trepidation. The couple would have to make the trek to Philadelphia for Cassini to pass muster before the assembled forces of the Kelly family.

Cassini was a worldly gentleman with unimpeachable manners that he took with him wherever he went. The Kellys were Irish-American provincials. To them, manners were something you showed to your own kind, not to the likes of this European dandy.

The whole weekend, Mr. Kelly said not a word to Cassini. He looked through him, showing by that cruel stare that, to his mind, his daughter's worthless beau did not even exist. Cassini had a right to expect some support from the woman he loved—a heartful hug, a word of caution to her father, an admonition to her brother—but she sat passive and quiet like her teenage self, saying not a word.

The Kellys called for a moratorium on the relationship, six months that Kelly and Cassini would not see each other. Kelly was a strong-willed, independent woman of means. She had made her way in adult life without her parents' support. Yet the Kellys sought to control their daughter. As much as Kelly tried, she could not find her way out of this maze.

Although Kelly did not formally agree to the hiatus, the relationship was never quite the same. A prima donna in his own right, Cassini became jealous and diffident, smelling betrayal everywhere. He was right to be suspicious. During the making of her latest film, *The Country Girl*, she had an affair with her costar, William Holden, and others also sweetened her nights.

Kelly felt she needed her diversions. She made six films over fourteen months, six films where she had no time for a life beyond the set, six films that defined her. When she exited that long tunnel, she discovered that she had become a great star and she was alone. "Looking back, I'm not sure how I survived," she reflected years later.

Unhappiness welled up in Kelly and took over her being. She told an interviewer for a cover story in the *Saturday Evening Post* about her life in Los Angeles, "I have many acquaintances here, but few friends. . . . Fear covers everything out here like the smog." The millions of readers of the weekly magazine would have exchanged lives with her in a moment, and she sounded ungrateful about all she had. No matter, she was a truth-teller, and that was how she felt.

As an actress, Kelly controlled her emotions, but off-screen she often cried. Full of anger, sometimes she despised her so-called friends, if they were friends at all. One moment, she would not want to hear of Cassini, the next moment, she wrote him letters full of bountiful words of love ("I so hope that we shall never stop growing and developing our minds and souls and love for God and each other, and that each day will bring us closer. I love you and want to be your wife.").

Kelly believed the executives at MGM cared nothing for her. They shuttled her between studios on loan-outs, little better than chattel, running her from film to film with little concern for her emotional well-being. She would get even in the only way that made sense—walking away from it all, leaving them to their pathetic games.

As angry as she was at her life in filmdom, there was one film Kelly felt she had to make. That was *The Swan*, based on a 1920 play by the Hungarian playwright and novelist Ferenc Molnár. Set in a mythical central European country in 1910, Napoleon has left Princess Beatrix's family bereft of its lands and privileges. The only way to redeem themselves is for Beatrix's daughter, Princess Alexandra, to marry their distant cousin Crown Prince Albert. When the prince's mother dies, he will ascend to the throne and his wife will be queen.

Albert is making the rounds of the great houses of Europe, looking for a proper wife. In his continuing quest, he descends on the family estate. Alexandra is infatuated with her brothers' handsome young tutor, Dr. Nicholas Agi, but the commoner is not a suitable match. She does not love Prince Albert and scarcely knows him, but to please her mother and fulfill her family obligations, she agrees to marry the prince and become his queen.

This ending may have worked when the play was first made into movies in 1925 and 1930. In Kelly's era, it was almost unthinkable that a woman would give up her quest for personal happiness to please her mother and advance family fortunes. Yet the story resonated with Kelly in ways that seemed inexplicable, exposing part of her that Kelly herself likely did not understand.

Billed as a romantic comedy, there was little true romance in *The Swan* and only snippets of humor. Kelly played Alexandra with modest diffidence and dignity. Alec Guinness played Prince Albert. The British actor was nobody's idea of a matinee idol, making it almost unseemly that Alexandra would marry him. The clear choice would have been the debonair young French actor Louis Jourdan, who played the tutor, Dr. Agi. In most Hollywood films, in the last reel, Princess Alexandra and Dr. Agi would have jumped into a carriage and ridden off together to a new life in a new world. But that was not to be.

It is difficult enough making a film, and then you have to go out and promote it. The constant attention overwhelmed Kelly. The demands reached a new level when, in March 1955, she won the Academy Award for Best Actress for her role as the loyal bedraggled wife of an alcoholic actor, played by Bing Crosby, in 1954's *The Country Girl*. Her compelling performance suggested that, given the right roles, Kelly could become a great actress.

The Cannes Film Festival implored Grace to make an appearance in May at the massive event before *The Country Girl* opened in Paris. Her instincts were to say no, but she had the fondest memories of filming *To Catch a Thief* in the Mediterranean resort town. There was another reason she said yes. The actress rarely ate the same meal twice, but she had renewed her affair with Jean-Pierre Aumont. A widower with a daughter, the actor and war hero was a man of decided maturity and none of Cassini's hysterics. When Kelly arrived at the train station in Cannes, the Frenchman was waiting for her.

Even when people approached Kelly in what appeared to be the most generous and spontaneous of manners, they often had secret agendas. Thus, when she was invited to have a private meeting with Prince Rainier III of Monaco in his pint-sized principality, she had no idea that the magazine *Paris Match* had set it up to get photos.

Wedged between France and Italy, Monaco is a historical afterthought. The city-state is dominated by the twelfth-century palace and the Casino of Monte Carlo. Monaco's citizens include a liberal sprinkling of characters hiding away from the authorities in other countries.

Rainier was an hour late for his meeting with Kelly. A man of flawless manners, he made his apologies and showed Kelly the palace gardens. Having to return to events in Cannes, Kelly left after half an hour. If Hitchcock had been filming the scene, he would have had some understated foreshadowing, a wistful look exchanged between the two of them, a touch of a hand, but there was none of that. Kelly had Aumont on her mind. After the film festival, they spent time together in Paris, where their love deepened and marriage appeared a distinct prospect.

Kelly's mother and the Sisters of the Assumption had taught her impeccable manners. When she returned to New York, she wrote a thank-you note to Rainier. His letter arrived at about the same time. Thus began a six-month-long correspondence. Rainier wrote about his life, faith, and destiny, and she replied in kind. These were not romantic epistles. It was more like corresponding to a pen pal in a distant land.

Rainier had other matters to face of far greater importance than writing to an American movie star. If the thirty-two-year-old prince did not marry and have a male heir, France would take over Monaco. That would be devastating to the twenty thousand citizens who paid no income taxes, served in no army, and were safe from the laws of France.

The diminutive prince faced other problems. The buzz was off Monte Carlo. The rich were no longer coming to the casino in great numbers, gambling for high stakes. The Greek tycoon Aristotle Onassis had taken control of the Société des Bains de Mer et du Cercle des Étrangers that ran the casino. Onassis was not happy, but he had a solution. America was taking over the world. If Rainier married an American beauty, preferably a movie star, the rich would once again come to Monte Carlo, bringing treasure to the casino.

Rainier may not have known what Onassis was suggesting, but the idea was in the air. Sometime during his correspondence with Kelly, he decided he might marry her. Kelly was one of the world's most celebrated women, and the prince envisioned many benefits.

In recent months, twenty-six-year-old Kelly had often been so depressed that gray was the brightest color in her spectrum. As she always did, Kelly returned to Philadelphia for Christmas. It was a time when memories came back, and ghosts haunted the rooms.

As part of his December 1955 visit to the United States, Rainier arrived in Philadelphia for Christmas dinner with the Kelly family. The Kellys had treated other suitors who came to the house on Henry Avenue with overweening disdain, but not the prince. Mrs. Kelly even invited him to stay over.

Late in the evening, Rainier and Kelly went into one of the rooms and shut the door behind them. If one of Grace's earlier beaux had done that, Mr. Kelly would have thrown the reprobate out. This was different. It was like a medieval ritual with the king asserting his droit du seigneur over a courtier's daughter. When the couple finally emerged after two in the morning, the prince had dog hairs on his suit. Kelly's sister Peggy fetched Scotch tape so he could easily remove them.

Kelly and Rainier spent most of the next three days together, mainly in New York, after which he asked for her hand in marriage, and she said yes. The Kellys were elated. With their daughter a princess, they would rise far above the Main Line Philadelphians who spurned them. They were blessedly unaware of the irony. In the nineteenth century, millions of Irish left the Emerald Isle not only to evade the potato famine but because they no longer wanted to doff their hats to the British nobility who ruled their land. But here, two generations later, the Kellys were doffing their hats to this plump little prince and giving him their daughter.

Kelly hardly knew Rainier. She was not in the emotional state to make such a monumental decision. If Mr. and Mrs. Kelly loved their daughter for herself, not for what she could do for them, they would have insisted Rainier give the relationship more time. But that was not on their agenda. As for Grace, once she said yes, the plane was on the runway, and there was no point in asking if this was truly a destination to which she wanted to go.

Insistent on doing the proper thing, Kelly knew she must tell Cassini before her lover heard elsewhere. She asked to meet him on the Staten Island Ferry. "Why?" he asked as the boat sailed across New York Harbor. "How and when did *this* develop?" It had not developed, but arrived full-born. "Are you going to marry someone because he has a title and a few acres of real estate?" he asked. "I will learn how to love him," she said.

Cassini was genuinely distressed. He saw the impending marriage "as a capitulation, a decision to avoid the wondrous turmoil of life." Kelly had tired of Hollywood. She flailed out at the industry, but her blows struck nothing but air. No matter, she had reached the point in her career when, like Gable and Grant, she would soon have been able to assert far more control. In leaving her life as an actress to marry Rainier, she was giving up much, whereas in marrying her, the prince was giving up little but his bachelorhood.

Before the wedding on April 19, 1956, watched live by 30 million viewers across Europe and covered by 1,600 journalists, much had to be prepared. Undocumented stories assert that the Kellys paid a $2 million dowry to the prince, wiping out their daughter's savings, leaving her a near pauper as she entered the palace. Even if that is not true, she brought a great bounty to the prince. Theirs was a dynastic marriage: a prince of a dying European nobility marrying a queen of the rising dynasty of celebrity.

Auber watched all of this from Paris. "The Prince Rainier thing was her parents' doing, but she had a major love affair with Aumont," the actress said. "And when she looked so thin and so pale at her wedding, the newspapers called it love. But she was suffering. A financial arrangement is what it was."

With Kelly ensconced in the palace, just as Rainier had hoped, the glamour and allure of Monte Carlo returned, and the high-end gamblers as well. Hitchcock was bereft. He wanted her back, and Kelly was willing to come, but her husband would not have it. A story was put out that the people of Monaco did not want their princess to resume her career. Whether that was true or not, behind them stood the unyielding figure of Prince Rainier, who had the princess he wanted in the place he wanted her to be.

Even before Kelly met the prince, she wanted so badly to make *The Swan*. She could not say why, but now it made sense. At the end of the film, just before Crown Prince Albert walks off arm in arm with Princess Alexandra, he speaks these words to the woman who will be his queen:

"Your father used to call you his swan. . . . Think what it means to be a swan, to glide like a dream on the smooth surface of the lake and never go on the shore. On dry land, where ordinary people walk, the swan is awkward, even ridiculous. . . . So there she must stay, out on the lake, silent, white, majestic. Be a bird, but never fly. Know one song, but never sing it until the moment of her death.

"And so it must be for you, Alexandra. Head high, cool indifference to the staring crowds along the bank. And song never."

CHAPTER 7

All in Lavender

I f Grace Kelly wasn't returning to Hollywood, Hitchcock would have to create another star. Actresses were the key to Hitchcock's career, but they were much more trouble than their male counterparts. Time and again, as the director saw it, these women did things that made no professional sense. Bergman and Kelly threw away careers he had helped to build movie by movie by movie. No matter, the director had no choice but to do it again. He would take the right actress and make her into a star playing the roles Kelly would have played, a young woman who might even be worthy of his affection.

Hitchcock thought he had his ideal candidate in Vera Miles, whose countenance had some resemblance to his beloved Kelly. "I feel the same way directing Vera that I did with Grace," the director said as he signed the actress to a personal five-year contract.

Miles was a divorced mother of two daughters, and she bridled at Hitchcock's overwhelming attention. When he costarred her as the disturbed wife in his 1956 film *The Wrong Man*, he inundated her with flowers, messages, and requests for personal get-togethers. He never touched her or said things she found unseemly, but his interest disturbed her.

Hitchcock's fantasy took a disastrous turn when, during the filming, Miles married the actor Gordon Scott. It was even more damaging to Hitchcock's male ego that Miles had been taken away from him by a bodybuilding hunk who was Hollywood's latest Tarzan.

Despite that drawback, when the director gave Miles a successful screen test in November 1956, he had everything in place for her to star in the film that became *Vertigo*. It was a singularly challenging opportunity. The actress would be playing two roles. For much of the film, she would be a single woman named Judy Barton who was pretending to be an unhappily married woman called Madeleine Elster. Then she would simply be Barton. To convey both those characters successfully would require acting of the highest order.

Vertigo was based on the 1954 novel *The Living and the Dead* by the French authors Pierre Boileau and Thomas Narcejac. Their previous book had become the classic French film *Les Diaboliques*. In that movie, at the moment of denouement, a supposedly dead body rises out of a bathtub to confront the living. It is a moment Hitchcockian in its terror and surprise. No wonder the director chose to turn the authors' perverse new thriller into his film, moving the action from France to San Francisco.

In this psychologically complex drama, San Francisco businessman Gavin Elster (Tom Helmore) conceives an intricate plot to murder his heiress wife, Madeleine. To have a convincing alibi, he hires retired police detective John "Scottie" Ferguson (James Stewart) to follow his supposedly troubled wife. Unbeknownst to Ferguson, it is not Madeleine he is tailing, but Elster's lover, Judy Barton, pretending to be his wife.

Four writers (Maxwell Anderson, Angus MacPhail, Alec Coppel, and Samuel A. Taylor) worked on successive script versions over fifteen months, transforming the novel into a compelling screenplay. Hitchcock was there the entire time, making suggestions with all the gravitas of commands.

In the end, the screenplay they wrote wasn't simply a thriller. It was an intimate psychological drama touching on some of the most sensitive matters in human relationships. Some people seek in love things that emotion cannot give; they call obsession love and let it carry them to places they should not go.

The process of making the film became even more onerous and elongated when, in January 1957, Hitchcock had an operation to remove a painful navel hernia. The procedure was supposed to be routine, but the surgeons discovered colitis. That sent the director to bed for several more weeks. He was still recovering in March when, in terrible pain, an ambulance took him to Cedars of Lebanon for an operation to remove gallstones. This time, the fifty-seven-year-old director spent a whole month in the hospital.

Hitchcock had always been healthy, and the business unsettled him. While he spent restless weeks in bed, the production faced another problem. Miles had been vague when she asked for a delay in the shooting. She was not so equivocal two months later when she said she was pregnant and would not be able to play the role.

Some actresses reach a point in their lives where their maternal instincts overwhelm their professional drives, and they choose motherhood over the claims of stardom. Hitchcock never understood that and chalked it up to the emotional, unpredictable nature of the female sex. "Don't you know it's bad taste to have more than two?" he asked Miles.

Miles's pregnancy meant that Hitchcock would have to go out once again to find an actress to play the role, and find her quickly.

When he went to see Lew Wasserman at MCA, Hollywood's most powerful agent had only one actress in mind.

Kim Novak had made only six movies, but in 1956, theater owners declared her America's second biggest female box office draw. Hitchcock had seen enough of the actress's films to realize her contradictory allure. Novak had startling platinum-silver hair and, by that measure, was perfect to become Hitchcock's next blonde. With a throaty voice that sounded like sex itself, a provocative body, and slightly exotic Slavic-tinged features, she might have come across as just another Hollywood sexpot. But she had a girl-next-door familiarity, as if this appeal had nothing to do with her.

Director George Sidney, who worked with Novak on *The Eddy Duchin Story*, expressed those paradoxical elements: "She has the façade and the equipment of a bitch in the long shot. Yet when you look in Kim's eyes in a close-up, she's like a baby. There is a fire with the sweetness, a bitchery with the virtue, all in one package."

Novak did not have a reputation as much of an actress, but she would bring people into the movie houses the way Miles would not. Wasserman had no trouble convincing Hitchcock that Novak was his answer. The agent went to Harry Cohn, who owned Novak's contract at Columbia, and arranged to have her loaned out to Paramount for *Vertigo*.

Much of the press treated Novak dismissively. *Time*'s July 1957 cover story on the actress codified these resentments. "By ancient Hollywood practice, a star is made, not just born," the weekly said. "Kim Novak herself was virtually invented, the first top-flight star ever made strictly to order, for delivery when needed. When Cohn's underlings found her, she was a small-time model, somewhat overweight and utterly lacking in acting experience."

As the magazine saw it, Cohn deserved the accolades, not this actress whom he had created out of a gob of nothingness. Needing a replacement for Rita Hayworth, the Columbia head took this nondescript lump and transformed her into a cinema goddess. "If you wanna bring me your wife or your aunt, we'll do the same for them," he said.

* * *

Novak was a long way from her home on the West Side of Chicago. As a child, she enjoyed going to the nearby train station to meet her father when he returned from his night shift as a dispatcher for the Chicago, Milwaukee, and St. Paul Railroad. She took his empty lunch box, and as they walked home, she tried to reach out to him, but he never responded in the way she hoped.

The child was too young to understand that her father was mentally sick. He was so depressed and so absorbed in his demons that he could not connect with her emotionally in ways that mattered. All she had was her father's partial, uncertain love. She sought that love elsewhere for the rest of her life. No matter how intense and sincere it might have been, it was never enough, and she constantly feared it would disappear.

Novak's Czech-American parents, Blanche and Joseph Novak, sought to live lives of perfect symmetry in a lower-middle-class neighborhood full of turmoil and trouble. When their first daughter, Arlene, was born in 1930, it was proper that her new sibling be a boy. Instead, Marilyn Pauline was born on February 13, 1933. The Novaks hid their disappointment as best they could, but the daughter the world would know as Kim Novak was second born and second best.

It was not easy being Catholic in a tough Jewish neighborhood during the war years. This was no bucolic melting pot, just two groups wanting nothing to do with each other. Some of the Jews struck out against those they thought supported Hitler. On occasion, they maligned those from countries like Czechoslovakia who felt the German jackboots on their necks.

"I often got knocked down, buried in snow, and pied with moldy deli pies," Novak recalled. Whenever she walked out the front door, she had no idea what taunt might greet her or which missiles could come winging her way, hurled by someone Jewish. Although it was frightening to her, she came to understand this righteous, if wrongly focused, anger. "These were young innocent Jewish kids trying to seek revenge for the murders of their kin," Novak reflected. "And it didn't help to have a grandpa whose first name was Adolf."

Novak's public school applied a crude triage, putting the lamest students in the back row. There Novak resided among "the jerks." As she sat there, her mind constantly drifted, sometimes dreaming that she was Jane, swinging from tree to tree on vines with Tarzan. These days, she probably would have been diagnosed with attention deficit disorder. Scrawny Novak sat ignored by her teachers, just as her parents often paid no attention to her. "My parents made me feel I was the cause of my troubles," she said. "They offered little support or encouragement. I don't know that I ever recovered from those experiences."

Novak's mother worked in a bra and girdle factory. When Kim developed a voluptuous figure at an early age, Blanche took no pride in her daughter's womanly appearance. Mrs. Novak knew her family lived in a dangerous world and decided Novak must cloak her beauty. The mother insisted her daughter wear her hair in pigtails and no makeup. Novak was so shy that she could hardly look at a boy, but she did what her mother told her to do.

Mrs. Novak was not wrong in fearing for her daughter's safety. Novak said she was raped, a trauma that affected the rest of her life. "It was in my early teens by multiple boys in the back seat of a stranger's car," she said.

Novak gathered up her clothes and said nothing to her parents, but kept this unbearable pain and terrible secret within her. That was not an unusual response. Victims of sexual assault often blame themselves. They wrongly think they have provoked their assailants and slink away in shame, telling no one.

When Novak looked back on her childhood, she saw that her primary inheritance of those years was a sickness that plagued her life. "I inherited my mental illness from my father, but the rape must have added to it," she said. As a middle-aged adult, Novak was diagnosed with bipolar disease and obsessive-compulsive disorder, but she had been sick for years. Darkness would rise up in her like a thunderstorm out of a cloudless sky, and then everything would clear, and she would become almost giddily exuberant.

That was the great struggle of her life, no less a challenge because she did not understand why she felt the way she did and acted at times in ways that appeared irrational. The sexual assault taught her in one terrible moment that she could trust no one fully, least of all the cunning blandishments of men. Her illness taught her that she was alone, going places others did not go. She hid all this the best she could and struggled onward.

Mrs. Novak pushed her shy, self-doubting daughter to go downtown to join the Fair Teens of Chicago. The modeling club taught teenagers how to dress and wear makeup. When Novak saw one self-assured, well-dressed girl after another entering the event, she almost turned away, but eventually joined the others. Unlike these teenagers, whose mere presence intimidated her, she won modeling gigs and beauty contests such as Miss Rhapsody in Blue and Snow Queen.

Novak's startling beauty was as much a curse as a blessing. She was so gorgeous that others decided she must be stupid, superficial, and mindlessly vain. People looked so intensely at her beauty that they did not see her. Men stared at her, wanting only one thing.

Women observed her with disdain for this creature who outshone them.

Few people noticed that Novak had an artistic soul. The teenager was a talented artist and wrote poetry. She received scholarships to Chicago's prestigious Art Institute. Her parents knew nothing about the creative world. If they did, they could have nurtured her, offering her a life in which her creativity was applauded. Instead, she spent years battling the unfair reputation of a talentless wannabe trading on her looks.

As a teenager, Novak was in love with love—the tingling sensation of attraction, the one way out of her unhappy world, a golden door to bliss. Like the manic side of bipolar disease, love was to her an incredible rush of emotion overwhelming everything in its path. She sought that high continually, moving from one young man to the next, seeking feelings that would take her out of the often mundane realities of her daily life. Engaged twice before she left her teenage years, she approached these relationships with feverish intensity before they tumbled down.

After high school, Novak attended junior college. When she was twenty, she was named Miss Deepfreeze of 1953. Holding that title, she headed west on the *Sunset Limited* with several other models to promote refrigerators on appliance shows across the American West. San Francisco was the last stop. Novak was ready to return to Chicago, when one of the models suggested they go to Los Angeles.

Hollywood beckoned young women by the thousands, but Novak had no interest in becoming an actress. She signed on at the Caroline Leonetti Modeling Agency, hoping to get modeling work, the one thing that she thought could bring her easy income. If the wolfish stares Novak got on the street were anything to go by, she looked sensational. But the agency told her that, for professional modeling, she was a good twenty pounds overweight, and the bookings did not come.

During Novak's early time in Hollywood, Jane Russell had her own weight problems playing a Texas heiress in *The French Line*. The excruciatingly foul musical comedy was an object lesson in what can happen to an actress who lives by her beauty alone. Russell had risen out of the hay in her first film, *The Outlaw*, shot when she was only nineteen years old, to become one of Hollywood's leading sex symbols. Her newest film had no higher purpose than to show as much of Russell's body as the censors allowed.

In twelve years, the camerapersons had moved from exposing Russell's body to disguising it. It would not do to have svelte chorus girls standing behind thirty-two-year-old Russell in the musical scenes; the contrast would be devastating. So RKO sent the call out for "plump extras," and Novak was one of those who responded.

In Novak's one scene, she stood on a massive staircase in a strapless gown among sixteen other chorines dressed in evening clothes. The other women used their moment to project themselves on the screen. Novak faded into the background.

It was a different matter on the set itself. Among the extras, Novak's beauty stood out like a star in a moonless sky. One who noticed was Max Arnow, Columbia's casting director, who had come to the RKO set that day looking for talent.

Arnow brought Novak to Columbia for a screen test. Richard Quine, a young director assigned to get the best out of the would-be actress, saw that Novak was projecting little into the camera but her insecurities. He remembered the stunning Jean Louis strapless gown that Rita Hayworth, the queen of Columbia, had worn in *Gilda*. The director asked for it to be brought from the wardrobe department.

Dressed in that gown, Novak stood transformed. There was not an angle that did not produce exquisite images, not a shot that wasn't printable.

The only opinion that mattered was that of Harry Cohn, the head of Columbia Pictures.

When Cohn went into his private screening room to see Novak's screen test footage, it had hardly begun when the mogul started condemning Novak as a worthless pretender. As far as he was concerned, the woman wasn't acting. She was speaking and hardly doing that. He could barely understand her mumbles. "This girl has probably never ever read the funnies out loud," Cohn told Arnow. Given her childhood, that was probably the truth.

"She will never be able to act, Harry," the casting director told Cohn. "But that just doesn't matter. She's got star quality."

It was not Cohn's aggressive crudity that brought him success but that he knew what moviegoers wanted to see when they went to the Bijou on Friday night. And he saw, whatever Novak's limitations, that she was a woman of transcendent beauty who just might have something to intrigue moviegoers. What did it cost to sign her to a short-term contract for a measly hundred dollars a week and see where it went?

That was a minor expense compared to the other money spent to turn Novak into something she was not. It took nothing to change Novak's first name so she would not be butting against America's leading lust object, Marilyn Monroe, but everything else cost money. Her teeth were whitened and straightened, her hair dyed into what became her signature platinum blonde. She was sent off to a gym, given extensive acting lessons, and put on a stringent diet that quickly led to a loss of fifteen pounds.

The publicity department created an image for the creature the studio had invented. They put out the story that an agent discovered Novak riding a bicycle in Beverly Hills. It wasn't quite the famous tale of Lana Turner being plucked up while sitting on a stool at Schwab's Pharmacy on Sunset Boulevard, but it wasn't bad. The publicists sent the story out accompanied by a photo of Novak in skintight, short

black shorts and a blouse unbuttoned to the waist. There was no bicycle to be seen.

Novak saw herself disappearing, covered over by this being that
the studio invented. In small ways, she tried to hold on to bits and
pieces of herself. Joan Crawford was a Hollywood legend. Thus Novak
had to have big, bold lips like Crawford in *Mildred Pierce*. As soon as
she left the studio, Novak wiped Crawford off her face.

Novak had wildly inviting looks, but she was still a starlet with an
uncertain future. The road to anything beyond that led through Harry
Cohn's office. "Send the dumb Polack in," Cohn yelled to his secretary
as he pressed the button to open the door. "Send in the fat Polack."
Novak was neither fat, dumb, nor Polish, but Cohn did not care. It was
just a way to rile her up. "You're nothing but a piece of meat in a
butcher shop, and you should never forget it," he said to this woman
who stood before him in all her flawless beauty.

Cohn treated the Columbia studio as his harem, but kept his hands
off Novak. She thought she knew why. "People that were under contract to him he didn't want to have any kind of relationship with because he wanted power," she reflected. "And I think he felt that if he
did get involved, he would be giving up power."

The studio figured they needed a gimmick to set Novak apart,
and they deputized publicist Muriel Roberts to find one. She came up
with the idea of calling Novak the "lavender blonde." When the actress got her own apartment, everything was done in purple, including
the bathroom fixtures and the car out in the driveway. She was told
that whenever she talked to a reporter, she should bring her love of
lavender into the conversation. For an interview in New York City on
a sweltering ninety-one-degree August day, Novak wore a lavender
skirt, a lavender sweater, a thick lavender coat, and what she called
lavender hair. "The color was designed especially for me, and it's

called 'lavender champagne,'" she said, speaking in what the interviewer called "a lavender champagne voice."

The Columbia head wanted control over Novak totally, and not just the color that surrounded her. The studio had Novak live at the sorority-like Studio Club, a Hollywood home for single actresses and others in the film business. Cohn had security watching over her there and wherever she traveled in Los Angeles. The Columbia head wanted to know precisely where she was going, what she was doing, and whom she saw. "He'd have people watching what I'd be doing," Novak said. "And so he'd say, 'Why do you stop to talk to those people at the coffee thing? You don't do it. You just go to the set and do your job.'"

Soon after she arrived in Los Angeles, Novak began dating Mac Krim, a wealthy theater owner. With his own expertise in the business, Krim was not only her devoted lover but an unofficial manager, watching out for her career. Cohn was not amused that this man should intrude in the mogul's fiefdom.

From the moment Novak appeared as a headliner in her first film, Cohn knew his little gamble had paid off. *Pushover* was one of those forgettable films that often graced the bottom half of double bills, but the patrons left the theaters talking about the spectacular-looking actress. "I put Kim Novak at the top of the newcomer list," the powerful Hollywood columnist Hedda Hopper wrote in January 1955. "She has magic, too, and glamour, and is beautiful with a lyric blond loveliness."

The Man with the Golden Arm (1955) made Novak an acknowledged star. The controversial drama focused on the then forbidden subject of drug addiction. The film tells the story of an ex-con drummer (Frank Sinatra) trying to kick the habit with the help of Molly (Novak), a hostess at a strip joint.

Novak had been thinking about marrying Krim, but the allures of Sinatra were too much to resist. She began what she later admitted was an affair with the edgy singer. Observing that she was almost patho-

logically timid, Sinatra gently nudged her into a creditable performance that, without his efforts, would probably not have happened.

Novak was getting a reputation as a prima donna who made life
difficult for others on the set. In *Picnic*, she played an innocent provincial girl brought to sexual awakening by a handsome stranger (William
Holden). She spent much of the time in her dressing room preening
before the mirror when she was not trying to put the other actresses in
her shadow.

This activity did not go unnoticed by director Josh Logan. He had
seen women like this before. They were there because of their looks
and they knew it. "Girls such as Kim Novak come from insecure back-
grounds, and it is their beauty that seems to them to be the one thing
which enabled them to rise above their meager pasts," Logan said.
"There is no respect for them—as individuals—only for their beauty."

All the world asked from Novak was her beauty. She gave it, and
she was derided for being what she was, simply because of the hap-
penstance of her looks. No matter how many acting lessons she took
and how hard she tried to get her parts right, the best compliment she
received was that she had finally reached the "heights of adequacy."

Yes, Novak was difficult. She stayed in her dressing room on the
set of *Pal Joey*, keeping the kindly Rita Hayworth waiting for an hour
and a half. Was she playing the diva that day, sending a message to an
actress who was her better, or was she so distressed, so full of self-
doubt, that she could not get up? Was it her ego taking hold or her
disease? Did she sit in front of her mirror looking at herself because
she was admiring her beauty or uncertain that it would pass the test
demanded of it?

Part of the press treated Novak with the disdain they showed to
almost no other star. "Nobody talks more about Kim's suffering psyche
than Kim herself," wrote *Time*. "She has given hundreds of interviews
with a couch-side slant, readily analyzes 'my inferiority complex' and

'my insecurity' and, digging back, rattles on about her childhood as if she were the only adult who ever had one."

The Columbia publicity office surely did not consider a discussion of Novak's childhood traumas as a fit subject for interviews. She spoke about these matters because she was consumed by her emotional struggles and could not be quiet. Novak's life was beyond lonely. She had her myriad beaux and her claque of admirers, but were they true friends? Where were the people with whom she could discuss her life in the same intimate detail as she did with random journalists? The reporters were not there to help her. It was a matter of her occasional desperation that she spoke as she did.

Novak felt she was being mercilessly exploited by Columbia. By loaning her out to various studios, Columbia was making a formidable amount of money. For the five-week shoot of *The Man with the Golden Arm*, Columbia paid Novak $125 a week. At the same time, United paid Columbia $100,000 for her services. That Novak raged with anger over this was not as simple as greed. She wanted a big enough slice of the pie to fill her stomach. As she saw it, she was being shown a lack of respect and a shameless disregard for her as a human being and her artistic efforts. It was psychologically debilitating to go into the studio each morning believing it was for just another day of being exploited.

Given all this, Novak would have done better if she had been able to live some measure of an everyday life. But Cohn sometimes had her working on two films at a time, six or seven days a week. That made things even worse by taking her at times close to exhaustion.

Novak's dark spirits were never far from her. It would have helped if her parents had been a bedrock of support. Her father saw only her first two films and refused to see others, where she might display herself in what he considered shamefully provocative ways. Dismissive of her success, he told *Time*, "I would just as soon have her living here and married to a truck driver." Her father had always wanted a car, but when she bought one for him and offered to drive with him from Chicago to Los Angeles, he said he suffered from migraine headaches and never went with his daughter.

Novak's romantic life was as melodramatic as any of her films, flamed to red heat by interviews musing on various men like a contestant on *The Bachelor*. Poor loyal Krim had to read in the newspaper that he was still her "steady boy friend but I'm not sure whether or not I'm in love with him." Italian count Mario Bandini pursued her across Europe, plying her with bouquets of devotion. "The count is extra special," she told a reporter in a voice of breathless intimacy. "The count was so sweet. He kissed my hand."

And then, of course, the ultimate stage-door Johnny, Aly Khan, came knocking. The playboy son of the spiritual leader of the Nizari Ismaili Muslims moved seamlessly from Rita Hayworth to Grace Kelly to stand before Novak's door bearing more than roses. And others were wooing the actress beneath her windowsill, shouting their words of endearment. How was a girl to choose?

It was one thing for Cohn to behave toward Novak with dismissal and disdain when she was a nobody, but the Columbia head treated her pretty much the same when she became one of the biggest-selling stars in Hollywood. His misogynistic sprites led him to act this way toward a woman who brought him millions of dollars. He slashed at her, demeaned her, damn all that she meant to Columbia's bottom line.

Cohn called Novak into his office to tell her that he was loaning her out to Paramount. "It's a lousy script, but it's with Alfred Hitchcock, so I'm going to let you do it," the Columbia head told her.

Four talented writers had worked on the script for many months, and it was in superb shape. Even if the screenplay had been mediocre, it wasn't the thing to say. Hitchcock was one of the most celebrated directors in the world, and the role she was scheduled to play could bring Novak critical plaudits. Cohn's remarks weren't about the script, but another attempt to make Novak feel uncomfortable. He had such subliminal anger toward the actress that he could not help himself.

When Novak went in to see Edith Head about the outfits she would wear in *Vertigo*, it should have been a routine meeting. Key to the wardrobe was Madeleine's tailored gray suit, the outfit that defined her as a character both in the novel and the script.

Novak would have none of it. "There are two things I don't wear," she lectured the costume designer. "I don't wear suits, and I don't wear gray." She also wasn't going to wear the black shoes Head had set out for her. "I did complain a bit," Novak recalled. "I am I suppose perhaps a bit opinionated."

Head told the angry actress, "I think it's time for you to meet Mr. Hitchcock." Novak knew almost nothing about Hitchcock when approached to star in *Vertigo*, and this was her first meeting with the director. He could be brusque with actors who troubled him with matters he thought should not be his concern. He could not afford to act that way this day. He had not yet shot a day of *Vertigo*, and he had to get this problematic actress under control. To do so, he used all his acumen.

"Yes, my dear," Hitchcock said, full of concern, "I understand from Edith you were having a little trouble with your costumes. Why don't you sit down here next to me and tell me all about it?" Head had already told him Novak's complaints, but he let the actress rant. And rant she did, her words crossing back and forth across each other, repeating the same narrow points again and again.

Hitchcock could have asked her to close it down, but he continued looking at Novak with rapt attention. He even encouraged her by punctuating her comments with "Mm-hmm" until she petered out. Then he said, "Now you'll follow Edith Head. She'll take all the dimensions, and you will, of course, wear the gray suit and the black shoes." And that was that.

Shortly thereafter, Hitchcock invited Novak to his house on Bellagio Road for dinner. The director had this ritual event with his female stars, in so doing setting the parameters of their relationship. Each occasion was decidedly different. Bergman had a worldly European patina, and Hitchcock treated her with a measure of equality. Before arriving in Hollywood, Kelly had traveled in rarefied social circles. Hitchcock's superb wines and fine food were a perfect match for the Philadelphia-born actress. Thus he deferred to her from her first visit to his home.

Hitchcock was not a man of second chances. If things started badly with him, they rarely got better . . . and they hadn't begun well with Novak. Unlike Hitchcock's previous blond actresses, she was a provincial full of massive insecurities. The director believed she required different treatment. Living in the boldly egalitarian United States, Hitchcock had to temper his snobbish disdain for the unenlightened, but those sentiments were still there. In this instance, he used them to try to break Novak down and turn her into a being who would do precisely what he wanted.

When Novak arrived, the maid led the actress through several rooms full of paintings by artists such as Utrillo and Dufy until they reached Hitchcock, standing in the grand salon with a bottle of twenty-year-old Chardonnay in his hand. "Did you know this was one of the best years for Chardonnay?" he asked, knowing perfectly well she had no idea.

Anyone who has ever been unsure of how to use a fish knife or crack a lobster without making a mess at an important dinner would appreciate the excruciating feelings Novak experienced that day. Hitchcock could have tried to make his nervous guest comfortable. He did the opposite. He wanted to grind a sense of social inferiority into Novak so deep that she would let him do his job without a peep.

Rather than talk about the movie they were about to make,

Hitchcock moved from subject to subject on matters about which Novak knew almost nothing, from the celebrated art on the wall to the
gourmet delicacies on the table, and from tales of Hitchcock's travels
to the vintage wine in the crystal glasses.

The screenwriter Samuel A. Taylor was there that day, and he
watched the director he admired act in ways that struck him as unfair
and ugly. "He succeeded in making her feel like a helpless child, igno-
rant and untutored, and that's just what he wanted—to break down her
resistance," Taylor said. "By the end of the afternoon, he had her right
where he wanted her, docile and obedient and even a little confused."

When Novak came back from a vacation that delayed the start of
production, she still did not return to the set. Paramount was paying
Columbia $250,000 for her services and Stewart's on another picture,
when she was getting $1,250 a week. She would not work until the
studio increased her salary to almost $3,000 weekly. Hers was in some
measure a worthy fight, but to Hitchcock her action could be con-
strued as further evidence that she was a selfish, petulant woman concerned only with herself.

A few weeks later, when Novak got her money and reported to the
set, casting director Arnow noticed how subdued the feisty actress had
become. "She became docile, obedient, and not just a bit confused,"
Arnow recalled. "Hitchcock wasn't even polite to her."

When Novak read the script, she realized it was the most challenging
role she had ever attempted. Naturally enough, the actress had ideas
of how the character should be played, and tried talking it out with
Hitchcock. She had no idea he could not stand it when actors came
to him with what he considered pretentious, irrelevant ideas about
their roles.

"Kim, this is only a movie," Hitchcock told Novak. "Let's not go too deeply into these things." The director was not treating the actress with special disregard. He expected all his actors to do their jobs without grasping his hand to help them walk. Hitchcock was convinced his mini-lecture "worked like a charm clearly: all she needed was to feel secure, to have the weight of responsibility taken off her shoulders."

Despite what Hitchcock thought, when Novak walked away that day, she was even more apprehensive. When she started a new project, she was often terrified that she could not do what she was supposed to, but this was the worst. She never had anybody to guide her. Almost always alone on things that mattered, she sought her own answers.

One line in the script resounded especially with Novak: "I want you to love me for me." How many times in her life could she have spoken those words? It made her realize that she could play Judy Barton as *her* story.

To keep her man, Judy must turn herself into someone else and play a false role from morning till night. That was what Cohn and his kind had forced Novak to do. As for the men who said they loved the actress, whom did they love, Marilyn Novak from the West Side of Chicago or cinema's lavender queen?

The filming of *Vertigo* began in San Francisco at the end of September 1957. Novak had been to the city by the Bay on her refrigerator tour as a model, and if it was not quite a homecoming, it was a place she loved. There she met up with James Stewart, who would be playing opposite her.

Stewart's role as retired police detective John "Scottie" Ferguson is as complicated and nuanced as Novak's. Suffering from acrophobia, Scottie is so afraid of heights that he has had to leave the police force. Because of a fall, he is wearing a corset, an item of clothing generally associated with women. Although he has a physical disability, his acrophobia, or vertigo, is a metaphor for a man afraid to climb the heights of life. Unable to perform his manly profession, he sits back impotently, living out a voyeur's life. In all this, Scottie is kin to another troubled Hitchcock man, Jeff Jefferies, the role Stewart played in *Rear Window.*

Scottie is approached by an old college friend, Gavin Elster, who tells him his heiress wife is possessed by a spirit of the past and is going to all these strange places. He wants the retired officer to follow her to try to make sense of it all.

Vertigo rests on the performances of Novak and Stewart. Not only do their complex characters have to be believable, but the two actors must mesh together. Stewart saw that Novak reeked of self-doubt. He reached out to her to help her to be comfortable within herself and bring life and substance to her role. "Thank God I had Jimmy Stewart with me in that picture," Novak said. "He treated me so well. I learned a lot about acting from him."

For two weeks, the crew traveled across San Francisco and its environs filming exterior shots, a wonderful travelogue of the city, as Scottie follows the supposed Madeleine wherever she goes. Hitchcock began filming at Mission Dolores, the oldest building in the city. Tailed by Scottie, Madeleine walks through the Spanish-style church and stands before the grave of Carlotta Valdes, the ancestor who haunts her.

As a small indication of the meticulous way Hitchcock went about filmmaking, he spent a day and most of a morning filming a sequence that lasted three minutes in the final film. It took at least twenty setups to get the shots Hitchcock wanted, out of which came twenty-eight pieces of film to be edited together.

After Novak fell over a tombstone, Stewart helped her get up, saying jokingly, "You might try lifting your feet." She could have spoken a mouthful about why she had fallen. It was likely the black shoes Hitchcock had forced her to wear. Not only did she find them ugly, but they pinched her feet. Novak could have asked for a larger pair, but the shoes constantly reminded her of the discomfort of pretending she was someone she was not. "Feeling the shoes didn't really fit was so right for the character whom I was playing," Novak said. "It's Judy trying to become what this man who is offering her all these things said she should be."

As for the gray suit, to Novak it was little better than a prison uniform. She would have cringed wearing such an outfit in real life. But like the tight black shoes, the gray suit helped her become the uptight character she was pretending to be.

It was a convivial group making the film, all except for Novak, who kept to herself in her dressing room. "Kim was sort of aloof, and nobody got to know her," recalled Clarence Oscar "C. O." Erickson, the production manager. Her behavior may have seemed arrogant, but it was more a measure of her self-doubt.

The cast and crew stayed at the premier Fairmont Hotel in the city's heart, while Hitchcock spent as much time as he could in his vacation estate an hour south overlooking Monterey Bay. During the San Francisco shoot, Hitchcock and Alma invited a group for dinner at their second home. It was a royal summons not to be spurned, and it was unsettling when, an hour into the event, Novak still had not shown up. She called finally and said she was lost. Even with the proper instructions, she took another hour to arrive.

Hitchcock had seen divas before making their dramatic entrances well into the proceedings, but this went well beyond that. For Hitchcock, it was just another chit against Novak. "He got very upset because he thought I didn't take it seriously enough to be there on time,"

Novak said. "I got lost. I think he thought it was an excuse because I was late."

The exterior shots had gone well, but this was a film about the relationship between two people; their dialogue would make or break *Vertigo*, and little of that had been shot. Thus, there was a measure of both anticipation and nervousness when the cast and crew returned to Los Angeles to shoot the rest of the film on sets at the Paramount studios starting on October 16, 1957.

Hitchcock decided to make the initial meeting between Madeleine and Scottie the first scene he would film with Novak. After saving Madeleine from committing suicide by throwing herself into the rushing waters of the Pacific, Scottie brings her back to his place in her pale green Jaguar.

The director eroticized the scene. Madeleine lies asleep naked in Scottie's bed. He has obviously undressed her and tucked her under the covers, an act of incredible intimacy toward a woman with whom he has never spoken. Scottie's bachelor apartment looks out onto Coit Tower, a large, angular building on Telegraph Hill. Hitchcock considered it "a phallic symbol." To the director, practically everything but a penis was a phallic symbol.

Novak came in that morning ready to begin what would surely be a difficult day. She was enough of a professional exhibitionist to unbutton an extra button when photographers took publicity photos, but being nude on the set of a film was not easy for any actress to contemplate. And that was just the beginning of a complex sequence between the two characters.

When Novak walked into her dressing room, she was startled to see a plucked chicken hanging upside down on her mirror. As she tried to make sense of this, she turned and saw Hitchcock, Stewart, and a few other men outside her door laughing. The director was always making practical jokes that a dispassionate observer would consider in awful taste. But it was beyond thoughtless to upset Novak on this of all mornings.

Novak had no sense of what the chicken meant. She would have understood a dead fish on her dresser as a Mob symbol of her life being in danger. Rotten eggs would have been a criticism of her acting. But a plucked chicken? "I didn't know what I was supposed to do," she said. "So I pretended I got the joke, but I didn't ever."

The actress moved beyond shock to play the scene that depended overwhelmingly on her. Madeleine comes out of Scottie's bedroom wearing his red silk bathrobe. As she talks with Scottie, she appears guileless and bewildered over what has happened. "You shouldn't have brought me here," Madeleine tells him, inferring that her host has done something improper.

Madeleine leaves without saying goodbye. Later, she tells Scottie of a recurring dream that haunts her sleep. Scottie realizes she is describing Mission San Juan Bautista. He vows to take her there. "You'll remember when you saw it before, and that will finish your dream and destroy it," he tells her. "I promise."

That afternoon, Scottie and Madeleine drive a hundred miles south to the historic mission. Madeleine sits in a surrey in the livery stable in a trancelike state, wearing her gray suit. Scottie thought bringing her here would shock her back into life, but her memories are not of a recent visit but of a hundred years ago. He tells her he loves her, and she responds with the same words. They embrace, but she says it is too late and runs toward the Cloisters.

Madeleine enters the church and proceeds up the tower stairs. Scottie follows as quickly as he can. Hitchcock filmed the scene with immense concern. Although the two characters seem to be rushing helter-skelter up the stairs, they are in a dance of death. "He wanted the rhythm on each step to hit at a certain point in the dialogue," Novak said. "That's why he used a metronome. It was an awesome thing to do."

Scottie tries to walk upward, but vertigo grabs hold of him and he can go no farther. As he stands halfway up the stairs, Madeleine shouts from high above, and then a gray-suited body falls onto the gray tile roof.

Scottie knows if he had been able to charge up those stairs, Madeleine would not have killed herself. He is so disturbed that he enters a sanitorium. When he gets out of the hospital, he retraces all the places Madeleine visited while he was tracking her.

Scottie knows Madeleine is dead, but he keeps thinking he sees her. One day walking downtown along Grant Avenue, Scottie passes a group of shopgirls. He is startled at the looks of one of them. She is a brunette, not a blonde like Madeleine; her makeup is almost gaudy compared to his love's understatement; her body in her green wool dress is voluptuous; and yet something about her evokes Madeleine. He follows the young woman to the downscale Empire Hotel and knocks on her door.

The woman's voice is in-your-face abrupt, its nasal tones far removed from Madeleine's restrained intonations. She tells him her name is Judy Barton, a moniker as pedestrian as everything else about her. She says she arrived from Salina, Kansas, three years ago and works at Magnin's.

Scottie invites Judy out and leaves to give her an hour to get ready. As she sits on her bed in the modest room, reflecting anxiously, we see the scene in the tower at San Juan Bautista when the supposed Madeleine runs up the stairs, fitfully pursued by Scottie. When she reaches the bell tower, Gavin Elster is there, holding his wife's dead body in his arms. As the Madeleine look-alike, Judy stands wearing the same gray suit. Elster pushes his wife's body out between the arches to fall to the roof far below.

Judy goes to her writing desk and pens a note to Scottie, explaining that he is the victim of Elster's elaborate murder conspiracy and that she has been part of it. To keep Elster's love, she has helped draw Scottie into this sick fantasy and led him to San Juan Bautista for the staging of Madeleine's death.

Elster knew that with Scottie's vertigo, he would not be able to climb the tower stairs, and it would be a perfect crime. Only, there was one mistake. "I fell in love," Judy wrote. "That wasn't part of the plan." Judy knows that if Scottie sees her letter, everything will be over. Hopeless, she tears up the note.

Scottie cares about Judy only to the extent that he can remake her as Madeleine reborn. He buys her the precise gray suit Madeleine wore, the same black pumps, and has her hair dyed Madeleine's shade of blond, her eyebrows plucked, and her makeup lightened. Then Scottie waits in Judy's hotel room for her to return as the creature he has created.

Vertigo is a psychological drama about the tragic places this thing called love can take people. In this tale of erotic obsession, Scottie transforms Judy into the image of his lost love. To play Judy, Novak reasserted her youthful Chicago self, including her accent and an unpretentious assertiveness. She felt strangely liberated playing Judy. Unlike Madeleine, Judy is real.

Novak saw how her character resonated with so many women's lives. "Judy surrendered herself to being made over," Novak reflected. "So many women do that. You so much want the love you feel for somebody to be returned that you are willing to be anything he wants if that will make him love you. But how long can you pretend to be someone else?"

Men so often seek to remake the woman they love. They want her to wear specific clothing items and act in ways foreign to them, and they pout if she is reluctant. "It was so real to me, the coming out and wanting approval in that scene," Novak said. "It was like, is this what you want? Is this what you want from me? My whole body was trembling. I mean I had chills inside and goose bumps all over just because it was the ultimate defining moment for anybody when they're going to someone they love and they just want to be perfect for them. And that's what I think makes it contemporary. It's about that thing that goes wrong in love, when you're attracted to someone and suddenly you need to change them."

When Judy returns to her room wearing the gray suit and blond hair, Scottie is not thankful she has made herself over for him. Instead, he is irritated that her hair is down, not in a bun like the way Madeleine wore it. To placate Scottie, she goes into the bathroom and transforms herself into Madeleine's precise image. Then Judy walks slowly toward him. It is a moment of startling sensual intensity. Hitchcock said she should have come out of the bathroom naked, and in a sense, she has. There is nothing left of Judy Barton. She has given up everything in the name of love. Scottie almost salivates at what he has crafted.

Scottie and Judy embrace in an epic Hitchcock clinch that goes on for a minute and thirteen seconds before she collapses in his arms. The scene is steamy and all-encompassing as the camera circles them, but not what it seems. Hitchcock considered Scottie a necrophiliac; if so, he is embracing a corpse. And what about Judy? She says she is in love with Scottie, but he does not love her or want her to reappear. She is as distorted in her misguided love as he is.

Judy has done everything Scottie asked her to do to remake herself and is in a giddily happy mood. She wants to go to dinner at Ernie's that evening, and as she gets ready, she reaches into her jewelry box and pulls out a necklace. As Scottie affixes it around her neck, he realizes this is Madeleine's necklace. Grasping that Judy has conned him into complicity in murder and destroyed the singular love of his life, he becomes a man without pity, consumed with revenge.

Instead of going to Ernie's, Scottie suggests they drive south of the city to a different place. At some point, Judy realizes Scottie is taking her back to San Juan Bautista and fears the denouement facing her there.

As Novak plays this scene, she thinks there is still hope for their love: "When Judy suddenly became more and more aware, 'Oh, my God, he's taking me there,' I think she felt at this point, 'Well, surely, I can make him understand.'" That is how Novak looked at love, no matter how often it failed her. But sometimes there is only a one-way road, and there is no getting off. That is the road Judy is traveling.

When the couple reaches the mission, Scottie tells Judy he has come here to complete his cure. "One final thing I have to do, and then I'll be free of the past," he says. Against Judy's will, he pushes her to climb the stairs of the church tower. Despite his vertigo, he walks to the top along with her. As they climb, Scottie confronts Judy about her deceitful part in this drama, and she confesses.

"I loved you so, Madeleine," Scottie says. Not a slip of the tongue; Judy is nothing more than a device.

"I loved you, Scottie," Judy says, and in her way, she did.

A nun appears out of nowhere, a black angel hovering in the shadows. When Judy sees the nun, she plunges to her death, falling where Madeleine's body fell.

By the look on Scottie's tortured face, the past still holds him in its rigid grip, and will never let go.

* * *

The shooting was almost over when Aly Khan invited Novak to the Helpers Charity Ball on the Wednesday evening before Thanksgiving. The playboy prince was in town to see his daughter Yasmin from his short-lived marriage to Rita Hayworth. Novak was never going to marry the staggeringly wealthy son of the Aga Khan, but he was a great dancer, gave her the use of his apartment in New York, and had other attributes that drew women to him.

Although her closets were full of clothes, Novak felt she did not have anything appropriate for this special evening. So she borrowed Madeleine's glorious green gown and Judy's brown wig and set out dressed like a Hollywood princess in her white Corvette with red leather seats to pick up the Muslim prince. Novak drank more than usual before leaving the gala to drive Khan to LAX for his flight.

The evening was still young, and Novak was dressed to party. Tony Curtis and Janet Leigh were having their own event after the ball. The Hollywood couple had told her that the director Richard Quine would be there. That was all it took to get Novak to drive to their house.

"I was in love with Richard from the first time he did my screen test," she said. "I don't think he knew I was in love with him." Novak used the word "love" the way adolescents do, employing it to describe momentary infatuations or attractions. With Quine, there was another problem. The man was married, but that did not trouble Novak as she arrived at the Curtis/Leigh home.

Although Quine was not at the party, there was another man who had come solely to see Novak. Sammy Davis Jr. was a singular entertainer who could hold his own on Broadway or a Las Vegas stage. Davis had lost his left eye in an auto accident. He radiated easy, ingratiating charm. That was a necessary attribute for a man who was often the token African American at Hollywood events, where his mere presence affirmed one's liberalism.

The summer before, Davis had appeared with Novak on *The Steve Allen Show* and had been wildly attracted to her. "You know, I reached a point with the indignities, the injustices, the nastiness, the racial abuses . . . where I wanted to get the whitest, the most famous chick in the world and just show 'em," he told his friend and coauthor of his autobiography, Burt Boyar. "To show everybody, yeah, guess what I'm doing with her! How do you like that?"

Davis arranged to come on the *Vertigo* set to take pictures. The entertainer was no photographer, but to spend time with Novak he pretended to be an avid shutterbug. As he shot his close-ups of her, she asked slyly, "Did you ever think of taking off the lens cover?"

While talking to Davis at the party, Novak had a drink or two (or more), to the point that she was drunk and should not have driven home. But off she zoomed and had almost reached her Bel Air apartment when she skidded off the road, knocked over a fence, and ended up on the lawn of a neighbor's house. "I was out of it," Novak said. "I remember waking up in bed, and my car was parked crooked on the street below my apartment."

The following day, Novak was still trying to puzzle out what had happened, when the phone rang. "Where are you?" Davis asked beseechingly. "You're supposed to be here."

"What?" Novak asked, trying to make sense of this.

"You told me you were coming over for Thanksgiving dinner."

Now Novak remembered. "Oh, God, give me an hour, and I'll be there. Tell me where to go."

Sammy's grandmother Rosa had moved out to LA to live with him, and she was the center of the home. It was an unpretentious, often joyous place, with Rosa cooking pork chops and collard greens and Sammy spinning records.

"Sammy had an innocent boyish quality and a crush on me," Novak said. "We had fun together." Davis initially sought to become involved with Novak to get a modicum of revenge against the white race. He hadn't figured on falling in love with the actress. Knowing what was at risk, the couple saw each other surreptitiously for the next month, culminating in Sammy's Christmas visit with the Novak family in Chicago.

"Something inside of me rebelled when I was told not to see him," Novak later recalled. "I didn't think it was anybody's business. If he had been a bad man, a dangerous man, then the studio might have had reason—but simply because he was black?"

Their mutual attraction struck at one of the most fundamental fears in American society. In 1892, the crusading Black journalist Ida B. Wells wrote an anonymous editorial for the *Memphis Free Speech*: "Nobody in this section of the country believes the old threadbare lie that Negro men rape white women. If Southern white men are not careful, they will overreach themselves, and public sentiment will have a reaction; a conclusion will be reached then which will be very damaging to the moral reputation of their women." For expressing the idea that white women might want to sleep with Black men, a mob burned down the newspaper offices, and Wells fled Memphis.

That danger was not just in the past. In 1955, a Mississippi lynch mob murdered Emmett Till, a fourteen-year-old African American boy, for allegedly whistling at a white woman. There was a very real possibility that the segregated film theaters of the South would refuse to show movies starring an actress who was dating an African American in real life . . . and many in the northern theaters would squirm in their seats too. The prospect of Novak and Davis dating wasn't just different—it was dangerous, for both of them.

Sammy's longtime friend Amy Greene believed Novak got involved with Davis to get even with Cohn. "It was just a blatant, sexual, fun relationship," she said. "Her entire life was programmed by Harry Cohn. All of a sudden Sammy came into her life." Perhaps on some unconscious level, Novak sought her own revenge, but after all the pressures of *Vertigo*, she was having a good time with Sammy.

That good time ended on January 1, 1958, when Chicago columnist Irv Kupcinet wrote about a romance and a possible marriage. Novak denied it vehemently, but nothing could stop the frenzy of the story.

Cohn was beyond livid. He had his Mob friends tell Davis that if he did not end his relationship with Novak, he would lose his one good eye. Davis had two good ears, and he listened. On January 10, 1958, the entertainer married a Black chorus girl, Loray White, whom he did not even know. They separated seven weeks later. Cohn had ended the crisis in his typically crude fashion. He died a few weeks later.

In playing her dual roles in *Vertigo*, Novak did a superb job, worthy of the highest accolades and of serious consideration for an Academy Award nomination. She got none of that, partly because Hitchcock dismissed her performance. It was a strange thing for him to do. He shared in the *Vertigo* profits. In putting Novak down, he was putting his film down. The director patronized her in a way he would never have a male actor.

"She doesn't ruin the story," Hitchcock told *Time*, the director's idea of a compliment. He told Hedda Hopper, "She was hopelessly inept when I started with her." He told another columnist, "Perhaps I should just say modestly that under my direction, she isn't lousy." Even when he had a modicum of praise for Novak, it was twisted upside down. "If I had used a truly gifted actress who could really create two distinctly different women, *Vertigo* wouldn't have been nearly so effective," he told another reporter. That wasn't true, but there was no one to defend her. Critics and Hollywood journalists were in awe of Hitchcock, and they picked up on his words as received wisdom.

The production planned a spectacular premiere in San Francisco and brought up scores of journalists from Southern California. Novak's suite at the Fairmont was decked out in lavender, from the sheets to the bathroom telephone, but the press had no interest in publicizing the actress's supposed favorite color. They had Novak's latest scandal to write about, which was far more intriguing. She had been seeing Lieutenant General Rafael Trujillo Jr., son of the Dominican Republic dictator, who had supposedly given her an array of expensive gifts, including a Mercedes-Benz. When she descended from her suite to a press conference, the reporters asked her about Trujillo, not *Vertigo*.

Hitchcock had the dubious pleasure of reading stories that focused on Novak's romance, not his film, then moving on to reviews, some of which were not the sort the director generally received. Those had a common theme: *Vertigo* was too long, too languid, and too complicated.

It took decades before critics came to appreciate Hitchcock's film as a masterpiece. In 2012, the British Film Institute's *Sight and Sound* critics' poll named *Vertigo* the greatest film ever made, a placement it held for a decade before falling to number two.

Those accolades came far too late to advance Novak's career. It did not help when the most prominent director of the age dismissed her. Add to that the stories about how difficult she was and rumors about interracial dating. Novak had roundly condemned Cohn, but now that he was gone, no one was getting her good parts, and she moved from one forgettable role to another. She starred in several films that did little more than exploit her sexuality in sadly obvious ways. As her status in the industry slowly declined, she married a British actor, Richard Johnson. The marriage was over scarcely before it began, and Novak was once again single.

Novak purchased a house in Big Sur overlooking the Pacific, but other than that, the actress's life appeared to be cursed. In November 1965, while filming a movie in France, she was so seriously injured when she fell off a horse that she had to be replaced. The following

August, she hurt her hand when her car fell down a 120-foot embankment in Santa Maria. That December, near her Bel Air home, she collided with another car on Sunset Boulevard.

Two days later a great mudslide descended on her house in Bel Air, taking down trees in her yard and inundating some of her living room furniture in wet muck. It was all too much, all too terribly much. Grabbing up what she could, Novak jumped into her white Jaguar and headed down the hill as a tree fell, nearly taking her out.

"I got back on the highway and started to drive too fast, up to Big Sur," she said. "I ran down to the beach and threw off all of my clothes and just scrubbed in the water. And it felt so good. It was the most cleansing, healing thing. And I started laughing and dancing in the waves, and by the time I got into the house, I slept like I never slept before."

Novak understood it was time, past time, for her to leave Hollywood. "I wanted to express my feelings," she said. Novak felt boxed up playing roles off-screen as much as on-screen. In seeking her feelings, she was seeking herself. As idyllic as Big Sur first appeared, it was not far enough away from the clamor of modern life or close enough to the feelings she sought. So a decade later, she moved to a country house on the Rogue River in southern Oregon.

Equine veterinarian Robert Malloy came to treat one of Novak's horses. He was a good man doing good work, and she fell in love and married him. She adored his sense of humor, not jokes picked up somewhere, but a warm, amusing take on life. And when he laughed, the ends of his lips turned up as if he was smiling twice.

Novak and Malloy lived in a redwood house in a forest at the center of a forty-three-acre ranch. They had horses, llamas, dogs, and a pet snake or two. Novak loved to ride her horse through grand vistas of trees and water with no other humans and their doings in sight. She often went with her husband when he hurried off to deliver an animal or save a wounded creature. And sometimes, when he could not be there, she did his work, including bringing horses into the world.

Much of the time, Novak painted, her creativity stoked on tokes of marijuana. Some of her swirling images are reminiscent of Edvard Munch. She painted a haunting portrait of her father with deep-set, sorrowful eyes, a biography on a canvas. Novak did not make art to win a new kind of renown. She painted because that's what she was and what she did, and in an attempt to paint her way out of sadness.

Novak still had terrible mood swings. They came when they chose to and departed in their own good time. She went to a doctor, who diagnosed her with bipolar disease and put her on medications. He helped her understand why she'd acted the way she had during those years in Hollywood. She still had massive emotional ups and downs, though not as bad as they once had been. But she had her feelings now. They never left her, and that freed her.

"Life is what you make it in the long run," Novak said. "I don't mind going down into that dark tunnel. I've been there so many times. But as long as you're looking for the light, you'll find light, you know, at the end of the tunnel. And it's all okay."

CHAPTER 8

A Delicate Balance

itchcock had been toying with the film idea he called "The Man on Lincoln's Nose" for most of a decade. The protagonist would be falsely accused of an assassination at the United Nations. He would flee and end up hanging from the sixteenth president's nose at Mount Rushmore. That was about all he had when he hired Ernest Lehman to write the script that became *North by Northwest*.

Lehman was a quiet man with all the charisma of a toll booth operator. Despite his unassuming aura, none of Hitchcock's other screenwriters surpassed him in the sheer literary quality of their work. At the age of forty-two, Lehman counted among his achievements writing the novelette and cowriting the screenplay for *Sweet Smell of Success* (1957), a dark drama about a corrupt New York columnist played by Burt Lancaster.

The screenwriter's challenge for this new project would be to tamp down his natural style and create what he hoped would be the basis for the ultimate Hitchcock film. The director couldn't stand flowery words that, to his mind, got in the way of pure cinema. To help Lehman write the script, Hitchcock didn't prattle on about the plot or suggest soliloquies where the characters unburdened their troubled souls. Instead, he presented Lehman with scenes he hoped to intersperse through the film.

A man hanging for dear life on Lincoln's nose. That was a winner, only why was he up there? "Get the lovers trapped on Mt. Rushmore," Hitchcock said, leaving the screenwriter to figure out how Roger O. Thornhill and Eve Kendall end up hanging from the side of the mountain. Then the director had an idea for a startling scene on a Detroit auto assembly line. The camera would show the making of a car from gestation to popping out finished at the end, only somewhere along the route, a dead body turns up. Lehman went so far as to go to Detroit to set up that idea, but he could not figure out how to make it work.

Hitchcock had yet another idea. "I want them on ice," he said. As the director laid it out, Eskimos are ice fishing when one of them pulls up not arctic char but a human hand. Hitchcock had no idea how Thornhill and Kendall got up to Alaska perched among bundled-up Eskimos and just whose hand it might be. That was for Lehman to work out. The screenwriter did not have to go to Alaska to realize that scene would not make it onto the screen.

During the writing of the screenplay, Alma returned home one afternoon from a doctor's appointment. She told Hitchcock she had been diagnosed with cervical cancer, the disease so progressed that she was to enter the hospital the following day for surgery. The Hitchcocks had a long-standing invitation with one of the screenwriters of *Vertigo*, Samuel A. Taylor, and his wife, Suzanne, to dine at Bellagio Road that evening. Alma went ahead cooking a sumptuous dinner, never giving any sign that she had other things on her mind than a social evening.

As Alma went through the life-threatening episode, she showed a kind of stoic strength that Hitchcock viewed as uniquely female—the ability to carry on and display almost no visible signs of stress, even in trying times. Hitchcock never understood that facility, nor did he seem to comprehend that it did not mean women *felt* less, simply that they (or at least, his wife) did not always show it.

Hitchcock, on the other hand, fell apart at the news of Alma's diagnosis, devastated at the prospect of losing his wife of thirty years. Unwilling to sit in his house alone while she recovered, he went out in the evenings to a restaurant near his Bel Air home. And he did what he always had done when he felt unbearable emotion. He trenched down enormous quantities of food. When Alma got better and came home, he stopped going to the restaurant and never entered its portals again.

Hitchcock was fortunate during those long days, when he could not show his newest project his total focus, that Lehman was capable of going ahead on his own. A master craftsman, Lehman wrote a script full of witty romantic patter that moved along as quickly as the *20th Century Limited* on which Thornhill and Kendall travel from New York to Chicago.

With Lehman's screenplay cooking like a filet mignon grilled to perfection, Hitchcock turned to casting, starting with the main character, New York advertising executive Roger O. Thornhill. *North by Northwest* is a caper tale of mistaken identity. When confused by foreign spies of being an American intelligence agent (who does not exist) and falsely accused of murder, Thornhill sets off on a frantic chase to find the imaginary agent across much of the United States.

James Stewart thought he could play Thornhill to perfection, and he lobbied Hitchcock for the role. The director wrongly blamed Stewart for the initial commercial and artistic failure of *Vertigo*, saying the actor had been too old to play a romantic lead. Hitchcock himself had chosen Stewart to play Scottie in *Vertigo*, but someone had to be blamed, and it could not be Hitchcock. Casting Stewart adrift, he turned to the one actor whom he believed could play the part superbly.

Cary Grant was in semiretirement, but with the help of an unprecedented contract—including a cut of the profits—he agreed to play Thornhill. Fifty-four-year-old Grant was four and a half years *older* than Stewart, but that math did not interest Hitchcock.

Then came the perennial problem of finding an appropriate female lead. Kelly would have played the glamorous undercover agent to perfection, but he could not get Princess Grace to leave the palace for the familiar shores of Los Angeles. He might have signed Novak for the role, but he had no intention of working with the actress again.

Hitchcock decided to offer the role to Elizabeth Taylor. The sultry star was going through a kind of renaissance and would bring moviegoers into the theaters. While he waited for a response, the director sent a script to another actress, Eva Marie Saint. When Taylor's agent turned the project down, Hitchcock was in a fix. The film was about to start shooting, and he still did not have a female lead.

Saint had just given birth to her second child, Laurette Hayden, on July 19, 1958, when the actress's agent, Kurt Frings, called to tell her Hitchcock wanted to consider her for a starring role in his new film. The thirty-four-year-old actress had won the 1955 Academy Award for Best Supporting Actress in her first film, *On the Waterfront*. Since then, she had starred in three other films.

Convalescing from giving birth, Saint had plenty of time to read the script Frings sent her.

Even before she read a word, the actress knew she could not possibly do the film. As hard as it was to give up the opportunity of working with Hitchcock and Grant, no way was Saint going to leave this precious bundle in her arms to traipse from New York to Chicago to the hills of South Dakota, ending up on the face of Mount Rushmore.

As Saint read through the pages in her rental home on Stone Canyon, focusing on her intended role as the duplicitous Eve Kendall, she saw that *North by Northwest* was overwhelmingly Thornhill's film, doubly so since Cary Grant would be playing the male lead.

Saint had a reputation for never strutting around playing the grande dame. Even if she did not show it, she had a considerable ego, but she was shrewd. She could say things to her husband, Jeffrey Hayden, that she would never have said to Hitchcock. "I don't know, honey," she said to Hayden. "I don't come in until about page seventy."

Saint's director/producer husband loved the screenplay. "Honey, I think you should find a quiet spot," Hayden told her. "I'll take care of the children, and I want you to really think about this and reread this script." She did so and afterward called her agent to say yes, she would like to do it.

Nothing was definite when Hitchcock invited Saint to his Bellagio Road home for lunch in August to talk about the role. This was a big moment, and the actress called her mother in New York to tell her. "Mom, I don't know what to wear," she said. When she was growing up, her mother had made her two daughters' clothes, and Saint valued her opinion on this and almost everything else.

"Well, honey, I happened to read something in the dentist's office about Hitchcock, and he loves beige," Mrs. Saint said.

On the day Saint drove up the long drive and knocked on the Hitchcocks' massive front door, she stood dressed in beige from toe to head. She also wore the white gloves she donned whenever she had an important meeting.

As Hitchcock and Alma greeted Saint, the actress had no idea she was far from the director's first choice for the role. Even as Hitchcock greeted her, he was worried about how it would work out if he gave her the role. In *On the Waterfront*, the actress played Edie Doyle, a figure of moral courage in the gritty drama of a stark struggle between good and evil on the Hoboken, New Jersey, waterfront. Taught as she was by the nuns, Edie's Catholic faith leads her to stand up against the Mob-led union that killed her brother. Edie wears no apparent makeup, and until she is sexually awakened by Terry Malloy (Marlon Brando) and lets her hair down, her blond hair is in a tight bun. Representing female virtue in a cruel, manly world, Edie is akin to Amy Kane in *High Noon*. Both roles celebrate the idea that a man must be brave and true if he is to merit a good woman.

Hitchcock believed Saint looked "mousy" in her role, the same criticism he made of Kelly in *High Noon*. Both actresses played courageous women true to themselves. But Hitchcock acted as if a woman who did not gussy herself up to attract the pleased glances of men was worthy of little more than dismissal. As he looked at Saint, he fancied he would have to create someone totally new out of this modest creature in beige who stood before him.

The other actresses Hitchcock invited to lunch over the years had been impressed with the celebrated art on the walls and the vintage wine and delicate crystal on the table. Saint was not disdainful toward such objects, but she did not consider them the mark of a person. Her father was a Quaker. He had taught her it was not things that mattered, but how a person acted. She had a baby at home, and that taught her even more about what was important in life, and it wasn't a bottle of Chardonnay.

What impressed Saint was something totally different. "Everybody was very kind, and everybody was so grateful that I came," the actress recalled. "It was like having a meal with your family."

Hitchcock and his wife gave Saint a beckoningly warm embrace, but her role in *On the Waterfront* stuck in the director's craw. He would never have made such a film. Its mere existence seemed to trouble him.

"You don't cry in this one," he told Saint. The director had no interest in squandering his life making teary movies about the deprived. If he could not clean Saint of her excursion into that coarse world, she would be a disaster. He seemed not to appreciate that Edie was a character that Saint played. It was only a performance, a great one at that, and she had left it behind with her humble costumes.

Aware of the emotional frailty of actors, Hitchcock could not let the actress see how uncertain he felt about her. Instead, he went to the other extreme. Saint left Hitchcock's home that day thinking, "One of his greatest gifts as a director was that he made you feel you were the only perfect person for the role, and this gave you incredible confidence."

Soon after Saint got back home, she received a call from her agent. "Well, you're Eve Kendall," Frings said.

* * *

Saint had not sought movie stardom. She came to Manhattan in 1946 after graduating from Ohio's Bowling Green State University with dreams of becoming a stage actress. Her aspirations had been buoyed when she took lessons at the Actors Studio, full of many of the best actors of her generation. Despite her training, it was hard getting roles.

Then an amazing thing happened. Saint was chosen to play Lieutenant Ann Girard in the Broadway play *Mister Roberts*, starring Henry Fonda. It was about a tyrannical captain on a supply ship in the Pacific during World War II. Lieutenant Girard was the only woman in the cast. It was an incredible opportunity for a young actress in her first Broadway role.

As opening night on February 18, 1948, drew near, there was an extraordinary buzz, the kind of excitement that happens only every few years. It had greeted *Oklahoma!* in 1943, but since then there had been nothing quite like it. No way would such an anticipated play fail, and she, Eva Marie Saint, would be a unique part of a show that would end up running 1,157 performances and become a movie.

Saint could almost hear the opening night ovations as she took her modest bow, when a few days before the premiere, director Josh Logan took her aside. He had painfully decided she was too sweet and pure to play a nurse coming on a ship among rowdy sailors. "We think we've got a hit, but we're going to replace you," Logan said. "We'd like you to stay on as understudy."

"Yes," Saint said meekly. She waited to cry until she got to her dressing room, but she had to stop weeping because, one after another, the other cast members came to say how sorry they were. Then she was alone, with nothing left to do but take the subway to the family apartment in Queens, where her mother had already put a star on her bedroom door.

As the train shuttled eastward, Saint asked herself how much more of this she could take. Was it time to end the dream, to give it up for good, and go ahead with teacher training? As she thought about her choices, it was as if she were observing another person, trying to figure out what Eva Marie Saint would do.

Saint's parents had provided her with a bedrock of support from the day she was born. They weren't seeking meaning for their own lives through their daughter's success, pushing her to achieve a modicum of celebrity so they would have bragging rights. Nor did they feel that since they had brought her up and paid for her college education, she should give up her impossible dream and become a teacher. They were there for her, whatever she chose. It was one thing to say that, another to mean it, and they meant it.

Saint's father was a salesman who traveled the northeast for B. F. Goodrich, selling tires. Mr. Saint was proud he earned a decent living providing for his wife and two daughters. When he came home, he had tales to tell and wonderful things from a distant world, like maple syrup from Vermont. Saint's mother had been a schoolteacher, but she had put that aside to be a full-time wife and mother. She found fulfillment through devotion to her family. The highlight of the day was the evening meal, when the family sat down together.

After the disappointment of *Mister Roberts*, Saint hid her pain deep within and set off the next day, auditioning for other roles. An actor is a small-time entrepreneur, constantly putting herself out there, suffering rejection, and getting up and going on. A few young women like Kim Novak are plucked out of obscurity without ever seeking stardom. For most, the road to any measure of success is so arduous that only those who believe they can do nothing else are best to attempt it.

Saint did not appear to be one of those with the relentless resolve needed. She seemed a polite, gentle young woman elbowed aside by actresses far more aggressive than her. But look closely. Her sweetness hid a core of steel, so much stronger since so few realized she had such strength. She may not have been the first in line for auditions, but she was always there, and back she came again and again. In the early years of television, she started getting callbacks, and small parts, and soon she was a frequent presence on network dramas and in advertisements.

The money was good, and Saint was able to get herself a small apartment in Manhattan. There was only one problem. She was lonely. Saint often thought of her parents and how they had met. Wounded in World War I, her father had spent four months in a hospital in Paris. One day after he got back stateside, he was looking for a post office. Seeing a pretty woman seated on a porch, he asked her for directions. When she told him, he looked her in the eyes and said, "I'm going to marry you."

Saint was making the rounds one day, handing out her résumé and seeking auditions in offices at Radio City Music Hall. She wore a purple corduroy coat that stood out from the blacks and grays of a New York winter. Jeffrey Hayden saw her, or maybe she saw him, and he asked her to have a cup of coffee with him. She said no, but when he asked her to dinner, that was a decent enough offer to accept.

The young actress was seeking a certain kind of mate. Saint had not been in the business long, but had seen enough to realize acting couples took jealousies home each evening. She was delighted to learn that Hayden was not one of her breed. He was an aspiring director/producer, and she felt that might work.

As much as Hayden was attracted to her, Saint was the aggressor, pulling him into her world and what she needed. She wanted a man she could trust completely and share everything with, and she had found him. They married in October 1951 and took an apartment in Greenwich Village, where Saint took care of the housekeeping.

The marriage did not lessen Saint's desire for a role on Broadway. In 1953, she got her opportunity in Horton Foote's *The Trip to Bountiful*. It may have been only a cameo, but the stage set where she wanted to be. The *New York Times* critic found the play thin, but singled out Saint for her "sweet characterization of a soldier's wife."

As small as Saint's part was, the Outer Critics Circle, an organization of out-of-town reviewers, gave her the annual award for Best Supporting Performance—Drama. The award party was one of those few events each year when actors, directors, and producers reunited. The occasion was a chance for Saint to schmooze and make the contacts she would need to get a role in another play. But that wasn't her. She and her husband sat apart on the side of the room, looking to one observer "as though being together was enough."

The Trip to Bountiful lasted only a month on Broadway, but it was long enough for the producers of *On the Waterfront* to see her and offer

Above: Alma Reville and Alfred Hitchcock around two years before their 1926 wedding.

Left: The Hitchcocks at home with their prized Sealyham Terriers.

Below: Alfred Hitchcock at dinner with his associate Joan Harrison beside him, along with his wife, Alma, and daughter, Pat.

Above: June Howard-Tripp and Ivor Novello clinch in a publicity shot for Hitchcock's silent classic *The Lodger*.

Right: The stunning British actress Madeleine Carroll.

Below: Madeleine Carroll and Robert Donat handcuffed together in *The 39 Steps*.

Above: Ingrid Bergman was not always the most comfortable of mothers.

Left: The fresh-faced beauty of Ingrid Bergman.

Below: Ingrid Bergman and Cary Grant kissing in *Notorious*.

Above: In 1956 Grace Kelly married Monaco's Prince Rainier and retreated behind the palace walls.

Left page, top: Grace Kelly's character is falsely convicted of murder in *Dial M for Murder*.

Left page, bottom: Alfred Hitchcock staged the ball scene in *To Catch a Thief* to display Grace Kelly in a splendid gown.

Left: The sultry-looking Kim Novak was a big star in the mid-fifties.

Below: Kim Novak portrayed two characters in *Vertigo* alongside James Stewart.

Above: Eva Marie Saint tests a suit to wear on the *20th Century Limited* in *North by Northwest*.

Below: Eva Marie Saint and Cary Grant dining on the train in *North by Northwest*.

Above: Janet Leigh holding her daughter Jamie Lee Curtis.

Below: Early in their marriage, Janet Leigh was madly in love with her husband Tony Curtis.

Above: Tippi Hedren was terrified as birds attacked her in *The Birds*.

Right: Ingrid Bergman hosted the 1979 American Film Institute tribute to Alfred Hitchcock.

Below: All hands were on Tippi Hedren when she played a compulsive thief in *Marnie*.

her the part that brought her to a Hollywood life and a starring role in *North by Northwest*.

* * *

Saint was hardly home from lunch with the Hitchcocks when she had to pack and fly to New York City for the first part of the shooting. Her first task was to select a new wardrobe fit for her character.

Grant needed a wardrobe too, but the director treated him differently. Whatever words the screenwriters put in the actor's mouth, Cary Grant played Cary Grant, and he played him perfectly. No clothes designer could come close to Grant in understanding the clothes he should wear to project his elegant, understated persona. Grant showed up each morning wearing precisely what he thought he should wear in that day's scenes, and he always got it impeccably right.

Hitchcock treated actresses differently. He had precise ideas about the image he wanted them to project and insisted on clothing them the way he wanted. Novak had thrown a fit when the director insisted she don the gray suit in *Vertigo* that defined her character.

Saint was far more conciliatory and would have been fine wearing the outfits the team at Metro-Goldwyn-Mayer prepared for her. When Hitchcock saw the clothes, he said MGM was "dressing her up like a waif" in someone's misbegotten idea that he was filming a new version of *On the Waterfront*. It just wouldn't do.

On one of her first days in Manhattan, Hitchcock took Saint to Bergdorf Goodman on Fifth Avenue. The director watched with rapt interest as one model after another paraded by wearing the store's finest. As Hitchcock selected Saint's wardrobe, the scene had erotic undertones similar to those in *Vertigo* when Scottie chooses Judy's clothes. "I called him my sugar daddy," Saint recalled. "The only one I ever had, the only one I ever wanted."

"I acted just like a rich man keeping a woman," Hitchcock said. As much subdued sexual pleasure as that might have merited the director, what he was doing was perfectly fitting for the character he was creating. "You're a kept woman," he told Saint, and he kept drumming that into her week after week.

The director took this wisp of a blonde, so déclassé in *On the Waterfront*, and transformed her into the svelte, sexually provocative woman of his imagination. Saint had nothing to do with her outfits but to say thank you.

When Hitchcock looked back on making *North by Northwest*, he remembered choosing Saint's clothes the way another director would recall staging the most dramatic scenes. He forgot nothing of it, from "a heavy black silk cocktail dress subtly imprinted with wine-red flowers in scenes where she deceives Cary Grant" to "a charcoal brown, full-skirted jersey and a burnt orange burlap outfit in the scenes of action."

Hitchcock concerned himself with every aspect of this marvelous creature he believed he had built out of nothing, from the way she wore her blond hair and her makeup to the collar of rubies he chose for her to accessorize her cocktail dress. Kendall was a woman who lived her life through the largesse of a rich man. She had one person she had to please. It would not do for her to dress so provocatively as to attract too much attention. The single-strand necklace was fine. Only the sophisticated would realize what an expensive piece of jewelry it was.

As for the makeup, this kept woman could not look like the young women who went to the movie theaters across America each weekend. He insisted Saint wear far heavier makeup than was natural to her, especially around her eyes. "He didn't want the wide-eyed all-American look," the actress said.

Saint knew Hitchcock's reputation, but she saw nothing of the director who enjoyed making actresses uncomfortable. During the course of the filming, never once did he push her to do things beyond her physical capacity or tell any of his randy tales in her presence.

"How could you tell a dirty limerick to someone who's named a Saint?" she said with lilting laughter. "Maybe he was influenced by that." The actress was joking, and then again, she wasn't. She had this pristine, proper manner, nothing priggish about it, that sent out a signal that one must act toward her with a measure of decorum. She was clearly a lady, and ladies should not be confronted by the rude blandishments of men.

Hitchcock would never have suggested that he had created a male actor, but he boasted that he had been Saint's Svengali. "I've done a great deal for Miss Eva Marie Saint," he told a reporter during the shooting in New York. "She was always a good actress, but she is no longer the drab, mousy little girl she was. I've given her vitality and sparkle. Now she's a beautiful actress."

A male actor might have confronted Hitchcock about his demeaning comments, but Saint chose a different response. She ignored it and pretended it did not exist. Never once did she criticize the director. She didn't hear what Hitchcock said when he disparaged her. And when she could not help but hear, she ignored it, believing only the good was worth remembering.

Grant brought with him his own wardrobe, but he carried with him his own problems too. Fifty-four-year-old Grant's days as a romantic lead were about over. He was being paid an enormous sum plus a cut of the profits to deliver the Cary Grant moviegoers loved. If he could not do that, the audience would cut him dead, and so would Hollywood.

In trying to maintain a veneer of youth, Grant treated the tiniest blemish on his face as a crisis and insisted on perks to maintain his image like no other actor in Hollywood. He had his own makeup team and a person who applied the coloring that gave him the face of a Miami Beach lifeguard. "He used to tease about that," Saint recalled. For onerous physical scenes, he had a double who looked so much like him that on several occasions Saint said "Hi, Cary," as she put her arm around the man.

Despite his accomplishments, or perhaps in part because of them, Grant was amazingly self-doubting. Hitchcock had worked long enough with actors to realize that the best are often the most uncertain about themselves. Even before the shooting of the first scene, Grant complained not only about the script but that the whole project would be a disaster. Hitchcock knew the way out of this was to say nothing and to move confidently ahead.

In Los Angeles, people had mostly gotten used to Hitchcock, but in New York City he was a sensation. Cabbies yelled his name out as they drove by. Children rushed up asking for his autograph, and adults who viewed his weekly television show looked at him with awe.

Since *Alfred Hitchcock Presents* had debuted on television in October 1955, the director had reached a level of celebrity possible only in this new medium. Each program began with Hitchcock's face in profile, locked within a caricature he had drawn. Then he introduced the half-hour episode with droll comments that often made fun of himself in a way John Ford or Orson Welles would never have done. Nor would they have dressed themselves like Little Lord Fauntleroy or supposedly naked in a barrel.

There are few things as endearing as self-mockery, and the public adored him. Only Walt Disney was so revered. The popular series allowed Hitchcock to reconnect professionally with his former associate Joan Harrison, who produced the program along with Norman Lloyd.

One evening, Hitchcock took Ernest Lehman to dinner at Christ Cella, a New York steakhouse celebrated for its enormous portions and little more. After a number of martinis sufficient to limber up his vocal cords and open up his emotions, he put his hand on Lehman's. "Ernie, do you realize what we're doing in this picture?" he said in a whisper, announcing that what he was about to say was only for the screenwriter's ears. "The audience is like a giant organ that you and I are playing. At one moment, we play *this* note on them and get *this* reaction, and then we play *that* chord, and they react *that* way. And someday, we won't even have to make a movie—there'll be electrodes implanted in their brains, and we'll just press different buttons, and they'll go 'ooooh' and 'aaaah' and we'll frighten them, and make them laugh. Won't that be wonderful?"

There was no need to wait until that glorious moment to manipulate the audience. Lehman's script had so many twists and turns that moviegoers risked crimping their necks. As the film begins, Thornhill is having drinks with business associates in the Oak Room at the Plaza Hotel. He is wearing a suit so beautifully fitted that the clothing could have been invented for him.

Out in the Plaza's lobby, two lowlife thugs, Valerian and Licht, look pointedly out of place. As dumb as they are malevolent, the duo mistake Thornhill for American undercover agent George Kaplan, nemesis to a group of Communist spies. Anything goes in the Cold War, and the two conspirators kidnap the unlucky advertising executive and take him to their leader, Phillip Vandamm (James Mason), in a mansion in Glen Cove, Long Island. Vandamm is a sophisticated gentleman, handsome enough to be a leading man, but his sinister eyes tell us to beware of this evil mastermind.

Vandamm's top associate, Leonard, is about thirty years old, with what the screenplay describes as a "soft baby face" and "attitudes [that] are unmistakably effeminate." When Hitchcock cast Martin Landau in the role, the actor decided to play the character as outrageously gay. In love with Vandamm, Leonard will do anything to protect his boss and drive away any woman who gets close to him. In those years, gays were still so much in the closet that most moviegoers probably did not comprehend what they were seeing, an openly gay character in a mainstream film.

"Everyone told me not to do what I did, but Hitchcock loved it," Landau said. The actor had honed his craft at the Actors Studio. Saint had studied acting there too, but it was not her overwhelming identity, and, working with Hitchcock, she knew she should downplay such techniques.

For Landau, his experience at the Actors Studio was at the center of his being. As he had been taught, he sought to get totally inside Leonard, inhabiting the character. This could seem irritatingly self-centered to a director wanting to get on with things, but that wasn't Landau's concern. He worked out a crucial scene with Mason and walked on the set ready to portray every shade of his role.

Hitchcock was not about to indulge Landau. He systematically cut the scene into little pieces so that a frustrated Landau could not get the traction to play the role the way he wanted to. It was a funny bit of business, mildly sadistic, and Landau did not get the joke. In the end, Hitchcock got out of the actor what *he* wanted, and Landau's Leonard is a simpering lackey embracing his dirty work as a high calling.

Eve Kendall does not appear in the film until Thornhill flees on the *20th Century Limited*, and Saint had little to do in New York. The actress did not simply hang out in her suite at the St. Regis, but was often with her colleagues. She bonded immediately with Grant and gave him a nickname: Thornycroft.

When the two actors were not together, Saint communicated with Thornycroft by telegrams that were sometimes as clever as Lehman's dialogue. Grant telegraphed her one day at her hotel when he was out on the set working: "All right, all right. So now you're in the St. Regis. I'm still in the doldrums and in a tizzy. Thornycroft."

In the scene of Thornhill held captive in a Long Island mansion, the debonair business executive keeps an ironic distance from his desperate dilemma, speaking lines fit for a comedy club. Despite Thornhill's fervid denials that he is Kaplan, Vandamm remains convinced the advertising man is the secret agent who must be eliminated. Thus begins a series of misadventures for Thornhill that would have had Job raising a white flag.

In the end, Thornhill concludes that the only way to end his torment is to confront the evil leader of this pack of vipers. He does not know his name, but believing that Vandamm is Lester Townsend, the owner of the house where he was held captive, he goes to the UN, where Townsend is addressing the General Assembly.

When Thornhill pages Townsend, the man who answers is not the chief of his tormenters. Townsend explains he is indeed Lester Townsend, and has not been in his Long Island house for weeks. It is clear to Thornhill that his persecutors had camped out there.

Valerian has followed Thornhill and stands at the edge of the lounge. Hopelessly inept at his criminal assignments, he throws a knife at Thornhill that lands in Townsend's back, killing him instantly. As Townsend falls, Thornhill reaches to pull the knife out, looking to observers as if he is the murderer.

Now Thornhill is being pursued not just by Communist conspirators but by the American authorities. He flees, knowing the one way to unravel his terrible plight is to find Kaplan, whom Vandamm said is headed to the Ambassador East Hotel in Chicago and from there to Rapid City, South Dakota.

By this time, much of the audience should have been rubbing their necks from all the going back and forth, but this is a Hitchcock film, and when the director is at the tiller, the audience accepts even the most unlikely of events without a complaint.

At Grand Central Terminal, Thornhill sneaks onto the *20th Century Limited*, traveling overnight to Chicago. For forty-two minutes,

Thornhill has been chased up and down the screen by murderous pursuers, and not for one moment has this handsome man come across an attractive woman.

Schmoozing with a beautiful woman had not been the beleaguered businessman's concern, but as Thornhill hurries down the train corridor, he sees a gorgeous blond creature. Eve Kendall presents a svelte image in her clinging black suit and is flirtatious in the most inviting way.

The only direction Hitchcock gave the actress was to "do three things: lower your voice; don't use your hands; and look into Cary's eyes at all times." If Saint had considered the techniques she learned at the Actors Studio sacrosanct, she might have mocked such simple suggestions. But she was in Hitchcock's hands, and she did what he told her to do.

The techniques worked magically, in part because they were far more revealing of character than they might appear. Kendall's emotions lay deeply embedded within her. She needs no flailing of her hands to express feelings she does not have. "Every move I made with my hands, body or legs was calculated, more controlled," Saint said.

Kendall's voice is just as much in control. "I found, when I got excited, my voice is inclined to go up," Saint reflected. "A woman who wants to be alluring should be in control of the situation at all times. She shouldn't get excited. She lets the man get excited. She must be *intelligent*, but not show it too much—it's a fine line." That was the model not just for Saint's character, but for how women often felt they had to act to attract men in 1950s America.

Without even knowing Thornhill, Kendall helps the debonair suspected murderer avoid the police. When she goes into the dining car for dinner, Thornhill joins her. Kendall has impish eyes asking for adventure. Seated there, Saint and Grant are a resonant romantic duo. Their captivating, flirtatious dialogue creates all the sense of character needed. Kendall knows Thornhill is an accused murderer. To her, if anything, that makes him more interesting.

Kendall is the aggressor, speaking seductive lines that in most films would have been spoken by a man.

"I tipped the steward five dollars to seat you here if you should come in," Kendall says.

"Is that a proposition?" Thornhill asks.

"I never make love on an empty stomach," Kendall says. The censors would not allow such a provocative line. They made Hitchcock dub over the offensive words, making it "I never discuss love on an empty stomach." No matter, Kendall appears to be inviting Thornhill to her compartment for a night of lovemaking. In those years, onscreen or off, a well-brought-up young lady did not act so provocatively. To perform on the same level of sexual forwardness today, Kendall would have had to reach out under the table and grab Thornhill's crotch.

Kendall welcomes Thornhill to her compartment, where she secretes him away from the police. He has told her the details of his plight, and she offers to seek out Kaplan herself in Chicago, a dangerous suggestion. As she embraces Thornhill while telling him he must sleep on the floor, her eyes express catlike cunning. She gives a note to the porter, who takes it to another drawing room occupied by Vandamm and Leonard. The note reads:

What do I do with him in the morning?

Eve

Before departing from the train, Kendall agrees to call Kaplan at his hotel and set up a meeting with Thornhill. After speaking to someone in a phone booth at the LaSalle Street Station, Eve tells

Thornhill that Kaplan has agreed to meet him. He is to take a Grey-hound bus to Indianapolis, getting off at the Prairie Stop on Highway 41. It is a junction to nowhere.

The scene was shot not in Indiana but in Bakersfield, California. In the motel where the cast and crew stayed, Grant called Lehman into his room for a discussion. The screenwriter knew about the rumors concerning Grant's bisexuality, and finding the actor dressed in a towel draped over his midsection, Lehman became nervous. "We sat on the bed to go over the scene, and I remember carefully leaving the door of the room open," he said.

On the day the cast and crew headed out from the motel to film the scene, the temperature reached 110 degrees, and that was in the shade. Grant sat in the back seat of an air-conditioned limousine be-moaning his fate, and it had nothing to do with the weather.

The actor did not dare unload on Hitchcock, so he beckoned Lehman to hear his rant. Grant was outraged that his character had to speak an inordinate amount of dialogue to carry the story ahead. To his ears, the dialogue was absurd. "You think you've written a Cary Grant picture?" he asked the screenwriter, who had worked from day one to make sure *North by Northwest* was precisely that. "This is a Da-vid Niven picture."

Then Grant got out of the limousine to shoot one of the most famous chase scenes in film history. Hitchcock always wore a coat and tie, but that morning he stood waiting to begin shooting in shirt-sleeves. The only person in business wear was Grant, who looked as cool as a mannequin in the window at Saks Fifth Avenue. In the nearby field stood three acres of corn that the production team had purchased and replanted.

Thornhill stands alone in this isolated spot, far from the protec-tion of civilization. Except for the stand of corn, there is nowhere to hide. In the distance, a crop-dusting plane flies back and forth over land where there is no corn. Then the plane turns and comes for Thornhill, trying to run him down or kill him with machine-gun fire. He sprints desperately to the cornfield. Treating him like a cornered rat, the pilot lays down a thick blanket of crop-dusting chemicals, driving Thornhill back into the open. Pursuing his victim at any cost, the pilot crashes into a fuel truck that explodes, flames reaching into the sky.

In Chicago, the cast and crew took up forty rooms in the Ambassador East. Grant was used to being treated better than anyone else. The actor was mildly disappointed that he could not have his favorite suite. Judy Garland was doing a weeklong series of shows, and she was staying in it.

The servers, doormen, elevator operators, and concierges were in particularly good moods, since they had three-day contracts as extras in their hands. Many other hotel guests were not so elated, since they could not move around the lobby when Hitchcock was shooting.

One evening in early September, Grant took Saint to Garland's concert at Orchestra Hall. The singer-actress was an American phenomenon, and there were no empty seats in the auditorium. "Everyone in the theater was reading their programs, looking at the stage, waiting for Garland to come on, and then Grant walks in, and it's like God has arrived," Saint said. "Everyone turned to look at him. . . . He was like a god. He really was."

Saint was overwhelmed by the attention. "I just don't know how you handle this," she told Grant.

"Eva Marie, it enriched their evening because they were excited, and they'll tell friends about it," Grant said. "They'll say they saw Cary Grant. And that's a good feeling. I did something and made their lives a little brighter."

But the audience came to see Judy Garland. When she walked forward to the footlights at the end of the evening and sang "Somewhere Over the Rainbow," it was as if she had never sung it before. When she finished, the lives of everyone in the theater were a little brighter. They did not need Grant for that, but he needed them. Without their applause and twittering excitement, he would have been lost. He was as much on the stage as Garland, acting out the image he had created over three decades.

The evening was unsettling to Saint. It was a cautionary tale, one she never forgot. Walk too readily into the glare of celebrity, believing it will make you whole, and one day you turn around to look back and find there is nothing left of what you once considered yourself. And then you turn forward once again, a prisoner to this being you have created.

In the movie, when Thornhill returns to Chicago, he knows Kendall has set him up to be murdered. He follows her to an auction at the Shaw & Oppenheim Galleries, where she is seated next to Vandamm, who is touching her shoulder intimately. Thornhill realizes Kendall is Vandamm's mistress and has betrayed him in ways he can barely contemplate. When Thornhill sees Vandamm's henchmen ready to shoot him, he stages a scene that brings in the police, who take him away.

Instead of arresting Thornhill, the cops drive him to the airport, where an elderly gentleman known only as the Professor hurries the reluctant businessman toward a waiting plane. The senior CIA operative tells him they know Thornhill killed no one. As for Kaplan, he is a useful fiction devised by the agency to fool the spies.

The Professor's most devastating revelation is that Kendall is the American undercover agent. Because of her budding romance with Thornhill, she risks being discovered and murdered. Vandamm plans to fly out of the country the following evening from his home near

Mount Rushmore. To save Kendall from discovery, Thornhill must continue the Kaplan charade by flying with the Professor to South Dakota.

The restaurants and bars of Rapid City, South Dakota, were more used to serving drunken cowboys than sober movie stars, but one evening in mid-September, Grant and Saint went out on the town. Grant wore a white jacket and a Western bolo tie. He looked like a croupier at a Las Vegas casino. Saint was dressed in a speckled suit and heels and could have been headed for a ladies' luncheon at the Bel Air Country Club. The two actors could not stay out late because they had a long day of shooting ahead of them beneath Mount Rushmore.

For Hitchcock, much of the motivation in doing *North by Northwest* was to film a stirring chase across the faces of the four presidents. Alas, the US National Park officials were not going to have a group of motley actors rummaging up and down the historical monument and refused his request. That left the director to film just one day in South Dakota, mainly at the visitor's center beneath the gigantic images carved out of the mountaintop.

In the crucial scene shot that long day to prove her fidelity to Vandamm, Kendall pulls out a pistol and shoots Thornhill, who appears to be critically wounded. But the pistol contains nothing but blanks. After the body is taken away, Thornhill gets up off the gurney.

Kendall explains to Thornhill how she met Vandamm at a party and fell in love. When the Professor told her the truth about her lover, she became an American agent spying on him. "Maybe it was the first time anyone ever asked me to do something worthwhile," she says. It is a line Alicia Huberman could have spoken in *Notorious* and established Kendall as yet another of Hitchcock's stained heroines who must act to redeem herself.

From South Dakota, the cast and crew traveled to Los Angeles to film the interior shots at the MGM studios. Hitchcock was glad to be home. He was so intent on getting things *right* that he was always going off on location, but he was much more in his element on an enclosed set, where he could control everything. "I prefer a nice drawing-room picture with a couch to sit on between scenes," he said.

Hitchcock insisted the crew dress in white shirts and ties with everything on the set spotless and regulated. One day, it upset him to see Saint wearing one of the exquisite outfits he had chosen, pouring her coffee into a Styrofoam cup. "Eva Marie, you don't get your coffee," he admonished her. "We have someone get it for you. And you drink from a porcelain cup and saucer. You are wearing a $3,000 dress, and I don't want the extras to see you quaffing from a Styrofoam cup."

Most of the scenes between Grant and Saint were shot at the MGM studios. Speaking irreverent dialogue, they played off each other brilliantly. Grant would hit the ball hard at Saint. She would wallop it back just as strong, and he would rear up and slam it back hard across the net, and back again it would come. Saint was endlessly solicitous to Grant; he was the same to her, and both came out well.

One day, Grant noticed Saint squinting. One of his many perks was control over the lighting when he was on camera. To look his best, he needed to be well-lit, but he turned to Hitchcock and said, "Excuse me, that light is really too bright for me." He could have mentioned Saint, but he did not do that.

When Saint drove home each afternoon, she was still wearing not only Kendall's makeup but her persona. The actress could not abandon all she had learned at the Actors Studio. She inhabited her character in a way that would have appalled Hitchcock if he had known. It was harder to wipe that off than makeup, and when she entered the house, her three-and-a-half-year-old son, Darrell, saw this strange woman with a peculiar voice and marks on her face.

"Mommy, there's dirt over your eyes," Darrell said.

* * *

In the final scenes in *North by Northwest*, Vandamm retreats for a few hours to his Frank Lloyd Wright–like home behind Mount Rushmore before intending to fly presumably behind the Iron Curtain from a private airfield just below his villa. Kendall returns to join him. Thornhill gets Kendall a message telling her that the conspirators are onto her and plan to drop her body over the Atlantic.

As Vandamm walks with Kendall to the waiting plane, she flees with Thornhill, ending up on the sheer cliffs of Mount Rushmore, pursued by Vandamm and his cohorts.

The chase is Hitchcock's dream fulfilled, and it was all done at the MGM studios. Unlike Grant, Saint had no double to take risks climbing on the faux Mount Rushmore. "I slipped a little," she recalled. "The fellow there didn't catch me quite early enough, so when I slid, I was hurt. I still have a tiny scrape on the inside of my elbow."

As Thornhill and Kendall try to escape down the presidential faces, Valerian jumps down at Thornhill. The villain attempts to stab Thornhill, but falls to his death. Kendall and Thornhill also fall, but hang on to the sheer face. Thornhill calls out for help. Leonard comes forward and begins pressing his foot on the businessman's hands with a look of exquisite sadistic pleasure. A shot rings out, and Leonard falls to the earth far below. High above, the Professor stands with state troopers, including the officer who shot Leonard. Next to the Professor stands the captured Vandamm.

The drama is not over. As Kendall holds desperately on to Thornhill's hand, afraid she will not make it to safety, he is no longer pulling her up the cliff but into an upper berth as "the train rolls off into the night." That's the way Lehman's script ends, but Hitchcock added a fortissimo coda. At the final moment of *North by Northwest*, the train enters a tunnel, Hitchcock's metaphor for sex.

It was a close call who was more pessimistic about *North by Northwest*'s prospects: Lehman, who every time there was a knock on the door thought failure was calling, or Grant, who criticized the screenplay on the first day of shooting and never stopped. For the first sneak preview in Santa Barbara in June 1959, Lehman refused to show up to face the boos he was sure would be the overwhelming greeting.

The following day, Grant called. Lehman could not bear to listen to Grant's whining complaints that would surely make the screenwriter the primary villain. But it was Cary Grant calling, and Lehman figured he had to take the call.

"Wasn't it marvelous?" Grant enthused. "Did you ever hear such a reaction?"

North by Northwest did fabulous business and received largely strong reviews. These days, it is considered by many one of the best films of all time. Saint did not have an easy time deciding what to do after such a singular success. She liked stretching different parts of her artistic persona, and she agreed to play opposite Paul Newman in *Exodus*, a dramatic tale about Israel's birth, based on a bestselling novel by Leon Uris. Her character is a widowed American nurse. Hitchcock was appalled that Saint would play such a role. "I took a lot of trouble with Eva Marie Saint grooming her and making her sleek and sophisticated," he told Hedda Hopper in 1962, exposing his sentiments to the world. "Next thing she's in a picture called *Exodus* and looking dissipated."

Hitchcock could not stop complaining. "You go to work on these girls and teach them how to use their face to convey thought, to convey sex, everything," he told François Truffaut. "All the heartaches I've had and the pain and the emotion I've poured into the thing ends up nothing, the effort completely wasted."

Saint had a life, and it was not Hitchcock's. Her husband and two children accompanied her to the three-month shoot in Israel and

Cyprus. That would be the pattern of Saint's life, always considering her family. To protect her home life, she generally did only one film a year. In the summers, the family traveled east, where Saint and her husband, Jeffrey, had glorious experiences working in summer stock.

Saint kept her Academy Award statuette in a closet at her home in Southern California, and there were few signs that a celebrity lived there. Her most significant achievement—one for which there is no award—is to have maintained a long, honorable career as an actress while not sacrificing her husband, children, and family for a moment. Her marriage was a blessing from the day she married Jeffrey in 1951 to the day sixty-five years later when he died in 2016. She loved and nurtured him for all those years, and he did the same for her.

Now everyone is gone, not just Jeffrey, but everyone she worked with, everyone who helped her. It is challenging to live in Los Angeles no longer with her husband, but she does so. Her strength of character did not just descend upon her because she needed support. It is something her mother and father instilled in her, something her husband helped her build. It is something she built up herself over decades.

At the age of ninety-nine, Saint lives in an apartment on Wilshire Boulevard. Sometimes the only sound is the lawn mower beneath her window cutting the grass.

CHAPTER 9

There Really Was a Hollywood

A s long as Hitchcock was working on a film, he was encapsulated within a separate world that kept the demons that pursued him at bay. He understood this, and during his entire career, whatever movie he was directing, he was also preparing for his next film. Hitchcock did not succeed at that during the filming of *North by Northwest*. The movie was a sterling success, and no one would have begrudged him for taking a few months off. But he needed to get busy or the emotional bile would rise within him.

As the weeks went by, Hitchcock and his minions foraged wider and broader through books, magazine articles, newspaper clippings, and scripts, looking for the one idea that would work. One day in April of 1959, the fifty-nine-year-old director was reading the Criminals at Large column in the *New York Times Book Review* that ran periodically in the publication's back pages. That placement reflected the low regard in which the literary establishment held crime thrillers. Considering them unworthy of significant reviews, the *Times* lumped the books together, each meriting no more than a few sentences.

Hitchcock read no further than the first review, a novel called *Psycho* by Robert Bloch. The author based the main character on Ed Gein, a serial killer who lived in the countryside of Wisconsin an hour from Bloch's home. A necrophiliac and a cannibal, Gein supposedly paraded around wearing the decimated breasts and skin of his late mother.

Critic Anthony Boucher wrote, "The narrative surprises and shocks are so cunningly arrayed that it's unwise even to hint at plot and theme beyond mention that they seem suggested by a recent real-life monstrosity in the Middle West." That was how the director would have hyped one of his movies. The review titillated Hitchcock enough that he ordered the book and read it the following weekend.

In the novel, Norman Bates runs a seedy motel. One night a woman shows up and takes a room. She has stolen $40,000 from her boss. As tempting as it is to continue on with her ill-gotten fortune—$400,000 in today's cash—she decides to drive back home in the morning to return the money. Before going to bed, she takes a shower. As she does so, she "started to scream, and then the curtains parted further, and a hand appeared, holding a butcher's knife. It was the knife that, a moment later, cut off her scream. And her head."

That was the author's full description of the murder, but it was enough to set off Hitchcock's imagination. Like the director's nearly decade-long obsession to make a movie featuring a chase down the face of Mount Rushmore, he wanted to make this film because of that one scene. "I think that the thing that appealed to me and made me decide to do the picture was the suddenness of the murder in the shower, coming, as it were, out of the blue," he reflected. "That was about all." The transvestite mass murderer had been driven to his evil deeds by his mother. What was a Hitchcock film without a malevolent mother?

The executives at Paramount to whom Hitchcock took the project were appalled that the director would consider doing such an exploitative film. In recent years, they had been competing with quickie, low-budget horror films fit for drive-ins and second-run theaters that sometimes made more money than their big-budget movies. As the most famous director in America, Hitchcock had no business falling into their ranks. The Paramount honchos were so upset that, despite Hitchcock's status, they refused to finance the film or to let him shoot on their lot.

Hitchcock looked at the same facts as the Paramount naysayers and came up with a different conclusion. Never having been a pretentious filmmaker, he was intrigued by the idea of making his version of a horror film. Always a friend of the bottom line, he liked the idea that if he made *Psycho* cheaply, he might make big profits.

So what if Paramount denied him? Hitchcock would finance *Psycho* himself. He would prepare the project with the same meticulous concern as always. But he would shoot the film in black and white on the Universal lot with a crew from his television series, a down-and-dirty group of pros used to working quickly and on budget. To ensure Paramount would distribute the film, Hitchcock agreed to waive his standard $250,000 director's fee and instead take a 60 percent cut of the negative.

Psycho was a daring film for Hitchcock to make. Most aging directors would have sought a project resonating with their past triumphs, not a film that risked sending them down into the lower depths of filmdom from which there was likely no return.

After one disastrous attempt to hire a screenwriter, Hitchcock settled on thirty-seven-year-old Joseph Stefano, a former actor and rock music composer who wore his cockiness on his sleeve.

Stefano thought he had been hired to write a Hitchcock film, but this was something beyond the pale and the screenwriter told the director precisely how he felt. The serial killer Norman Bates was so despicable that he dreaded having to write that character.

"How would you feel if Norman were played by Anthony Perkins?" Hitchcock asked. That was practically all it took to bring Stefano on board. Perkins was an actor who exuded sensitivity in playing good men like the Quaker Josh Birdwell in *Friendly Persuasion* (1956). If Perkins took the part, the serial killer would have an empathetic side that Stefano could fully invoke in the screenplay.

That wasn't the only good news Hitchcock had for his writer. "What if we got a big-name actress to play this girl?" Hitchcock said. "Nobody will expect her to die!" The director mentioned a star, probably Lana Turner, whom Stefano thought would be a disaster. Then he mentioned Janet Leigh, and everything made sense.

Although the blond actress was not in Hollywood's highest firmament, Leigh had played in thirty-two films, consistently winning good notices. She had just costarred in Orson Welles's film noir *Touch of Evil* (1958). Playing Susan Vargas, a woman falsely accused of murder, Leigh held her own against such consummate screen stealers as Charlton Heston and Orson Welles. It was not much of a stretch to imagine Leigh playing the morally conflicted Marion Crane heading off with her ill-gotten gains on a road trip to death.

* * *

In 1929, when Jeanette Helen Morrison, who would become famous as Janet Leigh, was two years old, her parents moved from Merced up the road to Stockton in California's Central Valley. In his classic novel, *Fat City*, Leonard Gardner described the "stunted skyline of Stockton—a city of eighty thousand surrounded by the sloughs, rivers and fertile fields of the San Joaquin River delta—a view of business buildings, church spires, chimneys, water towers, gas tanks and the

Merced for a couple of weeks in the summer. Her parents figured, why not?

Jeanette and Kenny had only a few days to plot how she could stay in Merced. It slowly came to them that there was one way. They should get married. She was fourteen years old, younger than the age of consent. Despite that, Kenny's parents enabled the marriage, loaning the couple a car to drive to Reno for the ceremony.

By Jeanette lying about her age, the couple got a wedding license. When the newlyweds drove back to Merced, Jeanette's parents were waiting for them in front of the Carlyles' house. Fred and Helen took their daughter's bag, pushed her into the car, and returned to Stockton as Kenny stood bereaved on the sidewalk. That was the last time Jeanette saw Kenny.

Jeanette's parents would not let up on their daughter. There were good girls and bad girls and nothing in between. In one night, Jeanette changed not just from a good girl to a bad girl but to a terrible girl. Her parents ranted on and on as if they were the ones who suffered the most, not Jeanette.

"How could you do this to your mother?" Helen asked rhetorically. "Look at what you've done to us." When her parents paid for an annulment, that was another reason to condemn their daughter, for forcing them to spend money they barely had.

Even if her parents had not said a word, Jeanette would have felt guilty, but their constant admonitions left her stunted. Fearing she would be humiliated and destroyed if anyone found out, she held on to the secret with white-knuckled tightness. She lived a lie because she thought that was the only life left to her. At Stockton High, she played the good girl as well as any role in her life. Although she had her full share of beaux, none touched her.

In September 1943, sixteen-year-old Jeanette entered the College of the Pacific as a music major. The classrooms were full of eligible young men who were part of the V-12 program, training to become officers, a decided side benefit for coeds at the Stockton school. One of them was a dashing sailor, Stanley Reames. Not only did he share Jeanette's interest in music, but he formed his own dance band. Being around Stanley was like going to the movies as a kid and being transported to a different world. That's how exciting she found him, and they became a steady duo.

In the spring of 1945, Stanley asked Jeanette to marry him. That confronted her with two compelling questions. Did she love Stanley enough to want to spend the rest of her life with him? That she kept asking herself that question meant the answer was likely no. Then there was the matter of her previous marriage. If Stanley knew the truth, would he still want to marry her? She decided she did not want to risk finding out.

The couple said their vows in a lovely wedding in October 1945 in the Morris Chapel at the College of the Pacific. Only Jeanette and her parents knew the marriage was beginning with monumental deceit and the perpetual apprehension that one day someone from Merced would tell Stanley he was not his bride's first husband.

Jeanette's second wedding night was much like the first: an anonymous hotel room, and then the door shut, leaving her alone with her new husband, full of apprehension. She did not fake a virgin's pain. That was genuine, but it did not lead to the rapture that she remembered experiencing with Kenny. In hiding her past, she had struck a terrible bargain, and she could not bring herself to be truthful to this man beside her.

Fred and Helen had devoted much of their lives to their daughter's happiness. With Jeanette married, the couple packed their belongings, gave their car to the newlyweds, and headed off to a new life. No matter how far the Morrisons intended to roam, they ended up only 140 miles away at the Sugar Bowl Ski Lodge in the High Sierra mountains, where Fred worked as an assistant desk clerk and Helen as a waitress in the dining room.

When Jeanette and Stanley came to visit, the resort photographer took her picture on the slopes to be used to promote the ski lodge. It was the perfect image for the resort: a fresh-faced, unmade-up, laughing young woman radiant with health. Fred missed his daughter so much and was so proud of her that he kept the picture next to him on his desk.

The resort had its share of celebrity guests, including the retired actress Norma Shearer, who had been the queen of MGM during the thirties. Shearer noted Jeanette's photo. Most people passing the desk would have seen just another pretty face, but to Shearer, "that smile made it the most fascinating face I had seen in years. I felt I had to show that face to somebody at the studio." Seeing a potential star, Shearer asked for a copy along with other pictures. It said something about the actress's judgment that she was right and something about her character that she would take pleasure in connecting this unknown young woman with Hollywood.

When Helen told her daughter about Shearer's request, Jeanette did not think much about it. She had other matters of concern. Stanley had decided his band's moment had arrived. The couple borrowed money and drove to LA, where they resided in the threadbare Harvey Hotel. Stanley haunted the venues where the big bands played and put together a group strong enough to get an audition at MCA. Stanley's group was good, but the big band era was ending. He had come at a time too late.

That news was sinking in when, thanks to Shearer, Jeanette received a letter from Levis Green, an agent at MCA, asking to meet "to discuss possible representation." To look like a potential movie star, she swept her hair back and doused herself in heavy makeup. When Green took one look at her, he picked up the photo Shearer had given the agency and said that was how she should look for the meeting he was taking her to at MGM.

Without even a screen test, the studio signed Jeanette to a seven-year contract. Then, a few weeks later, with her new name of Janet Leigh, she went off on location to play the female lead in *The Romance of Rosy Ridge* (1947), opposite Van Johnson. Things did not happen this way. A newly signed actress spent months taking acting lessons and made her debut as a starlet in a modest role.

Leigh's rise was so brisk that even the *New York Times* took notice. "The town is showing unusual interest in the girl," the paper wrote in August 1947, "a slim 19-year-old blonde, because her story outshines in implausibility the most fantastic tale ever concocted by a screen writer assigned to create a Hollywood success story." If that was not unlikely success enough, no one who saw her powerfully emotive performance in *The Romance of Rosy Ridge* could have imagined her only previous acting experience was in Gilbert and Sullivan's *The Pirates of Penzance* in college.

Nearly four decades later, when Leigh published her autobiography, she wrote about her early years growing up as Jeanette Morrison in the third person, as if this were someone she had left long ago. Then, when MGM gave her a new name, she wrote the rest of the book in the first person as Janet Leigh. Her subtitle for that part of her memoir is "Pollyanna in Hollywood." In good times, Pollyannas are an upbeat joy, pulling everyone else up with them. In bad times they often do not know where to look or what to say or do, only to pretend the bad times do not exist.

Leigh locked her face in a smile. No one was more upbeat. Her hands clasped firmly over her ears, she heard no evil, even when it rang all around her. Her eyes taped shut, she saw no perfidy, even when it occurred in front of her. Everyone around her was good and worthy.

Like many Pollyannas, Janet's boundless positiveness was, in some ways, a career move, a useful way to survive Hollywood's rude struggles. Almost totally lacking in introspection, she rarely looked deeply within herself or at the world around her.

Leigh's parents quit their jobs at the ski resort and drove down to live with their beloved daughter in a small house in the San Fernando Valley. Her father had nothing but disdain for Stanley, who, as he saw it, moped around the house living off his wife, too lazy to get a job.

Leigh had more empathy for a despairing husband who thought his life over. As much as she tried to help him, she had other worries, fearing at any moment she might be exposed as a twice-married child bride, her career ending in woeful shame. Leigh started to have stomach and nerve problems. That was something else not to be talked about, but these health problems stayed with her wherever she went and whatever she did.

Leigh's father got a job before Stanley had even started looking at the help wanted ads, and the Morrisons moved out. That allowed Stanley and Janet to get an apartment in Los Angeles, where he finally found some measure of work. Leigh had not known if she truly loved Stanley when she married him. She knew even less now, but could not abide being a twice-divorced twenty-year-old woman.

When Leigh began a relationship with the actor Barry Nelson, it may not have been fully consummated, but it went far enough to frighten her and drive her back toward Stanley. But it was no good. In July 1948, after a little over two and a half years of marriage, she won a divorce after charging her husband with "mental cruelty." Clutching the document, Leigh headed off into a glorious, full-blown affair with Nelson.

Leigh proudly purchased a house in the San Fernando Valley, where she lived with her parents and pursued her career with focused purpose. Her father managed her money and doled it out to her like she was a profligate teenager.

With her inability to show adult control over her own life and display initiative on her own, MGM was the perfect place for the actress. Fancying itself the home of the largest array of stars in Hollywood, MGM nurtured its actors. The studio taught them how to dress and act. They gave actors under contract prominent roles in one film after another, elevating them with a massive publicity machine until they became stars not simply in the credit at the beginning of their films but in the eyes of millions of moviegoers. Leigh was natural for this system. Never a temper tantrum. Never a gripe that her salary should be bigger. Never a complaint about her choice of roles.

In those years, in Hollywood, there were the good girls and the bad girls, and only a treacherous no-man's-land in between. Leigh's colleague at MGM, Elizabeth Taylor, was a naughty girl. There were no vixen-like roles for Leigh. The studio developed the twice-married divorcée into a morally fastidious goody-goody girl, exemplifying the supposed values of repressed America in the early postwar years. Along with actresses such as Debbie Reynolds and Doris Day, Leigh represented the model to which teenage girls were supposed to aspire. Only terrible things happened if they headed out into the back seat of a coupe.

For the most part, MGM did right by Leigh, starring her in a wide range of films. Leigh would hardly finish one role, when she would be back in the studio again in something else. Among her early films, she played opposite Lassie in *Hills of Home* (1948), displayed her modest singing abilities in the musical *Words and Music* (1948), and was a bewitching Meg in *Little Women* (1949).

In April 1949, when MGM staged its famous twenty-fifth-anniversary photo, Leigh had every right to be seated among the fifty-seven stars. She was not as celebrated as Clark Gable, Katharine Hepburn, or Judy Garland, but she belonged at the end of the third row next to Mario Lanza.

As an MGM contract player, Leigh did not end her day when she left the set. In the evenings, she was expected to keep her name in the papers by attending an endless array of functions, including movie openings, charity events, corporate-sponsored soirees, and dinners at the homes of Hollywood stars.

One evening in 1950, Leigh showed up at a cocktail party given by RKO Pictures that was open to contract players from all the major studios, as well as reporters and photographers from the fan magazines and newspapers. Hollywood was as hierarchical as the Vatican. The idea at these events was to get your picture taken with someone higher up in the pecking order. Leigh entered the soiree like a boxer surrounded by her entourage to protect the actress and move her around the event. She was accompanied by the man she was dating, Arthur Loew Jr., the debonair heir to a theater chain fortune, a notable catch in most eyes.

As Leigh schmoozed with endless acumen, she was approached by a young man who introduced himself as Tony Curtis. As he was a nobody by Hollywood standards, by rights Leigh should have muttered a few polite words and turned away. But even in this room, where good looks were the only entrée card that mattered, she was taken aback by this "devastatingly handsome young man—beautiful, really— with black unruly hair, large sensitive eyes fringed by long dark lashes, a full sensuous mouth—and an irresistible personality." He was from New York City, announcing it with his accent, and was under contract to Universal, the Motel 6 of studios. She was in a totally different place. As the actress shimmied up the studio pole, she had purchased a new small house in the rarefied precincts of Brentwood, where she lived with her parents. That evening Leigh did something she rarely did. She gave Curtis her phone number at her new home.

Whatever motivations led Curtis to the party, the moment he saw Leigh with her exquisite face, "look[s] sweet and vulnerable," large breasts juxtaposed against a twenty-one-inch waist so small he could have put his hands around it, he had another agenda in mind, and it wasn't getting his picture taken with the actress.

Curtis had the good sense not to seem too anxious but to wait a couple of days before calling Leigh. When he did, he pretended he was Cary Grant. His accent was impeccable, and if Leigh had not heard about his celebrated imitation, she likely would have been fooled. His was a delightfully original way to connect with the actress, and she accepted his invitation to dinner.

That evening Curtis told Leigh the story of his life with the sort of intimacy and detail she rarely employed. The poor son of a Jewish tailor, Bernie Schwartz had grown up in New York. As a kid, Bernie roamed the city, his one contact with the privileged was shining their shoes in front of the St. Regis Hotel. Things had gotten so bad that for a couple of weeks, his parents put Bernie and his brother Julius in an orphanage, where at least they could get regular meals.

As Curtis went on in his extended monologue, he skirted around the details of the tragedy in his young life. When he was thirteen, he attended the American Legion parade on Second Avenue. His brother Julius was four years younger, not somebody Curtis wanted hanging around when he was with his friends. He pushed Julius away. Later that day, a truck ran over and killed his little brother. The death changed the family forever. His parents had a third child, but the departed Julius haunted their lives.

Serious about acting, Bernie had gotten the money together to take lessons at the Dramatic Workshop, along with other such future stars as Walter Matthau and Harry Belafonte. He had done some acting in Yiddish theater, when Hollywood discovered him. Universal signed Bernie for his face and overwhelming sex appeal, not his skills as an actor, and changed his name to Tony Curtis.

After that evening, Leigh and Curtis were in bed together faster than Gary Cooper's quick draw. During his first months in Hollywood, Curtis had slept with innumerable women, some of whom he barely acknowledged. Leigh was different. Scratch Curtis, and there was a poor, uneducated Jewish kid from Manhattan. He was in awe of Leigh. Although she had only a couple of years of higher education, to him, she was a worldly, college-educated woman with a firm grasp on a world he had hardly seen.

Something else drew Curtis to Leigh. Although the movie moguls were Jewish, most of the actors were not, and Leigh offered him entrée to a WASP world that he had only viewed from distant windows.

What drew Leigh to Curtis was his warm, effusive soul. Brash, bold, spilling his ironic wit over everything, the actor exuded life. Although Leigh had also grown up poor, she had been brought up as a princess in a palace compared to Curtis. She had never dated anyone like Curtis before. Being around him, she was passionately alive too.

Leigh and Curtis had not fully worked out whether theirs was an abiding love or just another Hollywood infatuation when they made their first public appearance, at the Los Angeles opening of *Ice Follies of 1950* in September of that year. Seeing them together, the fans jumped with exhilaration.

The next month, when the couple attended the premiere of *Harvey*, along with many of Hollywood's top stars, the excitement they produced by their mere presence was remarkable. "Sounded to us like the fans in the bleachers gave the biggest hand to Janet Leigh and her date, Tony Curtis, as they emerged from his car," wrote one Hollywood reporter.

The fans wanted to see two of their favorites in a love match, making real everything they saw in the movie theaters. If they could, they would have lifted them onto their shoulders and carried them through the streets of the city. The fans pushed Curtis and Leigh toward marriage, seeing the union as inevitable and natural. In some measure, the couple had to marry or disappoint millions of fans, but there was no question, Curtis and Leigh loved each other.

Despite the fans celebrating the couple's love affair, when they decided to take their marital vows, the negative reactions stunned them. The powerful producer Leonard Goldstein warned Curtis that he should back off. If he married Leigh, his growing fan base would blame him for betraying their love. They would cease pursuing him, destroying his career. MGM was no happier about the marriage. In one unfortunate moment, Leigh would destroy the fantasies of young men from Maine to New Mexico.

The worst of the negativity came from the most unlikely of subjects—Leigh's own father. Like others in her entourage, Fred Morrison had attached himself so closely to his daughter that he felt her stardust falling on him. As his daughter's business manager, he had a salary and status he had never had in his life. He did not want to risk that by her doing the incredibly silly thing of getting married once again. Her father and the others backed off, but if the marriage faltered, they were ready to come forward tsk-tsking the whole business with cries of "I told you so."

Curtis and Leigh married in a civil ceremony in June 1951 in Greenwich, Connecticut. The nuptials were greeted by an avalanche of publicity beyond anything the newlyweds thought possible. They were ambitious young actors using whatever it took to get where they wanted to go. And here, set before them, was this incredible tool that Curtis exploited to the fullest.

After starring in a series of swashbuckling sagas in duly named tights that outlined his body in ways that delighted the bobby-soxers, he knew how to egg his fans on while appearing unconcerned. At movie premieres, Janet moved quickly up the red carpet, turning away from the adoring fans, while Curtis held back, milking every moment. On one movie tour, the PR folks at Universal designed a breakaway shirt so that when teenage girls grabbed at Curtis, they would come away with a souvenir shirtsleeve.

This gigantic image of Hollywood's leading couple spread out across the movie magazines painted in shades of pastel. "KING AND QUEEN OF HEARTS." "JANET LEIGH'S MARRIAGE SECRETS." "OUR RULES FOR ROMANCE." "WHEN LOVE IS ENOUGH." How could their relationship possibly equal these two illustrious characters that hovered above them in silent rebuke to their more mundane lives? That set their marriage up for disappointment.

And then there was the problem with their peers. Jealousy is one of the fuels that propels Hollywood, and they were rebuked for their meteoric rise driven by publicity. Movie columnist Hedda Hopper called the couple "publicity mad exhibitionists, ambitious, tiresome and crude," a stunning rebuke from one of the most powerful figures in the Hollywood community.

Curtis openly enjoyed the adoration. Leigh played the aggrieved innocent off-screen as much as on. "I can unequivocally state that I have never asked to have my picture taken or to be interviewed," she wrote in her autobiography. "I only tried to comply with requests, whenever possible."

For Leigh, everything had to be perfect, and when it wasn't, she had to find some reason that left no fault on her. When the couple married, they purchased a property in Beverly Hills that Leigh furnished like her own dollhouse. It was a precious thing she fashioned, a symbol of all she had achieved. Leigh kept it impeccably clean and neat, as if expecting at any moment a photographer from a fan magazine to arrive to shoot life at home with Janet and Tony. She had what her daughter Jamie Lee called "a powerful drive for immaculate order and control."

Leigh's next project was her husband, and she proceeded to try to make Curtis a worthy resident of her dollhouse. When he asked for a glass of water, Leigh gave it to him. As soon as he took a sip, she picked up the tumbler from the coffee table and brought it back to the kitchen so it would not ruin the living room. Tony liked living in a beautiful residence too, but he didn't think it was World War III if he left a glass on the table or a sock on the floor.

At parties, Leigh stood apart from her husband, watching him. When he grasped a wineglass as if he were trying to strangle the crystal, she signaled Curtis that he should hold it gently by his fingertips. In her way, Leigh meant the best for her husband. She was doing everything she could to improve his social conduct.

Curtis saw it differently. As an actor deeply observant of human conduct, he did not need his wife to tell him how most people at the party held their wineglasses. He was making a statement that he was going to be himself. That meant if he chose to hold a glass as if he wanted to crush it, that was nobody's business but his.

Curtis felt like an outlier in Leigh's world. "After I married Janet, I sensed some antagonism from people in Hollywood, perhaps because this Jewish kid had married a shiksa screen idol," Curtis said. His marriage to Janet gave him access to the group of WASP actors around Debbie Reynolds, Hollywood's most elite social circle. He enjoyed being in their lofty company, but if he had to give up his Jewish identity, he did not want to be one of them. He signaled that in part by refusing to accede to their ideas of good manners.

One evening Curtis and Leigh were at a party at the New York residence of Cole Porter. Unlike most of his songwriter peers, Porter was a wealthy WASP, the most elegant composer of the age. Porter's minions had set out an array of cutlery around the plates. Leigh kept whispering to her husband, trying to get him to use the right utensil. The more she implored him, the more studiously he grabbed the wrong fork.

Everything at the dinner was done with refined taste, including the wineglasses. They were so delicate that when Ethel Merman gently squeezed hers, it changed shape. When, at the songstress's encouragement, Curtis attempted the same, the crystal shattered. "Don't worry, kid," Merman said, and broke her glass. The host smiled, but Leigh looked at her husband with dour disdain.

The one element that held their marriage together longer than it might have lasted was the birth of their two daughters, Kelly and Jamie Lee. They were both devoted parents, but Janet pursued her career as assiduously as her husband, and they were often off at dawn to the set or filming on location, and the girls knew their nannies as much as their parents.

Infidelity is, in some measure, a matter of opportunity. Curtis had endless women angling for a few hours in his bed. The wonder is not how much he betrayed his wife, but how long it took him to begin. He never talked about the first time, probably because he was not proud of it, but after a while, he acted as if he did not care.

Early in their relationship, Curtis had the wildest, most satisfying sex with Leigh of anyone in his life, and she presumably felt the same. That had slowly petered out to almost nothing, and Curtis reached the point where he hardly hid his assignations. Despite that, he was madly jealous of any man who showed attention to his wife.

In 1955, Leigh costarred in the musical *My Sister Eileen* alongside Jack Lemmon. The choreographer on the film, Bob Fosse, was a wildly seductive ladies' man. Although both were married, Leigh admitted years later "that an affair would have happened if we let it."

Curtis discovered what he thought was Fosse's love letter to his wife. Instead of confronting Leigh and possibly provoking a divorce, Curtis flew to Chicago and stayed at Hugh Hefner's Playboy Mansion. The visit worked wonders. "After a week of debauchery, I knew I was going to be all right," he wrote in his autobiography, *American Prince*.

The world thought Leigh had the perfect marriage. By sheer force of will, she had to keep up the veneer, hiding the truths that lay within. The gossip that her marriage was in trouble became a drumbeat so loud she could not cover her ears to block it out, and she did something that stars rarely did. She went on the offensive, writing a lengthy story for *Silver Screen* magazine, denying the reports and insisting that she and Curtis remained profoundly in love. She talked to other magazines too, pushing a tale she so desperately wanted to believe.

When Hitchcock sent Leigh the novel *Psycho* in October 1959 and asked her to play Marion Crane, the main female character in the film, she was open to a daring role she might not have so quickly accepted if her marriage had been a loving sanctuary. It was the same with her husband. Billy Wilder wanted Curtis to dress in drag in *Some Like It Hot*. At risk to his studly image, he didn't care.

Leigh's character dies a third of the way through *Psycho*. Many stars would have said no to such a diminished role, but it was Hitchcock, and thirty-two-year-old Leigh was game. She was paid only $25,000, a third of her usual fee, and did not even get star billing. It was simply "And Janet Leigh as Marion Crane" at the end of the other actor credits.

Like so many actresses before her, Leigh's first meeting with Hitchcock was at his house on Bellagio Road. He saw no need to try to impress her with his artwork and his cultured life. Nor did he seek to intimidate the actress, turning her into a malleable piece of clay. The director clearly thought Leigh would do what she was asked in the way he wanted her to do it.

Hitchcock set out for Leigh what it would be like acting in *Psycho*, and it was like nothing she had ever done. The elaborate storyboards were like comic books setting out every scene. The camera angles had also been meticulously set out. During the shooting, there would be no improvisation and no frenzied rewriting of the script. If Leigh kept precisely to the words her character spoke, she would be fine.

"I hired you because you are an actress!" Hitchcock said. That was not always a compliment from the director, but it was here. "I will only direct you if A, you attempt to take more than your share of the pie, or B, if you don't take enough, or C, if you are having trouble motivating the necessary timed motion."

Leigh's character, Marion Crane, lives a marginal, lower-middle-class life in Phoenix. For her, marriage is the only way up, the only way out, the only answer. Reaching the age where her prospects are fast diminishing, she knows she is squandering her life in a long affair with a divorcé who has seen enough of the charms of marriage. She is desperate for a way out.

To prepare to play Marion Crane, Leigh invented an entire life for her character, everything from her family to the schools she attended, the food and movies she liked, every possible perspective including her fears and dreams. Growing up in Stockton, Leigh knew women struggling with all sorts of difficulties. She had fled that world, but if she could remove the veneer of glamour she had so laboriously applied to herself and go back emotionally to the town in which she was brought up, she might not just play Marion but *be* her.

When Leigh walked onto the set the first day, no one had any idea that her life with Curtis had deteriorated into a cold war that sometimes exploded in curses and rebukes. A movie set had always been a sanctuary for Leigh, and she entered it with a feeling of joy and anticipation. But her troubles were still deep within her, and they would come forward to help inform her portrayal of Marion.

Hitchcock was notorious for giving his actors almost no advice and tearing their heads off if they dared ask him too many questions. He treated Leigh differently. She was so genial, polite, and thankful that Hitchcock could hardly be less than gracious. He did leave the grotesque mannequin for Norman's mother sitting in her chair in her dressing room. And he peppered her with dirty limericks and foul jokes until her face turned pink. "What he liked to do most," Leigh recalled, "was to make me blush, and that is not a hard thing to do."

Leigh even made her own contributions to the off-color stew. One day she asked members of the crew to place a toilet in her dressing room. Then she had them take a picture of her sitting on the john reading the script. Hitchcock was the king of potty humor, and he was rightfully amused; it was just the kind of thing he might have done.

Hitchcock did not have that much to say to inform Leigh's role beyond describing the character in Bloch's novel. "Here's your piece of the pie," he said. "What you bring to Marion other than what I want is fine. You can do almost anything with Marion, and I won't interfere, so long as it's within my concept."

Unusual for him, Hitchcock took the considerable trouble of walking Leigh around the sets, explaining the various camera angles to her. Leigh's character was the key to *Psycho*. She may have been gone from the film after only forty-nine minutes, but she hovered over the entire movie and all the other characters. If Leigh got it wrong, the film would not work.

* * *

Bernard Herrmann's pulsating score plays during the credits for *Psycho*, a stunning overture full of menace and anxiety. The film has not even begun, and nobody is going out for popcorn.

Then there is a long, sweeping shot of downtown Phoenix. This is no vacation paradise, but a nondescript, shabby American city deposited in the Southwest. "The very geography seems to give us a climate of nefariousness, of back-doorness, dark and shadowy," Stefano writes in his script.

The camera zooms in on a half-opened window. The grubby venetian blinds are the shades of infidelity. Marion Crane lies on the bed in the cheap hotel room in her white bra and slip, her large breasts provocative. It is not a designer bra, but one any American woman could purchase. Hitchcock felt Leigh was self-conscious about her large breasts, and tried to move the scene along quickly.

Above Marion stands the tall, lean figure of Sam Loomis, played by John Gavin, wearing pants and bare chested, holding his shirt in his hand. Seeking a final embrace before leaving, Sam gets back in bed and reaches out for Marion. Never before in a Hollywood film had anyone dared to show a scene like this: a single man in bed with an undressed, unmarried woman on a Friday afternoon after a carnal interlude. Leigh's sexually enticing manner is frightening in its intensity and neediness.

Gavin was unsettled about playing this overtly sexual scene. Like a shy teenager who can't bring himself to kiss his date good night, the actor was uncomfortable exposing his sexuality in this public forum. Hitchcock tried unsuccessfully to get Gavin to perform more robustly. In the end, Gavin's failure was a plus, signaling the truth of Sam's character. As adept as he may have been in seducing Marion, he is equally adept at avoiding getting so wrapped up in her life that he leaves no room for escape.

Although Sam says he must wait to marry Marion until he has paid off his late father's debts and no longer has to pay alimony to his ex-wife, he has enough money to fly down to Phoenix regularly from the fictional Fairvale, California, where he runs a hardware store, to get it on with Marion. "Sam, this is the last time," she tells him, but it's unclear if her resolve is strong enough to take such a definitive step.

Dressed in a white shirtwaist dress that Leigh purchased off the rack in LA, a uniform for a proper woman of the time, Marion enters the Lowery Real Estate office and sits at her secretarial desk. Shortly afterward, her boss, George Lowery, enters with his half-drunk client, Tom Cassidy, a Texas oil leaseman.

"A gross man, exuding a kind of pitiful vulgarity," in screenwriter Stefano's words, the elderly man sits on Marion's desk and brags as he leers at her. Pulling out a thick stack of hundred-dollar bills, Cassidy says the $40,000 will buy a house for his eighteen-year-old daughter, whose wedding is the next day. Lowery looks askance at the massive amount of cash. This is dirty money the sleazy Cassidy has not declared on his taxes. To get his commission, Lowery is ready to take it.

Lowery tells Marion to put the money in a safe-deposit box at the bank. She places the envelope with the money in her white purse. Instead of driving to the bank, she goes home. The envelope sits on her bed next to a half-filled suitcase as she stands above it wearing a black bra and slip. There is no dialogue, only Herrmann's subtly foreboding music.

After finishing dressing and packing, Marion looks at the envelope on the bed. She is clearly tempted to take this lowlife's money. Why does she hesitate? Is it morality or fear of getting caught? Marion picks up the money and puts it in her black purse, ready to leave Phoenix.

With Hitchcock, it's the juxtapositions that matter—virtue with vice, demureness with abandon, the neatness of the bills with the squalor of the crime, and white with black. Much of it is obvious, but it works because generally people dress for the part they are playing.

Psycho rises and falls on the audience identifying with this woman who has just committed a major felony. Marion drives out of the Arizona city, entering the endless vistas of the American West, underscoring her aloneness and the secret she carries with her. The highway is the ultimate metaphor for American life. People travel to seek new lives, flee the old, or, like Marion, do both simultaneously.

After sleeping at the side of the road, Marion is awakened by an officer of the California Highway Patrol, who has observed her parked car. The policeman wears dark glasses on his smooth face. He is the face of authority feared by Hitchcock, the grand inquisitor who can make anyone confess.

Marion does not have the soul of a criminal. She has no business doing what she did and gives off a scent of guilt. "Am I acting as if there's something wrong?" Marion asks beseechingly. "Frankly, yes," the trooper says, his politeness hiding an underlying threat. After showing her papers, Marion drives on, followed discreetly by the officer.

In Bakersfield, Marion stops at a used-car lot, where she trades in her car with its Arizona license plates for a secondhand vehicle with California plates. The cop is parked across the street. As Marion drives away in her new car, he stands watching her alongside the car salesman and the mechanic who checked out her former vehicle. That is her life, either driving from or toward men who dominate her life.

Leigh had her secrets that she held as tightly as Marion that she could draw on in playing the role. The actress feared her career would be destroyed if the public learned she had married when she was fourteen years old. And then there was her marriage to Tony. That was false too; if that was exposed, she worried her career would be profoundly hurt. At whatever cost, she knew she must maintain the façade. All of that played one way or another into her characterization of Marion Crane.

Most of Leigh's presence in *Psycho* is without dialogue, making her challenge to create a compelling character an enormous one. To help her achieve that, Hitchcock worked with her far more closely than he did most actors. He sat next to her in his black suit, making one suggestion after another. After a while, she became so confident and trusting in her relationship with Hitchcock that she started coming to him with her ideas. Others had tried that and been roundly rebuked in put-downs bordering on the uncivil.

"Mr. Hitchcock, about my speech in tomorrow's scene," Perkins said, interrupting Hitchcock's reading of the London *Times* that he had airmailed to him every morning.

"Uh-huh," Hitchcock said, not even looking up from his newspaper.

"I've had a few ideas that I thought maybe you might like to listen to," Perkins said beseechingly.

"All right," Hitchcock said, as if he had much of a choice.

The actor laid out the way he wanted to do the scene and waited for the director's reaction.

"Oh, they're all right," Hitchcock said, not quite the enthusiastic response he was hoping to receive.

"But . . . but . . . but . . . you might not like them," Perkins said, giving Hitchcock carte blanche to tear his ideas apart.

Hitchcock did not like repeating himself. "I said they're all right," he said curtly. And then, perhaps thinking he was being a little bit too abrupt, he put down his paper and turned toward Perkins.

"Have you given it a lot of thought?" Hitchcock asked. "I mean, have you really thought it out? Do you really like these changes you've made?"

"Yes, I think they're right," Perkins said with a measure of determination.

"All right, that's the way we'll do it."

Hitchcock was helpful to Leigh, but she was the one who overwhelmingly forged the mesmerizing character of Marion Crane. In her public life, Leigh's face was a mask showing little of substance, but in the film, her face reads like a novel, telling tales within tales, exposing Marion's fear and guilt as she slowly realizes the magnitude of what she has done. Leigh creates a Marion Crane that the audience cares about. It is not that they excuse the theft, but they want her to come out of this well.

When an oppressive rain begins to fall, overwhelming the beleaguered windshield wipers, the audience wants Marion to move beyond the storm and enter the sunlight. A neon vacancy sign for the Bates Motel appears out of the gloom, a momentary sanctuary.

Marion runs through the rain into the office of the seedy motel. No one is there. She hurries out and looks behind the motel, where a gray Gothic house rises into the dark sky. The building was probably modeled after Edward Hopper's *House by the Railroad*. The great American painter was a poet of loneliness and estrangement, and the building rises apart from everyone and everything.

Marion sees a figure in a lit window. She runs back to her car and honks the horn with urgency. As she does so, a man comes out of the house and hurries down the steps, carrying an umbrella.

Unlike Marion, Norman Bates seems to have nothing to hide. In a self-deprecating manner, Norman explains that, since the building of the new highway, the motel has become a backwater, and she is the only guest. In checking Marion in, Norman's hand hovers over the board with keys for the twelve rooms before settling on number one, next to his office.

Then, in a genial manner, Norman invites Marion to have dinner with him in the house. She says yes, but soon overhears Norman and his mother screaming at each other as she tells him no strange woman is to have dinner in their house. Norman returns carrying a tray with a pitcher of milk and sandwiches for them to have dinner in the office parlor.

As Marion listens to Norman talking about his strange, isolated life, something else resonates with her. As she gets up to return to her room, she says, "I have a long drive tomorrow, all the way back to Phoenix. . . . I stepped into a private trap back there—I'd like to go back to try to pull myself out of it." She has decided to return the money and face whatever justice brings her.

Marion's bathroom is white, the color of purity. She takes off her bathrobe and enters the shower. She knows she is going to return the money, and the water pours down, washing away her sins. She doesn't have to scrub herself as intensely as she does, but wants to do so. Everything is clean and fresh; she opens her mouth in sheer pleasure. It is a feeling she has not had for a long time, and she stands luxuriating in the moment.

A shadowy womanly figure appears through the opaque shower curtain. The curtain is thrust aside, and as Marion screams, she is stabbed again and again and again. Herrmann's shrieking violins underscore the moment, music that will forever be remembered as crucial to this most memorable of movie murder scenes.

The horror is evoked without once showing the knife penetrating Marion's body. As she dies, she reaches out and grabs the shower curtain, pulling it down ring by ring. Marion's blood mixes with the water and runs down the drain, and the camera focuses on one of her eyeballs. It looks like that of a slaughtered cow.

There is no vulnerability like nakedness. For the shower scene to work, Hitchcock needed Marion to be nude. Leigh was not about to take off all her clothes. He had to find someone else. That was why Hitchcock sat in his office early in the shoot, looking at a statuesque redhead standing before him in her underwear. Twenty-one-year-old Marli Renfro danced for her living as a showgirl in places as diverse as Manhattan's Latin Quarter and Las Vegas casinos. As a nudist, she was more comfortable standing before the director naked than some actresses would have been fully clothed. Her figure was so stunning that a few months later, she would be *Playboy*'s cover girl.

Hitchcock kept looking at Renfro's feet. Beautifully pedicured, they were just what he sought. Convinced that she was perfect to be Marion's body in the shower, he asked her to talk to Leigh.

In the actress's dressing room, Renfro disrobed again and stood like an object for sale. Leigh acted in a manner Renfro thought was disdainful and dismissive. The actress considered Marion Crane *her* role. She did not want to share it with anyone else, even if it was just shots of Renfro's body.

As Renfro walked onto the set the first day of shooting the shower scene wearing a white robe, she saw a large sign: CLOSED SET—NO ADMITTANCE. RED LIGHTS FLASHING!!! That reassured her that her privacy would be respected, but then she saw bleachers full of reporters and Hollywood columnists sitting there as if watching a ball game. They had been invited to see her. She felt they were disappointed that she wasn't a stripper prepared to gyrate in front of them. Refusing to get upset at their peering eyes, she slipped off her robe, nude except for a moleskin patch, and began doing warm-up exercises.

The studio paid Renfro $500 for what was supposed to be a couple of days' work, but Hitchcock kept calling her back for seven days. For Renfro, it was like an athletic competition, standing hour after hour with the water raining down. As well as the moleskin patch had been applied, it couldn't hold up to all this, and Renfro asked Hitchcock if she could take it off. That was impossible, the director told her.

Sitting wearing a diffident expression, Hitchcock talked to the nude model as if he were having tea with Queen Elizabeth. Of course, he would not have told the queen the dirty jokes he passed on to Renfro. At one point, Hitchcock asked Renfro to cry out. She wasn't an actress, but she did her best and heard her voice among the death screams when she saw the finished film.

Although the shower scene lasted only a minute and a half, Hitchcock was such a perfectionist that he shot it again and again, editing it down into one tiny cut after another. Leigh is in the shower scene too, the camera exposing only her upper body, just above her breasts. Her cry in her death throes is beyond compelling.

Marion's sister, Lila (Vera Miles); her boyfriend, Sam; and Milton

Arbogast (Martin Balsam), a private detective hired by Cassidy to re-trieve his money, set out to try to learn what happened to Marion. On his second visit to the motel, the detective enters the house. Climbing the stairs, he is stabbed to death by a womanly figure dressed like the person who killed Marion.

Sam and Lila drive out to the motel on their own. Lila goes to the house, seeking out the mother they have been told has been dead for ten years. In the cellar she finds Mrs. Bates in a gray wig and long dress. As Lila turns her around, she sees it is not a living person but a grotesque skull and skeleton. As she screams in horror at her discov-ery, a womanly figure stands at the top of the stairs holding a shining knife, poised to plunge it into her. At that precise moment, Sam ar-rives. As he fights this would-be assassin, the wig falls off, exposing Norman.

The film ends with a four-minute-and-forty-second soliloquy by psychiatrist Dr. Fred Richman (Simon Oakland), who spoke to Nor-man in his cell. Dr. Richman says that after murdering both his mother and her lover, he assumed Mrs. Bates's identity. Norman no longer exists.

* * *

Every few years, there is a piece of art—a novel, a movie, a play—that resonates so deeply with the American psyche that everyone seems to have seen or read it or at least knows about it. Moviegoers formed lines outside theaters across America to see *Psycho*. They screamed out at the shower scene in an overwhelming chorus of hor-ror and left the theaters shaken by what they had seen. And they never forgot it. In 2022, *Variety* named *Psycho* the greatest movie of all time.

Leigh was nominated for an Academy Award for Best Supporting Actress and won a Golden Globe. Curtis was also on a roll, with an

Academy Award nomination for his role in *The Defiant Ones* (1958) and the popular and critical acclaim of *Some Like It Hot* (1959).

Curtis luxuriated in his success, but his wife did not. Curtis felt Leigh was jealous of actresses like Elizabeth Taylor, who had reached a level of fame she would never attain, and yet at the same time felt overwhelmed by the celebrity she had achieved.

Leigh started drinking. She was a lousy drunk, snarly and belligerent, stripped of the veneer that protected her. As she downed her drinks, her relationship with Curtis became largely disdainful distance or intimate shouting matches. The slurs and accusations were sometimes thrown out in front of their two daughters.

But the show that was their marriage had to go on. For their tenth wedding anniversary in June 1961, they staged a party extravagant even by Hollywood standards. The couple built a dance floor over the pool, a dais for the orchestra, and a platform for tables to hold the 250 guests, which included the film elite, from Frank Sinatra to Doris Day and Gene Kelly to Jack Lemmon. The last guest did not leave until after 5:30 in the morning.

And then they were alone. Nothing was left of their love but tattered remnants. They fought over money, but it was really about control. When Curtis wanted to buy a Rolls-Royce, it may have been a silly extravagance, but he was a big star, and his accountant could figure out a way for him to buy the vehicle. Leigh said no, they could not afford it.

He went ahead and bought the car anyway.

Then, on a Sunday two months after the anniversary party, Leigh's parents came over, as they often did. They had been fighting. Their faces were clenched with tension. Fred had an insurance brokerage business only because his daughter was a star. Not much of a businessman, he was in trouble and had come to ask for a loan. Curtis had enough of relatives hitting him up for money, especially when his wife tried to deny him his Rolls-Royce, and he turned down his father-in-law.

"These are my folks!" Leigh shouted. "If it was your family, you damn well would help."

Curtis was having none of it. "Oh, now it's okay to spend money!" he yelled. "Not if I want something, but if your dad does, that's all right."

"Go to hell," Leigh told her husband.

"It just went wrong right now," Leigh's father said beseechingly. "I can't help it. Jesus, do you think I like coming here and asking for a loan?"

Nothing was resolved when Leigh flew off to Nice as a guest of Mr. and Mrs. Joseph P. Kennedy to attend Monte Carlo's International Red Cross Ball, hosted by Princess Grace. It should have been a welcome respite, but Leigh carried all her problems with her.

Dressed in a gown that made her look every bit the movie star, Leigh walked into the Monte Carlo Casino for the ball. Her friend Sammy Davis Jr. was the headliner. When he did not receive the reception she felt he deserved, Leigh got up and walked to the powder room. There she began sobbing uncontrollably, her body shaking. It was terrifying to be like this, not knowing why it was happening or how to end it. When she finally got a measure of control, she left the event as it was hardly beginning and was driven back to her hotel room, where she lay filled with nameless despair.

On Sunday afternoon, Leigh was still suffering when Curtis called to tell her, "Janet, your dad died last night. He committed suicide." Some things you don't handle. They handle you. She fell into an emotional coma from which there seemed no release. It worsened when she arrived back in Los Angeles and learned that Tony had found her fifty-two-year-old father in his office next to a half-empty bottle of pills. Next to him lay a note, much of which became public.

Helen, I also just wanted to tell you one thing . . . Now maybe you can be happy because you have to have a man dead before you can be happy so—I hate you.

Leigh could not understand why her father killed himself. And why had he said these terrible things about her mother? Suicide is often about hate, but rarely is it this blatant. Leigh had tried to live a life that had nothing negative attached to it. And now her father's action tainted her. Leigh needed a loving husband, to hold and succor her. Curtis played the part, but it was only a part. She was alone, and there is no loneliness like a marriage gone bad.

Despite everything, Leigh, Curtis, and their two daughters sailed to Argentina, where he was filming *Taras Bulba*. The voyage gave them plenty of time to do their favorite thing: argue. Some couples fight so much that verbal warfare is their natural communication idiom. That's how it had become with the two of them, throwing invective and random objects at each other in drunken scenes. It did not help in Argentina when Curtis fell in love with his seventeen-year-old costar, Christine Kaufmann. That the girl was half Curtis's age and a minor, Leigh considered it more shameful business. Curtis didn't care. He was in love.

On their return to LA, the couple got into a fight that, even by their standards, was excessive. Between outbursts and drinks, Leigh went into her powder room to try to make up her tear-streaked face. As she did so, she downed a large number of red pills. Curtis rushed in and pounded on her back until she coughed up most of the drugs.

Given her father's suicide, there was something doubly ominous about Leigh's conduct. However Curtis felt about his wife of ten years and the mother of their two children, he surely should have tried to get her help and be with her until he no longer feared she would do this again. But he had traveled as far down the road as he was willing to go, and he wanted to be with his young mistress, whom he later married, and he left for good.

Right after the divorce, Leigh married Bob Brandt, a stockbroker and outdoorsman. Curtis speculated that his ex-wife may have begun their affair when she was still married to him. If that were true, few would fault her. Leigh retreated into her new marriage and a career that never again reached the peaks of *Psycho*. She wore the smile she always wore. Everything was perfect and always would be.

CHAPTER 10

A Pride of Lions

L ike millions of Americans, Hitchcock watched the *Today* show on NBC. On an October morning in 1961, he was viewing the program at the breakfast table with Alma when an ad appeared for Sego, a diet drink. He was mesmerized by the ash-blond actress who walked across the screen, turning as a boy whistled at her.

A connoisseur of the female form, Hitchcock was taken not only by this lady's stunning looks but also by her provocative stride. The model was only on the screen for a few seconds, but Hitchcock was mesmerized by what he perceived as her "jaunty assuredness, pertness, and attractive throw of the head."

By both her looks and manner, the woman could have been Grace Kelly's younger sister. Hitchcock had hardly digested the ad, no less his breakfast, when he asked his staff to contact her. He had this idea that he could turn this woman, whoever she was, into a star.

The model's name was Tippi Hedren, and she would always remember that particular Friday the thirteenth as one of the luckiest days of her life. Hedren had been a top New York model with the Ford Modeling Agency. For nearly a decade, her face had graced the covers of publications such as *Life* and the *Saturday Evening Post*, and she had been featured in all kinds of television ads.

Hedren was as photogenic as ever, but modeling was a profession for the young, and the thirty-one-year-old's bookings were thinning out. That was reason enough to move on. Beyond that, she was a divorced woman with a four-year-old, who desired trees and grass, not just the urban canyons of Manhattan. So she moved out to Los Angeles and rented a house in Westwood.

But Hedren got few modeling assignments in LA, her savings were draining out, and soon she would have to find some other kind of work to sustain her and her daughter, Melanie, in the upper-middle-class lifestyle to which she had become accustomed. That would not be easy for a woman with a high school education and no marketable skills beyond her looks. She was thinking of taking typing lessons, but that wasn't going to do it.

The timing could not have been more fortuitous when Hedren received a call from someone who said a "well-known director" had seen her in the commercial, and his agent at MCA, the giant entertainment agency, wanted to meet with her. Hedren was used to men using all kinds of means to get close to her, including the married Senator John F. Kennedy—who, after briefly meeting her in southern France, had an aide call her hotel room to say his car was waiting for her. If she had gone with him that evening, it is unlikely that he wanted to discuss the war in Indochina. Thus, she had no idea whether the "well-known director" had a legitimate interest in her or sought little more than a short-term assignation before casting her aside.

When Hedren went into MCA the following Tuesday, she went through a number of meetings before she learned Hitchcock wanted to sign her to a seven-year contract. She did not even think of calling in an attorney to check out the contract or attempt to up the dollar amount a little. She simply signed the document pushed before her.

Hedren's next step in this remarkable journey was to drive to the Paramount studios to meet her new employer and have lunch with Hitchcock. This ritual that the director went through with all his new actresses usually took place at his Bellagio Road home with Alma a quiet presence. Although his wife was not in the room this day, Hitchcock was there in all his showiness, attempting to impress Hedren with his erudite knowledge of art and his epicurean interest in food.

Hedren found Hitchcock "shorter and even rounder than I was expecting, and he was remarkably unattractive." She had hardly picked up her fork, when he was festooning the meal with filthy jokes and off-color limericks. It was not the kind of mealtime patter she was used to, but she did not flinch. No matter what Hitchcock said, she smiled her perfect model's smile.

Hitchcock never once talked about why he had signed Hedren, and she never asked. The hour-long lunch gave Hitchcock ample time to observe Hedren. He could be unremittingly tough, even cruel, in his judgments of women. The five-feet-four-inch-tall model was shorter than the statuesque actresses the director preferred. On the top of Hedren's head sat what he considered a grotesque beehive that overwhelmed her face. And her dress, was it turquoise blue or some other god-awful color?

Hitchcock would once again have to play Professor Henry Higgins, transforming Hedren into the woman of his cinema dreams, a lady of sophisticated coolness beneath which lay what he was sure was hidden sexuality overwhelming in intensity. This slight, 100-pound woman held her own with the director. Whatever he said, she had been there and done that or gave a telling performance that she had. Although Hedren was delighted to have a film contract, albeit one that paid her $500 a week for the first year, considerably less than what she was used to earning as a model, she had no grandiose illusions about her prospects.

Although Hitchcock was working on a new film, *The Birds*, about the omnipresent creatures attacking humans, she did not even consider the possibility that the director might cast her in the film, and doubly not in the starring role as Melanie Daniels, the petulant, self-involved main character. If Hedren were lucky, he would cast her in episodes of *Alfred Hitchcock Presents*, his half-hour weekly television show.

Before Hedren did anything, Hitchcock decided to give his newest acquisition a screen test, the entry-level exam for would-be actors that most directors would have insisted upon before signing a nonactor to a long-term contract. It wasn't a typical screen test knocked off in a few hours, but a sequence of three mini films overseen by the director's entire team, shot over three days. Costing more than $25,000, it was the most expensive screen test in Hollywood history. Edith Head designed a wardrobe that displayed Hedren at her best in the color footage. And Hitchcock and Alma spent hours giving Hedren a crash course in acting.

Hedren had the challenging task of playing scenes immortalized by Joan Fontaine in *Rebecca*, Ingrid Bergman in *Notorious*, and Grace Kelly in *To Catch a Thief*, three of Hitchcock's best films. For each segment, the director had the studio create special sets. The three actresses' shadows hung over every moment. Hitchcock was not going to make it even more difficult by having Hedren do her scenes with a hack actor. Instead, he flew in Martin Balsam, who had done a stellar job playing the private detective Arbogast in *Psycho*, from the East Coast.

After the screen test, Hedren waited several weeks, hoping she would get a call from the studio saying she had a part in Hitchcock's television series. When the phone finally rang, it was not with a part but an invitation to have dinner with the Hitchcocks at Chasen's, the celebrated West Hollywood restaurant.

This summons was as unusual as the screen test. Thursday evenings, Hitchcock and Alma almost always had dinner at the eatery that had been on Beverly Boulevard since 1936. They were in good company; other regulars at the see-and-be-seen establishment included Elizabeth Taylor, Cary Grant, Groucho Marx, and Frank Sinatra. But after all these years, the restaurant had begun to lose its edge, and some stars had started to move on to chic new places ringed by paparazzi. Hitchcock hardly noticed as he and Alma held court in the booth with their names on it. A creature of studied routine, he had no intention of enjoying his weekly dinner out anywhere else.

A snob as only a son of the British lower middle class could be, the sixty-two-year-old director did not have dinner with mere mortals. It was one of the highest social honors in Hollywood to be invited to the Hitchcocks' table. If Hedren had any idea how Hollywood worked, she would have guessed something special was afoot when Lew Wasserman was the other guest. The sinewy, owlish MCA executive looking across the table at her in his signature black-rimmed glasses was one of the most powerful men in the film industry. In Hollywood, business and social life blend seamlessly into each other. If Hitchcock's agent was spending a whole evening in this banquette, there was likely the smell of a deal in the air.

Hitchcock was like a little boy who could not keep a secret. The three of them had hardly ordered drinks before he turned toward Hedren, holding in his hands a gift box from Gump's, the expensive San Francisco store. She unwrapped the little package and stared uncomprehendingly at the beautiful pearl pin showing three birds in flight.

Before she could utter a proper thank-you, Hitchcock said, "We want you to play Melanie Daniels in *The Birds*."

Hedren shed tears of elation. Alma had tears in her eyes too. Even the taciturn Wasserman had wet eyes. Only the maestro of the moment had dry eyes. Hitchcock had that satisfied look on his face he had when he shot a scene that required only one take.

* * *

By the time of the dinner at Chasen's, Evan Hunter was well at work on the script for *The Birds*. The thirty-five-year-old New York author was best known for a series of police procedurals set in Manhattan's 87th Precinct, written pseudonymously as Ed McBain, that was a new television series. Hunter had also done some screenwriting, including a script for an episode of *Alfred Hitchcock Presents*.

That was where Hitchcock met the lean, brash writer and later asked Hunter if he would be interested in writing the script for *The Birds*. All Hunter had to go on was a story by the English novelist Daphne du Maurier, in which a Cornish farmer and his wife are inexplicably attacked by birds. The setting and the characters would have to be changed, and a whole new story written.

Hunter was soon flying out to Hollywood and renting a house in Brentwood, where he brought his wife, Anita, and their young children. One day in Hitchcock's office, Hunter looked up at all the honors on the walls, including everything but an Academy Award for Best Director. "You've got quite a collection there, Hitch," the writer said.

"Always a bridesmaid, never a bride," the director said.

Hitchcock may have been born in London, but his insecurity made him as American as a Dodger Dog. Beneath the glittery veneer, Hollywood was a cold, unforgiving place. What mattered were your latest box office figures, not your legendary past. By industry standards, Hitchcock was an old man, a relic of years gone by. All around him were hungry young directors seeking to supplant him.

Hitchcock considered Wasserman his closest friend in America. The agent had helped make the director a rich man, but Hitchcock knew the moment he could no longer bring bounty to Wasserman, the friendship would be over. "Wasserman wouldn't hesitate to stab me in the back," Hitchcock told his authorized biographer, John Russell Taylor.

Hunter believed *The Birds* was Hitchcock's attempt to win the esteem of his colleagues that he felt he had never received. The novelist was part of the package. "*The Birds* was going to be his bid for respectability," Hunter said. "He got a New York novelist to write it."

The screenwriter worked almost daily with Hitchcock. Both men were full of ideas and endlessly inventive as they produced something new and unique. The duo transposed the story from the Cornish countryside to Bodega Bay, an ocean-side village in Northern California.

Early on, Hitchcock and Hunter made what the screenwriter called "an 'artistic' decision" not to explain the bird attacks. They could have said the birds were getting even for their mistreatment by the human race, or amoral Communist scientists wired the birds to attack. For Hitchcock, that was all too easy. Without rhyme or reason, dark acts came out of the clearest of skies.

Before Hitchcock left for Christmas vacation in St. Moritz in the Swiss Alps, where he rarely left the Palace Hotel, he sent Hedren bushels of potatoes with a note saying that eaten in ample quantities, she would gain weight. With Hitchcock's Irish roots, he surely knew the humble tuber was the staple food of the Irish peasant; in Hollywood, if eaten at all, the vegetable sat on the side of the plate in sparse quantities. The director balanced the potatoes with a case of Dom Pérignon champagne.

* * *

Hedren had little in her early background to help her play the sophisticated, spoiled Melanie Daniels. Born Nathalie Kay "Tippi" Hedren in 1930 in Lafayette, Minnesota, a town of about two hundred, her Swedish-American father owned the general store and her German-Norwegian mother taught school. Lafayette was a traditional village not unlike Grover's Corners in Thornton Wilder's *Our Town*, where people were born, lived their lives, and died.

The Hedrens most likely would never have left the town, but the Great Depression savaged the smallest of villages as much as the largest of cities. Her father lost his business, and the family moved to the suburbs of Minneapolis, where her mother worked in a store and her sickly father just survived.

Hedren's parents were devoted to each other, but rarely showed any demonstrable affection. She had the same sort of Lutheran soul, cool and self-contained. Keeping emotional distance from others, she did not risk the costs of getting close. Hedren was so shy that she could hardly look at anyone, but her green eyes, blond hair, and shimmering good looks were so extraordinary that Donaldson's department store hired the young teenager as a model.

Soon the fifteen-year-old also had a desirable boyfriend, Richard McFarland, who was a year older and from a wealthy family. As far as Tippi was concerned, everything was going just dandy when, because of her father's declining health, the family decided to move to the sunshine of Los Angeles.

Hedren was beyond devastated. How would she possibly find another Richard? But unlike fourteen-year-old Janet Leigh, who defied her parents by marrying her beau, Hedren got on the train with her parents for the journey to California.

In LA, Hedren learned the crucial secret of her life. Beauty unlocked everything. After embracing only a few rays of Southern California sun, she began working as a model. Her looks were a magical talisman that brought her everything she needed—starting with a new beau, Jimmy Lewis, who like his predecessor was a year older and from a prominent family. Thanks to modeling, she knew how to walk, dress, and put herself forward.

It wasn't just boys staring at Hedren. It gave everyone a brief moment of pleasure to look at her. That's all it took for doors to open for her and for people to invite her into their lives. She did not have to know anything or learn anything, just to display herself in all her beauty.

Hedren entered Pasadena City College, but the classes were a tedious business compared to earning more than many of her professors did by smiling and wearing beautiful clothes as photographers shot her image. No way was she going to spend four years getting a bachelor's degree. After dropping out to model full-time, she soon realized New York was the place to be.

The Ford Modeling Agency was to that profession in Manhattan what MCA was to filmmaking in Hollywood. Eileen Ford only had to look at the portfolio Hedren sent her to invite her to take the train east for an interview. As soon as the modeling executive saw Hedren, she signed her on and sent her out working, earning $350 her first week. Hedren had thought of marrying Lewis, who yearned for her back in LA, but when things were over for her, they were over.

Grace Kelly had been a successful model in Manhattan when she was studying drama, but it was only a device to make money before she moved on to a full-time career as an actress. For Hedren, modeling was all she wanted to do, all she knew, and year after year, there was a necessary sameness to her life. If she lost the look in her portfolio that brought her so much business, her phone would no longer ring. The model's beauty was her calling card into the most elevated of circles, but that card could be taken away in a moment. Growing older was death before death, and she did everything to impede its first ominous signs.

Models like Hedren were natural narcissists, consumed with themselves. Dr. Frank Vaccaro, a Manhattan psychiatrist whose patients were primarily top models, observed that mindset for decades. "People assumed I sat there all day talking about sex," the retired therapist said. "That's not what concerned them. Their looks obsessed them. If they had a small blemish on their cheek, they were distressed beyond belief. That was their focus and what I spent my career talking about."

Hedren's assignments took her all over America and the world. She met all kinds of people on her travels and developed a classy, polished veneer. But it was just that, a surface no more profound than a snapshot beneath which lay her provincial, small-town roots. With only limited education and life experience, she could not converse on the same level as many of the people she met. Hedren was forever retreating into her beauty, the one certainty in her life.

As much as Hedren enjoyed her work, modeling was often a predatory business, with photographers and others hitting on women who were often teenagers or a few years older. But even as a young woman, there was a cool distance about her that said "Do not touch."

On her first acting job, playing a small role in a radio drama, twenty-one-year-old Hedren met eighteen-year-old Peter Griffith, a former child actor. A model would more likely date a man considerably older than three years younger, especially one whose best career days lay behind him. Hedren had to control every element of the world around her. With Griffith, she could do just that. She was the central figure in the relationship, and in 1952, they walked down the aisle.

The marriage worked well enough until Griffith joined the army and he became an MP in Korea. Hedren's husband was different when he came back. She was different too. They had a baby girl, Melanie, but that did not improve things. When Hedren realized her husband was seeking solace elsewhere with a multitude of lovers, she flew to Mexico to obtain a divorce.

Just as Hedren was starting her new life as a divorced mother, her career began a decline, and she decided to leave Manhattan. Hedren was living such an affluent lifestyle that when she and young Melanie took the train to a new life in LA, she brought her daughter's nanny, Josephine, along with a menagerie of pets, including a puppy, a kitten, and a bunny. She loved domestic animals. They asked for little and gave much. She arrived with no clear idea what she would do in California.

Then the call came from Hitchcock's office.

The director wanted to remake everything about Hedren, starting with her name. From now on, she would be "Tippi," her first name enclosed in quotations so she would stand out from everyone else.

To Hitchcock, actors were puppets in his hands. At times he had an almost disdainful attitude toward their craft, saying he wanted no more out of them but to speak the lines they were given. Hedren was a model, not an actor, and despite Hitchcock's condescending view of actors, he knew that would not be enough if he wanted her to succeed.

In *The Birds*, Hedren plays the spoiled socialite Melanie Daniels, the central figure on-screen for most of the film. Hitchcock rarely spent time coaching his actors, but he sat down with Hedren to talk through her entire role with meticulous concern, highlighting every nuance and detail. Hitchcock recorded the sessions and had the thirty-five pages transcribed.

As their discussions made clear, Hedren was a literalist. She looked at the script, saw what was there, and reached out for no meaning beyond the words. As a novice actress, Hedren sought protection in the words before her and saw no reason to add further complexity to her role.

Hitchcock was different. For him, the words were only the beginning. Melanie was not just a character he and Hunter had created. Melanie had grown into a real human being, and he talked about her in the rich detail of someone he knew intimately.

As the film begins, Melanie Daniels enters a pet shop in downtown San Francisco on a Friday afternoon wearing a chic black suit, black high heels, and black gloves. Everything about Melanie suggests she is a supercilious scion of wealth, the sort of woman Hollywood loves to skewer, to the immense pleasure of most filmgoers.

The handsome bachelor attorney Mitch Brenner (Rod Taylor) enters the shop dressed as formally as Melanie in a gray suit and tie, carrying his hat in his hands. He recognizes her as the young woman who got in legal trouble for breaking a shop window in a misguided prank. She achieved another measure of notoriety by jumping into a fountain in Rome.

In their first scene together, Melanie and Mitch go at each other in a flurry of insults. Hitchcock knew the temptation, especially to a novice, to play the fast-paced, witty dialogue over the top, the Marx Brothers come to San Francisco. That would not do. "It's high comedy," Hitchcock told Hedren in their taped discussions. "A high comedy is played like drama. It's the situation that carries you."

"Back in your gilded cage, Melanie Daniels," Mitch says as he puts an escaped canary back into captivity. Hitchcock added that line, making it clear that Mitch already knew Melanie's name and viewed her as a spoiled socialite living a narrow life. To the director, Melanie represents the sins of complacency all wrapped together in one stunning package.

With the threadbare excuse that she wants to deliver lovebirds to Mitch's sister, Cathy (Veronica Cartwright), for her eleventh birthday, the next day Melanie drives an hour and a half north in her open Aston Martin coupe to Mitch's weekend home in Bodega Bay. From her perspective as a woman, Hedren could not understand why the beautiful Melanie would do this.

"It may be that we have to justify why she goes sixty miles," Hitchcock said as they sat discussing the film. "Now, what justification can there be except that she wants to see Mitch again? And we can only do this by whatever expression—"

"But does she realize this yet?" Hedren interjected.

"What?" Hitchcock asked.

"That she wants to see him," Hedren said.

"Well, I just said she's gone to all this trouble—"

"I know," Hedren interjected again, "but I'm going according to the script that she doesn't quite realize that it's really Mitch she wants to see."

"What would she go to all this trouble for?" Hitchcock insisted. "I'm sure she wants to see him again."

For her visit to Bodega Bay, Hitchcock outfitted Melanie over the top in a lime-green designer suit, tan shoes, and matching gloves. On a shirtsleeve day, over her clothes she wore a fur coat, a symbol that she is rich and privileged, driving to a world beneath her. Her high heels are as absurd as stilts for a visit to this humble village.

Hitchcock flew up to Bodega Bay on a chartered plane with his film crew at the end of February 1962. While most of the cast and crew stayed at the utilitarian El Rancho Motel in Santa Rosa, twenty miles east of Bodega Bay, Hitchcock took up residence at San Francisco's luxurious Fairmont Hotel. That meant that, early in the morning, his chauffeur drove him the sixty-five miles to Bodega Bay. Along the route, schoolchildren stood holding up signs: MR. HITCHCOCK, PLEASE STOP! As busy as his day ahead was, he told the driver to pull over so he could sign autographs.

As Hitchcock set out to shoot *The Birds*, he was full of foreboding. The director did not like filming on location, where he could not control things the way he did in the studio. That said, he would have no choice but to stay in Northern California for more than a month.

The director wasn't about to tell Hunter, but Hitchcock felt the script was riddled with problems. "Something happened that was altogether new in my experience," the director told François Truffaut. "I began to study the scenario as we went along, and I saw that there were weaknesses in it."

Every night back at his suite at the Fairmont, Hitchcock went over the next scenes, often changing them, cutting several scenes, and adding one. It was not natural for him to do this, and he was fraught with fretfulness.

Hitchcock's problem was not just the script, but Hedren. If she failed, he failed. His colleagues and the critics would mock his impulsive decision to cast her as a disaster of the first order. When he signed Hedren on, he envisioned her as one of his classic blondes, her coolness hiding a smoldering sexuality. He was bedeviled about how he could get more emotion out of her. He goaded her by telling her the foulest of jokes just before he shot her scenes.

Then there were the birds. They bedeviled him too. He could not direct them. To get what he wanted, he was at the mercy of the special effects people. Beyond all his other concerns, Hitchcock fretted about money and all he was risking on this film.

As Hitchcock juggled all these problems, he could not let anyone know how apprehensive he was, or his fears might prove contagious, affecting the actors and crew. He had to play the grandiose, witty, confident Hitchcock as his actors played their roles. And he had to play it best to Hedren, or her self-doubt might grow to unmanageable proportions.

The narcissistic Hedren lived in a house of mirrors. Everywhere she looked she saw images of herself. As much as she liked to have things her own way, working with Hitchcock she had no choice but to defer to him, acceding to his wishes. Off camera, she lived with precise order. She had little to do with the other actors and crew, who shared comradely good times. Always polite, she kept her distance.

When Melanie arrives in Bodega Bay, she does not even know the name of Mitch's little sister. A kindly shopkeeper directs her to the home of the girl's teacher, Annie Hayworth (Suzanne Pleshette), who came to the seaside village in part because she had been involved with Mitch.

Seven years younger than Hedren, the black-haired Pleshette was a provocateur of the first order. Who else would have dared to sit on Hitchcock's lap, telling him jokes so dirty that even he might not have told them? "I had this insane sense of humor, completely bawdy, the antithesis of the Hitchcock woman, and he rather appreciated it," Pleshette says. "If he had this image of the Madonna and the whore, I certainly didn't fall into the Madonna character."

As much as the Broadway actress amused Hitchcock, he could not have his audience wondering why Mitch would give up this wildly attractive, emotionally up-front woman for the self-indulgent, pampered Melanie. To give Mitch a man's reasons, Edith Head outfitted Pleshette in dowdy, loosely fitting clothes, announcing her as a spinster schoolmarm without husbandly prospects. "The blonde he gives a mink, me he gives a schmatte [Yiddish for an old garment] and wedgies," Pleshette told Hunter.

That was just the first of the ways Hitchcock diminished Pleshette's presence. The cameraman did not light her properly and shot her at angles that showed her poorly. Pleshette knew what was going on, but she was a trouper and made no complaints.

To surprise Mitch, Melanie decides to rent a motorboat and sail across the bay to the house where he lives on the weekends with his mother (Jessica Tandy) and sister. Her mink coat and high heels are hardly a seafarer's outfit, but she guides the skiff through still waters.

The Brenner home and barn sit apart. The house is not even in the community, but in nearby Bodega Head. The crew found the century-old ranch house in such decrepit shape that it had to be rebuilt inside and out.

Sailing back across the bay after leaving the birds and a note in the Brenners' living room, a gull attacks Melanie. "This gull should strike when her mood is cozying itself up for another meeting with Mitch," Hitchcock told Hedren. "That's all she's thinking of . . . then boom, this thing arrives."

Mitch is waiting for Melanie when she arrives back at the dock. Taylor thought his character should jump down into the boat and succor the bleeding woman with tender concern. Hitchcock would have none of it. "He didn't have any experience of behaving like a masculine and rugged man," said Taylor. "He had no streak of tenderness for relationships between men and women."

Melanie drives to Annie's house to rent a room for the night and then goes to the Brenners' for dinner. As she arrives, without thought or apprehension, Cathy rushes up and embraces this woman she has never met before, thanking Melanie for the lovebirds.

In the story conference, Hitchcock challenged why a child would jump all over a grown woman whom she did not even know. "I really don't know much about their behavior," he said. "Do they [children] really fling themselves into people's arms?" He had a daughter and three grandchildren, yet he sounded as if children were an exotic species unknown to him.

As Melanie leaves to drive to spend the night at Annie's house in the village, the telephone lines are full of crows. When Melanie arrives at the house, Annie is sitting in the living room reading a newspaper. Over brandy, it is time for a little girl talk. As Melanie suspects,

Annie had a relationship with Mitch. His mother, Lydia, drove Annie away, as she did any woman who threatened to give him the kind of love a mother cannot give a son.

The relationship had not gone far. "Maybe there's never been anything between Mitch and any girl," Annie says. Mitch may look like the Marlboro Man, but he is another of Hitchcock's impotent male characters unable to assert himself as a full-blown, independent man.

As the two women are about to go to bed, they hear a knock. Annie opens the door and finds a dead seagull that has smashed itself against the house. Hitchcock considered the birds the true stars of the film. They were the reason he felt he did not need to cast expensive marquee-quality actors in the main roles.

In the months before shooting began, the production spent over $200,000 on mechanical birds, drone-like devices with motorized wings, and dummy birds. The faux birds were a feat of engineering, but could not create the terrifying presence Hitchcock needed. That meant they also used live birds, over twenty thousand of them.

The next afternoon, everyone goes to the Brenners' for Cathy's birthday party. Outside on the lawn, the birds make their first major attack. It took a week to shoot this short scene. Hitchcock thought of children as one of life's minor afflictions; he took no pleasure in spending days directing the ornery creatures.

When Hitchcock chose the child extras, he pointedly vetoed one obnoxious youngster, but somehow the production hired him anyway. All the minor players called the director "Mr. Hitchcock" except for his tiny nemesis. Every morning, the boy ran up to Hitchcock, slapped him on the back, and said, "Hello, Alfred." After a while, Hitchcock speculated wildly that his torturer wasn't a child at all, but a miniature man, and the woman who accompanied him was not his mother but his wife.

One morning, as they were about to shoot the children being

pursued by the birds once again, the boy asked, "Where shall I run, Alfred?" Hitchcock pointed toward the bay. "Run straight out into the ocean until the water gets over your head," the director said. "Then sit down until I call you."

Veronica Cartwright was the one child in *The Birds* whose company Hitchcock enjoyed. She and her younger sister, Angela, were highly successful actresses. In 1961, Veronica played Rosalie, a thief and a liar, in the filming of Lillian Hellman's play *The Children's Hour*. For Veronica, it was a wonderful game of make-believe, and she moved from that unpleasant character to the far more likable Cathy. Veronica was just another actor on the set.

"I would bring Hitchcock tea in a china cup and biscuits at four o'clock in the afternoon," she recalled. "And we'd just chat. He was wonderful to me. I never ever felt intimidated. And I could ask him any question."

At the outdoor party, the birds attack during a game of blindman's bluff. As the birthday girl, Cathy is the blindfolded child. The bird trainer Ray Berwick spread birdseed through Veronica's hair and got up on a ladder holding a seagull in his hand. When the trainer let go, the gull dove at his victim. "An actual bird hit my head," Cartwright said. "It wasn't a game to me. I took everything for real."

Berwick had loosely wired together the bird's beak to minimize the harm the gull could do. As the bird swept down, the wire holding the gull broke, and it flew away. "They had to stop shooting, and they went and got it," Cartwright recalled. "Otherwise, the gull would have starved to death."

During the attack, Melanie reaches beyond herself to help the children. After the guests go home, the Brenners and Melanie sit in the living room having dinner, but there is no respite from the birds. Hundreds of sparrows fly down the chimney and emerge through the fireplace into the living room.

The scene was shot inside a bubble on a set in the Universal studios in Los Angeles. The trainers placed 1,500 sparrows, finches, and other small birds above the fake chimney. On cue, the crew opened the cages and the birds flew down the ersatz chimney. A stream of air from hoses kept the birds flying around the living room. "Eventually, the birds settled on the floor," Cartwright said. "Jessica trod on a bird, and she was a basket case."

Hitchcock told the distraught Tandy, "Listen, Jessica, if one of them gets up your skirt, grab it! Because a bird in the hand . . ."

Having bonded with the birthday girl, Melanie agrees to stay overnight. In the morning, Lydia gets in her old Ford pickup, drops Cathy off at school, and drives to her neighbor Dan Fawcett's farm to see how he is doing. She finds Fawcett in his pajamas in his bedroom, lying dead with his eyes plucked out. Nearly hysterical and unable to speak a word, Lydia drives with maddening speed back to her home.

Hitchcock was like an orchestra conductor, obsessed that even the tiniest sound of the piccolo played out in fullness. For the scene at the farmhouse, he had the dirt road watered down so that when Lydia drove there, she could have been on a paved road. When she drives back after seeing her dead friend, a large plume of dust rises behind her.

To make Lydia less worried, Melanie drives to the school to pick up Cathy. In the schoolyard, hundreds of crows alight on the jungle gym. As the children flee down the hillside to the port, the crows pursue them, pecking at them.

Hitchcock shot the scene on location. The director did the close-ups later in the studio with the children running on treadmills. "Hitchcock had a little bit of a sadistic sense of humor," Cartwright said. "He kept us running and running, speeding the treadmill up. If you weren't in the front and you fell, you bowled everyone over, and we all fell down on this huge mattress. I don't know how many times we did this."

One girl cut her lip as she fell. Hitchcock saw that as a missed opportunity. "You could have spit it [the blood] out, and we would have used it in the film," he said.

"Are you nuts?" the child asked, a question no adult would have dared ask.

Hedren had no one on the set to whom she could confess her rightful insecurities. She wasn't a convivial, social person, and stood apart from the other actors. She loved her daughter, Melanie (who would grow up to be a film star herself: Melanie Griffith), beyond measure, but she did not want to bring her here. Better to leave her with the nanny in LA.

At first, Hedren viewed Hitchcock's interest in her with unmitigated delight. He was beside her for her every shot. As the weeks went by, Hedren became nervous. She could see how the men on the set had been told to avoid her, and actors like Rod Taylor confirmed they had been warned off. Hitchcock tried to dominate every aspect of her life. He wanted to oversee whom she saw, what she ate, and where she went.

When the director Peter Bogdanovich interviewed Hitchcock at the time *The Birds* was coming out, the director made no apologies for how he treated Hedren. "It's like this girl Hedren," he said. "Until I have launched them, they belong to me, and they better face that fact. You can't run around with men, you can't start having babies, one thing at a time, get the career going and then start to have the babies."

As authoritarian as that sounded, Pleshette saw that as the price of stardom. "I saw him take a girl who had an enormous responsibility in a major film who had very little experience, and yes, he was controlling," she said. "He wanted to mold her into his future star. He wanted her to look a certain way and sound a certain way, and move a certain way. I mean, this is what he did. This was a Hitchcock film. To think that it would be otherwise is ludicrous. We were all there to realize his vision."

In her autobiography, published more than half a century later, Hedren tells the story of driving with Hitchcock one afternoon back to the Santa Rosa motel. "The limo was just pulling to a stop at the entrance to the hotel, which was swarming with guests and valets and some of our crew members, when with no warning, he threw himself on top of me and tried to kiss me."

No one else ever came forward saying they saw Hitchcock do this. That does not mean Hedren made up the story. It may be that the director's action was not as dramatic as she, in retrospect, described it. Hitchcock was a repressed man who reached out to women in impulsive bursts and then retreated just as quickly.

As Hedren told it, the director became even more obsessed with her. When they returned to finish shooting the film in Los Angeles, she writes in her autobiography that she found him on occasion driving past her home. He did not drive, and he would have done this in a chauffeur-driven vehicle.

On one occasion, in a remote part of the set, Hedren writes, "He'd asked me to touch him, and I resisted the temptation to slap him and just turned and walked away." The further Hedren got from the filming, the angrier she became, and the greater her allegations. It may have happened just as Hedren said it did, but it is also possible the actress misread this. Hedren had the most literal of minds. Certain subtleties and nuances sailed beyond her. Hitchcock had a wicked sense of humor. He sometimes said things he really did not mean and would have been startled to have them acted upon.

Hedren's hairdresser, Virginia Darcy, was on the set all the time. She saw how Hitchcock behaved and largely dismissed it. "He would say shocking things to me, but I laughed and said, 'You can't say those things, they're not nice, you can get into trouble,'" she said. Hitchcock should not have been allowed to say such things to any woman. He could do so because that was the patriarchal Hollywood culture of the time, overseen by men used to getting their way in all things.

After running down the street with the children, Melanie ends up in the Tides Restaurant. She looks out the window and sees the birds attacking a gas station attendant. His hose falls from his hand. The gasoline spreads across the street, where a careless salesman lighting his cigar tosses a match, setting off a conflagration flaming down the road, presumably leaving the world with one less salesman.

Melanie flees into a glass phone booth, where the gulls attack her. She began the film in a gilded cage, and now she is just where Hitchcock wants her, in what he calls "a cage of misery." The mechanical birds smash themselves kamikaze-like against the glass, shattering it and spewing shards at Hedren. The rest of the day, the makeup team plucked tiny bits of glass from the actress's face.

"A part of me did wonder if I was being punished for rejecting him and doing it so publicly," Hedren writes in her autobiography. That was the actress's paranoia taking its walk through her pages. This is not something he would have done to the actress starring in his film, who had many more scenes to shoot. If he had done it, no way could he have gotten away with such an egregious action without others knowing about it.

Mitch rescues Melanie from the phone booth. After the birds fly off, the couple walk quickly up the hill to Annie's house, where Cathy has taken shelter. They hurry past the school, where crows sit aligned along the roof as if it is now their property. At Annie's house, the schoolteacher is lying on the ground outside, pecked to death by the birds. Inside, Cathy is safe, if emotionally shattered.

Back at the Brenners' that evening, it is time for the penultimate attack. To motivate the actors, Hitchcock has drums playing, beating out their tattoos during the shooting. The birds strike through a broken window and peck through a door, and then as suddenly as they arrived, the birds depart, and there is blessed silence.

Later in the evening, hearing a sound, Melanie walks gingerly up the stairs and opens the attic door. The birds have pecked a hole in the roof, and they assail her in a vicious, prolonged manner akin to rape. The only sound is the thrashing of their wings as the assault seems to go on forever, cutting her face, arms, and legs. Mitch pushes his way into the room and carries Melanie to safety. She continues to flail away at imaginary birds until she trusts him.

The birds' attack on Melanie is the most controversial scene Hitchcock ever filmed. Shot over an entire week, the two-minute scene is Hitchcock at his perfectionist extreme, oblivious to the pain and danger. At this point, the bird wranglers had suffered twelve injuries serious enough to send them to the hospital. And here they were for a whole week heaving birds at Hedren.

By the fifth day, Hedren was beyond exhaustion, almost incoherent. It was then that the handlers attached the bird to her shoulder that clawed menacingly near her eyes. She could take no more, and walked away. Against Hitchcock's wishes, she took the next week off, spending most of the time in bed.

Hedren thought Hitchcock was trying to break her, but he treated her no worse than he did the children on the treadmill. Beyond that, he was apprehensive about what he was putting Hedren through. "It was very hard for Hitch at this time, too," Hedren said. "He wouldn't come out of his office until we were absolutely ready to shoot because he couldn't stand to watch it."

In the film, Mitch bandages the almost comatose Melanie. He feels she must go to a hospital in San Francisco. As they exit the house, the birds are everywhere, covering the lawn. It is not just one species out there, but crows, gulls, sparrows, and others. The only sound is their cooing, ominous in its intensity. Mitch, Melanie, Lydia, and Cathy walk through the birds to get into Melanie's car. In the back seat, Lydia embraces the wounded Melanie with tenderness as they drive away through hundreds of birds.

It is a strange ending with no foreshadowing of what else the birds may do. Hunter had written several more pages, and there were suggestions that there should be a final scene of thousands of birds on the Golden Gate Bridge. Hunter believed Hitchcock was so exhausted that he simply packed up and walked away.

To drive the audience into the theaters, Hitchcock promoted *The Birds* as a horror film whose sole purpose is to scare the bejesus out of the moviegoer. It wasn't easy being out there hyping a movie receiving decidedly mixed reviews. A number of critics mocked Hedren's rudimentary acting skills. Worse yet, the audiences were not coming out the way they had for *Psycho*. But Hitchcock could not show his disappointment. Wherever he went, he was full of wry ripostes, playing the beloved Alfred Hitchcock character as he beat the drum for *The Birds*.

Hedren was out hustling too, and whatever her faults as an actress, the former model was good at selling the film. Hitchcock watched over her as closely as ever. When she arrived at the London airport, he sent a memo saying she was to "wear hair in French roll" and "get yellow out of hair." And he lectured her to "stay out of sun."

The actress might have balked, but Hitchcock had signed her to play the title role in his next film, *Marnie*, a complex character that would test her acting skills far beyond *The Birds*.

As untoward as Hedren later said Hitchcock had behaved toward her during the shooting, she was delighted to star in a second Hitchcock film. Her former stepson John Marshall was with Tippi in the seventies, well before she started criticizing Hitchcock. "Tippi always said she was pleased with *The Birds*," Marshall said. "If Hitchcock had acted badly, she wouldn't have done *Marnie*."

* * *

Hitchcock purchased the film rights to *Marnie*, by the British novelist Winston Graham, shortly after the novel was published in January 1961. The psychological thriller tells the story of a compulsive thief. The woman moves from employer to employer, stealing from them and traveling on. Despite pilfering from him (or perhaps partially because of it), her boss, Mark Rutland, takes a romantic interest in Marnie and marries her. Rutland helps Marnie discover the root cause of her malady, her criminal career coming to a presumed end.

After finishing *The Birds*, Hunter began writing the screenplay for *Marnie*, closely following the novel. One scene profoundly troubled him. When Rutland marries Marnie, he discovers on their wedding night that his bride is frigid. Believing he has his marital rights, he rapes her on their honeymoon.

Hitchcock loved the scene as written in the novel. It was one of the primary reasons he bought the movie rights. The screenwriter thought it so wrong, ugly, unnecessary, and excessive that he called Hitchcock to discuss how to proceed.

"We're going to lose all sympathy for the lead character," Hunter said. "No guy who claims to love a woman, sees her cowering in the corner, is going to rape her."

"When he sticks it to her, I want that camera right on her face," Hitchcock said.

When Hunter submitted his first draft in April 1963, the screenwriter wrote a lengthy cover letter, making his case again. "Stanley Kowalski might rape her, but *not* Mark Rutland," Hunter said, referring to the bestial character in Tennessee Williams's *A Streetcar Named Desire*. Then, to give Hitchcock a choice, he included two versions of that scene, a yellow version with the rape and a white version without it. Two days after Hitchcock received the script, he fired the screenwriter.

To replace Hunter, Hitchcock brought in another largely untried screenwriter, Jay Presson Allen, not telling her Hunter had preceded her. Allen's play *The Prime of Miss Jean Brodie*, adapted from Muriel Spark's novel, would become a hit in London, but she had never written a movie script. Nonetheless, it was a chance Hitchcock wanted to take.

A postfeminist woman in a prefeminist age, the willowy, irreverent Allen approached her work far differently than Hunter. The forty-one-year-old playwright did not consider directors the enemy who perversely changed the writer's immortal words. To get her way, she used a full measure of female guile. "Well, you have to let them feel it's *theirs*, or you won't get anything *you* want," she said.

The first weeks Allen spent with Hitchcock were an endless party. They talked about everything except *Marnie*. Allen was a convivial sort, and the sparkling blonde enjoyed being part of this social ambience, but it was bizarre. In her recollection, they spent two months together before Hitchcock first mentioned the book. She had the sense that the director was squandering all this time because he was working his way out of a depression.

One day at the house on Bellagio Road, Allen joined Hitchcock in the garden.

"I've had a wonderful dream, an amazing dream," he said. "Would you like to hear it?"

Allen approached writing in a highly psychological way. Of course she wanted to hear Hitchcock's dream.

"My penis was etched crystal, and it was extraordinarily beautiful and valuable," Hitchcock said. "My main concern was to keep it from the cook."

Allen told the director the obvious. Who was the cook in the house but Alma? By the measure of his dream, Hitchcock wanted to keep his business away from his wife. It was a strange apprehension, as it had been four decades since Hitchcock's etched crystal had entered Alma's kitchen.

As Hitchcock began talking about the film, Allen saw into his strange character. "He was addicted to all kinds of psychological perversities, and the Marnie character was filled with them, just filled with them," the screenwriter said.

Allen had a husband and child back in New York, but she soon realized Hitchcock wanted to control her very being. It wasn't about sex. It was about drawing her into the center of his world and keeping her there until he no longer needed her. "He liked to work with women," Allen said. "He would have had a harem of his own if he could have. He liked women who were on a par with him, who stood up to him."

Whatever difficulties Hitchcock had with Hedren during the filming of *The Birds*, *Marnie* was a new film and a new day. In October 1963, before the shooting of a single scene, Hitchcock spent three days going over the script with Tippi. As he had done with her for *The Birds*, the director recorded the sessions and had them transcribed into fifty-eight single-spaced pages. It was, in essence, a verbal storyboard, each scene described in intricate detail with precise instructions for the actress. For Hedren, it was a gift of immense value but, inexplicably, she said she never went back and referred to those pages.

Unlike *The Birds*, Hitchcock thought he had gotten everything right this time, starting with the screenwriter. Unlike her argumentative, macho predecessor, Allen worked seamlessly with the director, creating a script that did just what Hitchcock wanted it to do. Not only did she write compelling dialogue, she fleshed out the main characters with vivid, novelesque details. Thanks to Allen's efforts, during the shooting, Hitchcock would not be spending his evenings writing new pages.

Most of *Marnie* was shot on sets at the Universal studios in Los Angeles. Hitchcock had his own special series of rooms that was like a second home. Next to his quarters he placed Hedren's large dressing room. Making matters even more comfortable for the director, he had worked previously with almost everyone, from the hairdresser to the grips. Hitchcock was the king of decorum. On the set, hushed tones were the order of the day.

Hedren was tired of the Sturm und Drang days of *The Birds*, and was happy the only drama was on the pages of the script. Her character, Margaret "Marnie" Edgar, is a woman who makes a living stealing from her employers. With each successful heist, she changes her name, her hairstyle, and her hometown. On-screen for almost the entire film, Hedren must make the audience feel sympathy for an apparent sociopath.

Despite having no references, Marnie is hired as a secretary at Rutland Publishing in Philadelphia because the owner, Mark Rutland (Sean Connery), is attracted to her. Before she has worked a single day, the brunette clerk is figuring out how she can get the key to the safe full of cash.

The handsome widower begins dating this mysterious woman, treating her graciously and well. Marnie is so disturbed and such a compulsive thief that even Mark's love for her does not stop her from stealing thousands of dollars in cash from the company safe on a Friday afternoon after everyone has left the office.

"She doesn't have any feeling of exhilaration at all, does she?" Hedren asked as she discussed the scene with the director.

"No, not yet, because the feeling of exhilaration comes after the robbery," Hitchcock said. "She is calculating, cautious, wary. You have to have it in your mind that you're not going to get caught."

Mark tracks Marnie down and comes upon her, newly blonde and newly named, riding her steed, Forio, in the Maryland horse country. As angry as Mark is, his answer is not to take her to the police, but to insist that she marry him. Another of Hitchcock's flawed men, Mark does not do this out of missionary zeal, but so he can control Marnie as he does nothing else in his life. His father is the strong Rutland patriarch, and despite saving the failing family business, Mark barely has his own life. Marnie has no choice but to go along with it and let him dominate her.

On their honeymoon, Mark discovers that his bride is frigid, repulsed by her husband's touch. He tries to go along with her wishes to be left alone, but one evening on the South Seas cruise, he rapes Marnie. Unlike Hitchcock's boast to Hunter, it is the most decorous of assaults as his bride lies back, her countenance devoid of expression.

The rest of the film is about Marnie's attempt, with Mark's help, to come to terms with her malady. She tries in a fitful, sometimes desperate, manner to understand herself and, in so doing, free herself from the curse that holds her in its bonds.

At the end of the film, Mark and Marnie go to visit her mother in Baltimore. There Mrs. Edgar tells the story of how, in Marnie's early childhood, her mother was a prostitute. One evening during a thunderstorm, thinking she was protecting her mother, Marnie killed her client with a fireplace poker. Thus, Marnie's hatred of sex and fear of red, the color of blood.

In the early part of the film, Marnie is almost totally repressed, showing no emotion, and Hedren portrays her effectively. But her role becomes increasingly complicated. These are scenes that are a tour de force for an actress, allowing her to explore a complex pattern of emotions. As hard as Hedren tried, and as much as Hitchcock coached her, she was incapable of reaching the depths of character needed.

"It was very difficult for Tippi because her personal quality is not vulnerable," said Allen. "She's very beautiful, and she has a rather brittle quality. I'm not blaming her. I'm blaming Hitch because he was pushing her into something that was not her image."

Composer Bernard Herrmann had his own singular disregard for Hedren's qualities as an actress. He considered her "both untalented and exploitive of Hitchcock's obvious infatuation." To compensate for Hedren's inability to emote, the composer's biographer believes Herrmann wrote an "aggressively romantic score" for *Marnie*.

Hitchcock was devastated that, as well as he had prepared, the central figure of the film could not fully deliver. It was a further irritant when, during the shooting, Hedren became engaged to Noel Marshall, a divorced father of three children.

Hedren began dating Marshall at the time *The Birds* started shooting, but she had kept her affair secret. Marshall was a classic LA type who hung around the fringes of the film industry. Men like him manage car washes, run dry cleaners, and sell tiles, biding their time until the day they believe they will ascend to their rightful place as producers or directors. Often more charismatic and self-confident than the specimens they seek to replace, some of them eventually succeed, but most have everything needed for success except the requisite talent. Marshall had knocked around, doing everything from directing children's television to working at Sears, before he fell upon his latest gig as an agent for commercials.

Hedren blamed Hitchcock for almost everything bad in her life. She knew she did not love Marshall, but she told herself that being married to him might get the director to back off from his obsession with her. Hedren knew that Marshall did not love her either. She was the break he had been after for so long, the rocket ride out of oblivion.

Hedren told herself that entering into this loveless marriage was an act of principle. "When I say yes to something, I honor it, so when I said yes to Noel, I took the commitment seriously," she writes in *Tippi: A Memoir.*

Hitchcock had never changed his attitude that *his* actresses should not marry but focus solely on acting. For Hedren to marry Marshall was a double betrayal of her covenant with her craft and her obligation to her director.

In a strange attempt to regain command over his universe and to make Hedren jealous, Hitchcock began showering attention on Diane Baker, the attractive actress who played Mark's late wife's sister. He invited her to have lunch with him and showered her with the sweetest words of praise in front of Hedren. That he thought this would consume Hedren with jealousy and transform her on-screen into the Marnie he sought showed his limited understanding of the female psyche. "I was embarrassed for Tippi," said Baker, "and feeling sorry that he was turning his attention onto me in front of Tippi when Tippi was within ear range or sight."

The filming shut down over the Christmas holidays, and Hitchcock had plenty of time to view the rushes. As upbeat and celebratory as Hitchcock might be in public, in private he was brutally realistic about his own work. As he sat viewing the footage, his vision just was not there, not in the way he intended. Hitchcock knew that in a few days, he would be shooting scenes in which Hedren would have to emote powerful emotional qualities in ways that were sorely lacking in these rushes.

At the end of January 1964, Hedren asked to take Friday off to fly to New York City to receive *Photoplay*'s "most promising actress of the year" award and to appear on *The Tonight Show*. Johnny Carson was the king of late night. Most actors in Hollywood dreamed of sitting next to Carson for a few minutes of celebrity chitchat watched by millions. Hedren was not in the scene being shot that Friday, and she would be back on Monday morning ready to proceed as always. On the show, she would surely be asked about *Marnie*, giving the film a jolt of early publicity. Hedren saw no reason why Hitchcock would answer her request with anything but an enthusiastic yes.

As entranced as Hitchcock was at times with Hedren, he viewed her as a fickle actress who had to be constantly coaxed into a workmanlike performance. The director had spent weeks getting Hedren into the proper mindset to play Marnie. If she went jetting off to the East Coast, he felt it might take days to get her back in the proper mood. He could not risk that, plus it was doubtlessly pleasurable to show Hedren he was still in control.

Hedren felt she had given so much to this role and was asking so little. When Hitchcock told her she could not go, she was beyond livid. From the first day she met the director, she had been almost physically repulsed by him. He was this plump little troll who lived under a bridge, frightening all who sought to cross. She had known not to flinch or to show in any way what she truly felt.

This day, as others stood nearby, Hedren reportedly told Hitchcock what she thought. "You're a fat pig," she said.

Obesity was the curse that haunted Hitchcock, a malady he could not hide. But no one dared to mention it. In uttering those words, Hedren committed the sin against the Holy Ghost, the unpardonable sin. Nothing could mend the damage that was done by those four words, and he had few conversations with her after that.

A few weeks later, Hedren says he approached her in her dressing room with a sexual proposition so unspeakably crude that for the rest of her life she could not even repeat his words. Over their time together, Hitchcock told her jokes that would have made a state trooper blush, and she hardly reacted. What could he have said that was so unspeakable?

Hitchcock discussed the incident with his authorized biographer, Taylor. "It was quite likely that Tippi might have put a heavy construction on something which was just said in passing," Taylor said.

The screenwriter Allen's views were not unlike Taylor's. "I think he was having an old man's *crise de coeur* over Tippi," she reflected. "I don't believe that it was as extreme as has been indicated by some writers. I was there all the time, and I did not see that." Even if that was the case, his verbal entreaties were enough that in the #MeToo mood of today, he would have been fortunate if only his hands were slapped.

Hedren did not go out to promote *Marnie* and was pushed aside. She later blamed Hitchcock for getting other filmmakers not to hire her, destroying her career. The director held her contract, but he never once used her again. Beyond that, there is no evidence he set out to ruin her or did anything but move on.

* * *

When Hedren first met Marshall, she found her future husband's impulsive behavior exciting. She never knew what he would do next, but being married to him, it was exhausting and irritating. In their first five years of marriage, he jumped from managing her career to selling real estate, doing construction, and working again as a commercial agent.

Although Hedren had no more starring roles in major studio films, she found considerable work. In 1969, she and Marshall flew to Zimbabwe, where she starred in *Satan's Harvest*, a dreary film about drug trafficking in Africa. The following year they flew back to Africa, where Hedren starred in *Mister Kingstreet's War*, another mediocre film.

While roaming the outback of Mozambique, Hedren and Marshall drove past an abandoned gamekeeper's house inhabited by a pride of lions. That gave the couple the idea for a movie. A naturalist is working in Africa. The scientist's wife and children come to visit and find him sharing a house with lions and tigers. The plot may have been anorexic, but no more so than their model, the highly successful 1966 film *Born Free*, about a game warden and his wife living in Kenya bringing up domesticated lions.

No legitimate studio would back *Roar*. So the couple decided they would do it themselves. Without Hedren's celebrity, they would not have been able to raise any significant money to make the film. Still, from the beginning of this interminable project, Marshall assumed control. Standing firmly at the center of the stage, he wrote, produced, directed, and starred in what he thought would be an immortal movie. While making a passionate plea to save nature's proudest creatures, *Roar* would make a fortune.

The couple decided to shoot *Roar* on 180 acres of scruffy land that Marshall purchased forty miles north of Los Angeles in the Santa Clarita Valley. They needed to fill the land with animals born in captivity amiable to training, and they sought them out wherever they could find them.

At one point, by Hedren's reckoning, living on the property were "132 big cats, one elephant, three aoudad sheep, and a collection of ostriches, flamingos, marabous, storks, and black swans for background." These animals were native to three different continents. Only in Marshall's fantasy did they exist together.

At the center of the vast property sat "Africa House," a large open structure modeled on the building Hedren and Marshall had seen in

Mozambique. Elsewhere on their land, the couple and Melanie Griffith lived in a mobile home.

Early on in the process, when they were seeking money wherever they could find it, Tippi starred in *The Harrad Experiment*, a feature film produced by her husband. The movie is about a college where the students have sex with each other using techniques they learn in class. Harrad College would have had no trouble getting applicants, but it was a far cry from *The Birds* and *Marnie*.

The set was hardly the atmosphere for a young teenager just beginning to explore her sexuality. Nonetheless, Tippi brought Melanie on as an extra. One of the other stars was twenty-two-year-old Don Johnson, who began a relationship with fourteen-year-old Melanie.

Like many teenage girls, Melanie was a petulant, moody child who challenged anyone who tried to corral her. Hedren acted as if she were singularly cursed, the first mother to have such a daughter. In insisting on living her own life, Melanie was not unlike fourteen-year-old Janet Leigh, who ran off to Reno to get married. Leigh's parents would have none of it. They marched her back home and annulled the marriage.

Hedren's solution was to let Melanie do precisely what she wanted: to go off and live with Johnson in Los Angeles. Tippi never seemed to consider that she might have been committing child abuse/neglect and Johnson statutory rape. In 1976, eighteen-year-old Melanie made her own trip to Las Vegas with Johnson to get married. The knot unraveled within six months.

"I've thought a thousand times how much easier the lions were to handle than my daughter was back then," Tippi reflected. The lions she handled. Her daughter she let roam free.

No one with a real résumé in Hollywood would consider working on this bizarre, nonunion project that was eleven years in production, including five years of filming. Marshall hired novices who sought credentials that they hoped would get them jobs in an actual Hollywood project. Many of them lived in nearby mobile homes.

Growing a long, straggly beard like a lion's mane, Marshall asserted himself as the king of the beasts. He strolled through his domain, surrounded by lions and tigers. His aura was irresistible, and everyone, including Hedren, deferred to him. Marshall was the center of the film, wrestling with lions, cavorting with tigers, more daring than any circus animal trainer, a man above men, a hero among mortals. A wildly intemperate, impulsive man, one day he slapped one of his sons in front of the crew. He was far more controlling than Hitchcock ever had been.

The film had scarcely started shooting in October 1976 when a lion bit Marshall's hand, creating an inch-wide hole and the first of many trips of cast and crew to the Palmdale Hospital. The wound might have led to some weighty introspection, but it did just the opposite. The injury justified everything they were doing. They loved being with the animals. "It's special to have a seven-hundred-pound lion jump on you," said Marshall's son John, who had that pleasure many times.

Only Melanie looked straight on at what was happening. Already featured in several films, the teenager knew what a movie was, and she said she no longer wanted to act in *Roar*.

Two weeks later, a lion tore off cinematographer Jan de Bont's scalp. At the Palmdale Hospital, de Bont required 120 stitches. Another day, a lion bit Hedren in the head. She received her second Purple Heart when an elephant tossed her, fracturing her ankle. She was still on crutches when she went to the Palmdale Hospital with her stepson Jerry after a lion bit him. As the doctor worked over young Marshall, he saw gangrene had set in on Hedren's leg, and she needed a skin graft.

Despite all that she had seen, Melanie changed her mind and decided she wanted to come back and act in the film. One day she was there when Marshall was shooting a scene with two of his sons. A playful lioness pounced on Melanie from behind, swiping her paws against her face. Melanie came within inches from losing her right eye and required extensive plastic surgery.

The previous decade, Hitchcock had sicced scores of birds on Tippi during the filming of *The Birds*, an act she thought cruel and despicable. But that was nothing compared to Tippi willfully involving her daughter in this madness in which Melanie could have been scarred for life.

When the teenager got home from the hospital, Melanie told Hedren, "Mom, I'm not quitting. We'll finish this film no matter what."

Hedren could have told her daughter that enough was enough. This could not go on, not like this. But Hedren had become a full-time partner in what was not a movie but a cult. Despite all that her daughter suffered, Hedren said that, in returning, Melanie was "displaying great courage and responsibility, Melanie had grown up."

Marshall pushed and pushed and pushed. One day he insisted on twenty or more takes of one scene, shuttling the lions around. The animals were getting restless, but he kept going until one of the lions grabbed him by the back of the leg and hauled him off. That led to another ambulance visit to the new wing of the Palmdale Hospital that the crew called "The Noel Marshall Wing."

"It [*Roar*] is probably the most unbelievably crazy insane film that has ever been made," said John Marshall. "And it was shocking beyond belief that no one died." During the filming, the big cats wounded at least seventy cast and crew members, but it all finally ended, and everyone slowly woke up.

Roar found no American distributor and was a financial disaster. Hedren and Marshall's marriage was another victim. He moved back to LA. She stayed right where she was, calling the acres "Shambala" and creating a foundation to sustain the animal preserve. She married for a third time, but that did not last, and she was again by herself. She chose to live in a mobile home amid Shambala, awakened each morning by the roar of lions.

The great themes of Hedren's later life were her love for the lions and anger at Hitchcock. "Hedren was a calculating narcissist," said psychoanalyst Dr. Heath King. "Thus, her ability to relate best to animals. Lions are a symbol of strength, and they alleviated her inner fears and insecurity. As for her relationship with Hitchcock, it was totally symbiotic. Even when he was being obnoxious, she smiled and held back her true feelings. Years later, it finally erupted into acts of aggression. Hedren always avoided direct conflict, and it was perfectly in line for her to wait until Hitchcock died to attack him."

Hedren told her story first to a Hitchcock biographer, who painted the late director as a creature of darkness. Thanks to her extensive interviews, the book's portrait had credibility it would not have had otherwise, and it changed Hitchcock's image.

Then Hedren cooperated with a movie about the making of *The Birds* that took all of her allegations, blew them up to enormous size, and left out almost everything else. Even Hedren realized the portrait of Hitchcock was distorted. "It wasn't a constant barrage of harassment," she told a journalist. "If it had been constantly the way we've had to do it in this film, I would have been long gone."

Hitchcock starred Hedren in two films that some critics consider among his best works. For the rest of her acting career, she did nothing that was not quickly forgotten and lived through the fame she gained working with Hitchcock. Hedren's words about Hitchcock were not all negative. She sometimes talked about his greatness and all she learned working with him, but people remembered her charges.

CHAPTER 11

The Tribute

I n March 1979, Hitchcock received the American Film Institute Life Achievement Award at a dinner at the Beverly Hilton Hotel. The ballroom was full of 1,500 Hollywood notables, not just those who had worked with him, but many others who wanted to honor the seventy-nine-year-old director.

Ingrid Bergman was the mistress of ceremonies for the evening. When the sixty-three-year-old actress walked onstage, the audience stood as one. Everyone in the audience knew her story. When the wife and mother ran off with the married Italian director Roberto Rossellini in 1949, she left a shattered reputation behind. Few thought she would ever be accepted back. But after marrying the Italian and having three children with him, she left Rossellini and returned to the one thing she cared about above all others: her career as an actress.

Bergman was slowly dying of cancer, and it was a trying thing to host the event. Few people knew about her illness and what a performance she was putting on that evening. Bergman looked resplendent in her blue gown, her beauty a splendid aura shining out across the ballroom.

The actress had just completed work on *Autumn Sonata*, a film written and directed by her fellow Swede Ingmar Bergman. It is the story of a world-famous pianist, a woman so obsessed with her career that for seven years she has not seen her disabled daughter. The movie resonated closely enough with Bergman's life that it was an especially difficult role. It turned out to be her last film, and some consider it her finest performance.

Bergman loved the camera, and the camera loved her. CBS was filming the event for an hour-and-a-half-long special, but that was not for whom she was performing. Nor was it for her colleagues spread throughout the ballroom. No, her performance was for one person: Alfred Hitchcock.

The actress was not about to read the "awful" words on the cue cards written for her. She would say what she wanted to say her own way about this director with whom she had made three films.

When Bergman came onstage and looked out at Hitchcock sitting at a table with Alma on one side and Cary Grant on the other, she was stunned. "I saw Hitch, who is quite lame with arthritis, struggling so gallantly to stand up for me, and I had to try hard to keep from bursting into tears," Bergman said. "Tears then—and that was just the beginning."

As Bergman shared her sweet memories and gentle anecdotes focused on Hitchcock, his face was a death mask, devoid of even a hint of emotion. It was unsettling and not just to Bergman. Earlier, when Hitchcock walked into the ballroom to a sustained standing ovation, he took tiny, mincing steps as if he were on a ship's deck during a storm and feared he would be swept overboard.

The guests in the grand ballroom had no idea that behind Hitchcock's blank countenance lay emotions tearing him apart. All his career, he had held in check the demons that pursued him, using that as the energy of his creativity. But he was old and half sick, and he did not have the strength any longer to push away his devils.

Hitchcock lived through his work. He still had his bungalow at Universal and a small staff. But he was drinking earlier and more, and often he could not work. For most of his life he had covered his drinking with a veneer of culture and good taste. He did not do that any longer. He just drank. If he had been more animated, it would have been easier to tell if he was in a stupor.

Hitchcock had always controlled his obsessions to some measure, but he could not do that anymore. The target of this was a young secretary whose comings and goings he observed with untoward interest. "I remember her as a decent person who got enmeshed in a little local lunacy," said David Freeman, a screenwriter working almost daily with Hitchcock.

In the mornings, when Hitchcock was often already drunk, the secretary came into his office and shut the door behind her. Freeman thought she was likely partially undressing in front of the director. To get her to do this, the screenwriter believed Hitchcock was paying her enough money in cash so she could buy the newer used car that she brought on the lot. To Freeman, "the whole thing had a pathetic innocence about it." Innocent or not, it was a disturbing, dangerous thing for Hitchcock to do, but he seemed unable to understand the risk he was taking, and no one dared to confront him.

Then there was Alma at home. A marriage is proven in the worst of times, not the best. By that standard, the Hitchcocks' fifty-two-year marriage was strong and solid. Alma had suffered a series of strokes. She could not walk unaided and had the services of day and night nurses. When their daughter, Pat, did not bring dinner, Hitchcock and the day nurse cooked steak or chicken.

"It is very tragic because Alma spends most of the day in the big window seat in the living room," Hitchcock wrote a friend. "She has plenty to read and she has a miniature color television on the large coffee table.... Naturally, she never leaves the house, but I try to take her out one night a week to our favorite restaurant, but maneuvering her is quite a business."

For a while, Hitchcock was feeling so poorly that he was not up to going into Universal. Instead, he had Freeman come out to his house. At the studio, Hitchcock sat for hours like a recumbent Buddha, the only motion his mouth. But in Alma's presence, he got up and walked around with whatever animated energy he could still muster, spinning out his latest movie ideas.

"When Hitchcock saw Alma sitting there engaged in their discussion, I could just feel the years coming off his shoulders," Freeman said. "He was saying to his wife, 'Look, we can make another one. This can happen. It's worth living.' It was like a kid showing off for the girl."

One day Hitchcock slipped on a piece of carpeting that sat outside his shower and fell onto the floor of the white marble bathroom. Forget calling out to Alma. She could not get out of bed. The night nurse tried to get him up, but she was a wisp of a young woman and could not begin to lift his heavy form. So they called for the paramedics, and three of them marched into the house, set Hitchcock on a gurney, and wheeled him out. The tests at the UCLA Medical Center proved negative, but the episode unsettled him.

To do publicity for the AFI tribute, Hitchcock did several interviews, most notably with Charles Champlin of the *Los Angeles Times*. For decades Hitchcock had done a masterful job of using these occasions to promote whatever needed to be promoted. But this day, he talked about his pacemaker and his past.

"On next Aug. 13th, I will be 80 years old," Hitchcock said. "I must be one of the oldest still at it. It's a funny thing mentally how your mind travels back. You wonder what ever happened to so and so. Or I might see a set being put up and say, we did that in 1922."

On the morning of the tribute, Hitchcock received a telegram from eighty-one-year-old Frank Capra. The celebrated director wired his colleague to tell him he was in Palm Springs and would not be able to come to the tribute. Hitchcock could understand that all too well, and he sat crying. It was not about Capra. It was about him. He knew about journeys too far.

Champlin's piece in the *Los Angeles Times* that morning said that Hitchcock's "pleasure in this night's tribute is lessened by the possibility that Alma Reville Hitchcock, his wife and film collaborator for fifty-three years, who is partly paralyzed after two strokes, will be unable to attend." That was a reasonable assumption, but Alma would not let it be true. Her nurses dressed her, half carried her to the hotel, and sat her in a chair in the ballroom to await her husband's arrival.

Before Hitchcock walked across the grand ballroom, he had a task to perform. The producers were not taking any chances that he would falter in making his remarks. They had him deliver his talk to their cameras beforehand, the footage they later interspersed with his faulty speaking of the same words in the ballroom. Then his handlers took him to a suite at the Hilton, where their primary job was to see that he had nothing to drink. A knock at the door brought a gift of champagne from CBS. Hitchcock was on his way to downing both bottles like a naughty child when they took the champagne away.

None of the many tributes that evening was more eloquent and deeply felt than that of the French director François Truffaut. His collection of interviews with Hitchcock was a magnificent how-to book to be read and reread by anyone interested in the art of cinema.

With his lean good looks and long white scarf wrapped jauntily around his neck, Truffaut was a Gallic showman. "In America, you call this man Hitch," he said, his finger pointing out toward his honored friend. "In France, we call him Monsieur Hitchcock. You respect him because he shoots scenes of love as if they were scenes of murder. We respect him because he shoots scenes of murder like scenes of love."

The most profound tribute to Hitchcock came not from spoken words but from film clips. The director was not about story as much as he was about scenes; one after another, they appeared interspersed throughout the evening.

There were June Howard-Tripp and Ivor Novello in *The Lodger*, in a scene from half a century earlier that showed, at the beginning of Hitchcock's career, he was already making daringly inventive shots.

Then there were images from *Notorious*, as the formally dressed Ingrid Bergman and Cary Grant rummage in a wine cellar looking for the Nazi conspirators' secret.

Grant was just as sartorial supreme in his tuxedo in *To Catch a Thief*, next to the exquisite Grace Kelly, dressed in a shimmering blue gown. In another scene from that film, the fireworks above Cannes cannot compete with those between Grant and Kelly.

Grant was everywhere. There he was, running from a crop-dusting plane trying to kill him in the wilds of Indiana in *North by Northwest*. Later, in another clip, Grant and Eva Marie Saint almost die falling off the face of Mount Rushmore, pursued by Communist agents, another one of Hitchcock's signature scenes.

The actor was not the only one being chased. Tippi Hedren ran down the street with schoolchildren fleeing marauding birds in *The Birds*. She escapes, but Janet Leigh does not in *Psycho*, as her assailant knifes her to death in the shower, a scene terrifying no matter how many times one has seen it.

And what a moment it is in *Vertigo* when Jimmy Stewart looks for the first time at the woman he believes he has crafted in the image of his late love, played compellingly by Kim Novak. That romance ends tragically, but in the last reel of *Spellbound*, Bergman and Gregory Peck express their love with a kiss that fills the screen.

These shots from films made over the course of five decades in England and Hollywood testified to the compelling entertainment Hitchcock created and the unprecedented longevity of his career. He spanned the ages, always disciplined and full of close purpose, never losing focus.

Later in the evening, many actors who had worked with Hitchcock were introduced. Janet Leigh looked stunningly youthful in her long gown. Tippi Hedren was as blond and glamorous as ever. After the event, she would drive back to her trailer in the Santa Clarita Valley countryside to continue shooting *Roar* among the lions, tigers, and panthers.

To Hitchcock, the AFI evening was less a tribute than a requiem for a heavyweight. When it came time for him to accept the AFI award, he spoke the talk written for him. The words had a small measure of wit and were mildly self-deprecating with no purpose other than to garner a few chuckles.

It was a terrible waste of a unique opportunity. Hitchcock was crucial in developing the first truly democratic art form in human history. He had been there from the beginning, from silent pictures to talkies, from talkies to color, and then the big screen. Operating in a forthrightly commercial milieu without high artistic pretensions, Hitchcock produced numerous immortal films. A creature of cinema, there was so much he could have told this audience about his life in film.

The fault did not lie in the writer, but in the director himself. His art was often brilliant and always limited. He rarely reached out to tragedy or profound love, to passionate, singular emotions. He touched that neither in his art nor in his personal life, and he was not going to expose his feelings in this public arena.

This was likely the last time he would ever have an opportunity to speak to millions, and he would go out as he came in—pushing emotions away, using irony as his shield. Hitchcock was receiving AFI's Life Achievement Award, but when he read those words off the cue card, he said Life *Amusement* Award. It was unclear whether he had misread the words or improvised his own ironic moment.

Hitchcock had one moment of genuine feeling in his talk. "I will mention only four people who have given me the most affection, appreciation, and encouragement and constant collaboration," Hitchcock said. "First of the four is a film editor. The second is a scriptwriter. The third is the mother of my daughter, Pat. And the fourth is as fine a cook as ever performed miracles in a domestic kitchen. And their names are Alma Reville."

In the final minutes, Bergman returned to the stage. All she ever sought to be was an actress, but now she was also a writer and director. Wanting to end the evening on a powerful emotional note, she set out what she was about to do, ensuring the audience understood.

"Now, there's just one little thing I want to add before we finish this evening," Bergman began. Then she reminded the audience of the scene in *Notorious* where Bergman's character pockets the key to the wine cellar that holds the secret to the Nazis' evil plans.

"Well, you know what? Cary stole that key," Bergman said. "And he kept it ten years. And one day, he put it in my hand and said, 'I've kept this long enough. Now it's for you for good luck.'

"I have kept it for twenty years," Bergman declared, holding up the small metal piece. "In this very same hand, there is the key.

"I'm coming over," Bergman announced, signaling what she was about to do. "It has given me a lot of good luck and quite a few good movies too, and now I'm going to give it to you with a prayer that it will open some very good doors for you too.

"God bless you, dear Hitch; I'm coming to give you the key,"

Bergman repeated, doubly ensuring the audience understood. She had set it up perfectly, and as she threaded her way through the tables toward Hitchcock, the audience stood and applauded. Hitchcock managed to rise too.

Most of Hitchcock's films had a MacGuffin, a device that set the story in motion. The key Bergman carried toward Hitchcock was his final MacGuffin.

Bergman handed the key to Hitchcock and kissed him on the cheeks. Then in a motion that was spontaneous, deep, and true, she hugged him. Although Hitchcock did not like people to touch him, he reached out with his arms and enveloped the actress. Hitchcock was embracing not just Bergman but life itself.

CHAPTER 12

The Lives

JUNE HOWARD-TRIPP

June 11, 1901–January 14, 1985

After recovering from a ruptured scar brought on by the shooting of *The Lodger*, Howard-Tripp returned to a career on the stage. In 1929, she married John Alan Burns, 4th Baron Inverclyde, an heir to the Cunard shipping fortune. Burns took her to his castle in Scotland, where he denied her access to her theater friends and emotionally abused her. Their 1933 divorce was one of the most publicized of the day. In 1937, June married Edward Hillman Jr., whose family owned a Chicago department store. Promising her a life of solitude and beauty in Southern California, she was greeted by starlets, models, champagne, and endless parties. The couple twice divorced and twice reconciled, staying together until Hillman's death in 1966. June lived out her life in California, dying at the age of eighty-three. Her final professional role was speaking the voice-over in Jean Renoir's classic 1951 film, *The River*, about life along the Ganges in pre-independence India. The last words of the film and the last words of June's professional career are: "The river runs, the round world spins. Dawn and lamplight. Midnight. Noon. Sun follows day. Light, stars, and moon. The day ends. The end begins."

MADELEINE CARROLL

February 26, 1906–October 2, 1987

Although lucky in love, Carroll was unlucky in marriage. After divorcing Sterling Hayden in 1946, she married the French film producer Henri Lavorel. That relationship lasted no longer than the clap of a hand. In 1950, Carroll married *Life* publisher Andrew Heiskell, with whom she had a daughter, Anne Madeleine. In the ensuing fifteen years, although Carroll occasionally performed, her main role was as society matron. After her divorce in 1965, she eventually settled in a villa outside Marbella, Spain, where she lived the rest of her eighty-one years. Carroll did not look back wistfully at what had been. "Movie?" she said queryingly to a reporter, who chanced by one day. "Just say I got out when the going was good."

JOAN HARRISON

June 20, 1907–August 14, 1994

As the producer of the weekly television series *Alfred Hitchcock Presents*, Harrison hired many blacklisted writers and actors, giving them their first entrée back into the business. She also convinced a number of movie actors and writers to work in television for the first time. Although always discreet, she had time for many lovers, likely women as well as men. As she passed her fiftieth birthday, as youthfully stylish as ever, it seemed likely she would never marry. Then she brought in the celebrated British spy novelist Eric Ambler to write one of the weekly tales, and they began an affair. In 1958, she married the author, who was two years her junior, and brought her husband into her rarefied Hollywood life. Television had little room for a woman producer past the half-century mark. In 1968, the couple moved to Lake Geneva. Neither of them took much to the Swiss, and they ended up in London, where Harrison lived out her last twenty years, dying in 1994 at the age of eighty-seven.

Ingrid Bergman

August 29, 1915–August 29, 1982

Bergman's final role was as Golda Meir in a television movie. The actress looked nothing like the diminutive Israeli prime minister, but she transformed herself, shedding her beauty, adding an accent, and effectively portraying this feisty, willful woman who died of cancer. Everyone on the set in Tel Aviv knew Bergman was sick. Her arm was enormous and largely immovable, and she played the role in long sleeves, disguising the pain she felt. When she returned to her London home, her arm grew to a grotesque size. "I call him my dog," she wrote the Italian journalist Oriana Fallaci. "I joke with him. 'You are a dog, a nasty sick dog. Come on, let's go walking.'" In mid-August 1982, as sick as she was, Bergman flew to Sweden for a final visit. There she told an old friend, "I am not afraid to die. I've had a rich life. I am content." Returning to London, she died in her bed on her sixty-seventh birthday.

GRACE KELLY

November 12, 1929–September 14, 1982

When the gates of the palace closed behind Kelly on her wedding day in 1956, she began playing the role she would assume for the rest of her life: Princess Grace of Monaco. Missing her life as an actress, she would have loved to have starred in another Hitchcock film. She never talked about what regrets she may have felt in giving up her spectacular career. Kelly devoted herself to mothering her three children—Caroline, Albert II, and Stephanie—and to her charitable pursuits. In 1982, she was driving with Stephanie above Monte Carlo when the vehicle plunged off the narrow road, taking fifty-two-year-old Kelly to her death. The site is very much like the spot down the road in France where she and Cary Grant filmed a romantic interlude in *To Catch a Thief.*

KIM NOVAK

February 13, 1933

For most of her adult life, a black cloud hovered over Novak, periodically swooping down to fill her with despair. She has long since recognized her bipolar disease and obsessive-compulsive disorder. These days Novak deals with it the best she can, knowing the blackness will come again one day, leaving as suddenly as it arrived. She is an immensely creative woman, a singular artist. In her remote Oregon home, ninety-year-old Novak reckons with her fate.

EVA MARIE SAINT

July 4, 1924

Saint's daughter, Laurette, lives nearby in Los Angeles. Her son, Darrell, is a short plane ride away in San Francisco. She sees them frequently, if not always in person, then on Zoom. Her four grandchildren and two great-grandchildren also visit her in her luxury apartment. But for the most part, Saint lives her own life. A big Dodgers fan, she watches the team on television. As intrigued by politics as ever, she discusses the subject with her friends. During the pandemic, she acted in several plays on a podcast with Annette Bening, Matthew Broderick, Sarah Jessica Parker, and Marisa Tomei. She suffers from the minor indignities of age that any ninety-nine-year-old suffers, but as much as she can, she ignores such inflictions. Saint's motto is "Just keep moving."

JANET LEIGH

July 6, 1927–October 3, 2004

To have played the crucial role in *Psycho* was an accomplishment of a lifetime. In the following years, Leigh had roles in all kinds of movies and television dramas, including two horror movies, in which she played alongside her daughter, Jamie Lee Curtis, but nothing as celebrated as *Psycho*. Besides acting, Leigh wrote four books, including a bestselling memoir and an account of the making of *Psycho*. In her last years she kept quiet that she was suffering from vasculitis, a blood vessel disease. The seventy-seven-year-old actress died in her Beverly Hills home in 2004 with her husband and two daughters beside her.

TIPPI HEDREN

January 19, 1930

Shambala is Hedren's passion, living among lions and tigers far from urban civilization. These beasts are her friends, though she knows, given the right circumstances, they might tear her apart. Through her Roar Foundation, over the years she has watched out for her charges. Not only has the foundation fed the animals and given them proper medical care, but Hedren worked to pass the 2003 Captive Wildlife Safety Act, which prevents the sale and interstate commerce of lions, tigers, leopards, cheetahs, jaguars, and cougars. For these wild animals stolen out of their native environment, unable any longer to hunt and forage and be their true selves, Shambala is a place to live out their lives. So it is for ninety-three-year-old Tippi Hedren, who has withdrawn from public life.

ALFRED HITCHCOCK

August 13, 1899–April 29, 1980

In the months after the AFI tribute, Hitchcock realized he was not going to be able to direct another movie, and he ordered his Universal office shut down. He did so in an arbitrary, abrupt way without informing his loyal staff. As the passions of his life drained out of him, Hitchcock became totally self-absorbed, rarely seeing beyond himself. Hitchcock had an invalid wife, a daughter, three grandchildren, and a number of loving friends. But if he could not do the one thing he cared about, he believed he had no reason to live. And so this man of indomitable purpose took the intense focus that had served him so well for so long and applied it to his final task: to let himself die. He stopped eating, and drinking only a little water, until the eighty-year-old director succumbed on April 29, 1980.

Alma Reville Hitchcock

August 14, 1899–July 6, 1982

For Hitchcock's memorial mass at the Church of the Good Shepherd in Beverly Hills, Alma sat in a wheelchair. From the look on her face, she may not have understood what was transpiring or that her husband had died. Although she lived two more years, dying at the age of eighty-two, the fierce, inquisitive spirit that defined her was gone and she was incapable of reflecting on the epic journey of the life she shared with Hitchcock.

ACKNOWLEDGMENTS

I am fortunate to have written a book about such complex, fascinating characters. Most of the principals and their associates in *Hitchcock's Blondes* are gone. I was able to interview two of the actresses, Kim Novak and Eva Marie Saint. They were articulate and forthcoming, and I thank them for enriching this book. Novak's manager, Sue Cameron, set up the interview after my longtime friend, *People's* Liz McNeil, introduced us. Saint's publicist, Jeff Sanderson, was helpful and gracious from beginning to end.

Tippi Hedren has retired from doing interviews, but her former stepson John Marshall talked to me and was refreshingly candid. The young Veronica Cartwright was delightful in *The Birds*, and she's still delightful. Marli Renfro doubled for Janet Leigh in much of the shower murder scene in *Psycho*. She closely observed and helped me understand the making of that classic film. I wrote my biography of Ingrid Bergman, *As Time Goes By*, in 1986. I was able to use much of that research in this book.

When I started work on *Hitchcock's Blondes*, the first thing I did was to read the definitive biography of Alfred Hitchcock by Patrick McGilligan. The author spent years researching *Hitchcock: A Life in Darkness and Light*, and deposited his voluminous research at the University of Wisconsin–Madison. I was grateful when McGilligan gave me access to his documents. I could not have written *Hitchcock's Blondes* as I did without those hundreds of pages of material. Mary Huelsbeck at the University of Wisconsin Library did yeoman-like service gathering together the files and sending them to me. Jon Krampner gave me early access to his revealing biography, *Ernest Lehman: The Sweet Smell of Success.*

I had three researchers who rendered indispensable service. Will Coates did the bulk of the work, penetrating the labyrinth that is the Margaret Herrick Library in Los Angeles. In London, Mary Troath made some important suggestions; and in Boston, Mary Chitty worked her way through the Whitfield Cook papers at the Boston University Library. At the Margaret Herrick Library, Louise Hilton, Clare Denk, and Caroline Jorgenson were extremely helpful. Despite her busy schedule at the American Film Institute, Emily Wittenberg secured an important photo.

I also had several perceptive readers. As always, my wife, Vesna Obradovic Leamer, was my first reader, and that was just the beginning of how indispensable she is to my life. My dear friend Raleigh Robinson read the pages numerous times, always coming up with important suggestions. Marty Bell brought all the acumen he achieved producing plays on Broadway to these pages. Susan Nernberg, an avid reader, had valuable comments. My fellow author Mark Olshaker came up with the idea for the first chapter.

Michelle Howry, Putnam's executive editor, is an author's dream. She misses nothing and is always there backing me up. Her job is easier because she has such a diligent assistant in Ashley Di Dio. I'm fortunate too in having Katie Grinch handling publicity for *Hitchcock's Blondes* as she did for my previous book, *Capote's Women.* I also lucked out in a major way in having David Halpern at the Robbins Office as my literary agent. My Hollywood agent, Matthew Snyder at CAA, could sell bikinis to the Taliban.

Rob Sternitzky copyedited the manuscript with skill and sensitivity. Hilary McClellen did the same when she fact-checked *Hitchcock's*

Blondes. Among the people who helped me during the writing of this book or gave previous interviews were Dr. Heath King, Gregory Peck, Petter Lindstrom, Elsa Holm, Alf Kjellin, Larry Adler, Scott Eyman, Norman Lloyd, Robert Lacey, Oleg Cassini, Dr. Frank Vaccaro, Greta Danielsson, Daniela Mantilla, Antonio Mantilla, Alejandro Mantilla, Emilia Mantilla, Don Spencer, Nancy Lubin, Eric Dezenhall, Dan Moldea, Gus Russo, Mark Obenhaus, Joel Swerdlow, Bob Bates, Edward Leamer, Robert Leamer, Paul Friedman, David and Ronnie Fingold, Toni Holt Kramer, Jeff Jacobus, and Paul and Paulette Cooper Noble.

I must thank one other person. You. An author is nothing without readers. I am so thankful you are reading *Hitchcock's Blondes.*

NOTES

Unless otherwise mentioned, interviews were conducted by the author. For his research he often used the Kindle edition along with the original book. Materials from the Margaret Herrick Library are credited as MHL, those from the Patrick McGilligan Papers as PMP.

CHAPTER 1: A FAIRY TALE

1 **"Buddy and Tippi":** Tony Lee Moral, *The Making of Hitchcock's* The Birds (New York: Open Road, 2010), loc. 2579, Kindle.

CHAPTER 2: A NAUGHTY BOY

6 **have become a "poof":** Patrick McGilligan, *Alfred Hitchcock: A Life in Darkness and Light* (New York: It Books, 2004), 66.

7 **pulled out her glasses:** François Truffaut, *Hitchcock* (New York: Simon & Schuster, 1983), 39.

7 **"I think the northern Germans . . .":** McGilligan, *Alfred Hitchcock*, 83.

8 **"women form three-quarters . . .":** Sidney Gottlieb, ed., *Hitchcock on Hitchcock: Selected Writings and Interviews* (Berkeley: University of California Press, 1995), 73.

8 **"I have to consider whether . . .":** Gottlieb, ed., *Hitchcock on Hitchcock*, 75.

9 **"He was a loner . . .":** Dr. Heath King interview.

11 **"misogyny is a hopelessly simplistic and . . .":** James Bell, ed., *39 Steps to the Genius of Hitchcock* (London: British Film Institute, 2012), 52.

11 **"the agonized complexity . . .":** Bell, ed., *39 Steps to the Genius of Hitchcock*, 52.

11 **That fundamental fear of women:** David D. Gilmore, *Misogyny: The Male Malady* (Philadelphia: University of Pennsylvania Press, 2001), 3.

12 **His films received forty-six Academy:** "Alfred Hitchcock," Wikipedia, https://en.wikipedia.org/wiki/Alfred_Hitchcock.

12 **despite five nominations:** McGilligan, *Alfred Hitchcock*, 573.

12 **"He [Hitchcock] works exactly . . .":** François Truffaut, "Hitchcock—His True Power Is Emotion," *New York Times*, March 4, 1979.

13 **"The shower scene in *Psycho* . . .":** Sam Kemp, "Martin Scorsese on the Importance of Alfred Hitchcock Film 'Vertigo,'" *Far Out Magazine*, September 21, 2021.

13 **"a rather nervous man":** McGilligan, *Alfred Hitchcock*, 25.

14 **his "little lamb":** John Russell Taylor interview, Patrick McGilligan Papers at the University of Wisconsin–Madison, PMP.

14 **"This is what we . . .":** McGilligan, *Alfred Hitchcock*, 11.

14 **"the clang of the door . . .":** McGilligan, *Alfred Hitchcock*, 11.

15 **"She [his mother] was always a slightly . . .":** Taylor interview.

15 **"I would sit quietly in a corner . . .":** McGilligan, *Alfred Hitchcock*, 9.

16 **"And then—then, swinging . . .":** McGilligan, *Alfred Hitchcock*, 33.

16 **"Half a crown please":** McGilligan, *Alfred Hitchcock*, 33.

17 **A wee bit short:** Alfred Hitchcock, "The Woman Who Knows Too Much," *McCall's*, March 1956.

17 **"a trifle snooty to me . . .":** McGilligan, *Alfred Hitchcock*, 55.

17 **"I regarded myself . . .":** Christina Lane, *Phantom Lady: Hollywood Producer Joan Harrison, the Forgotten Woman Behind Hitchcock* (Chicago: Chicago Review Press, 2020), 37.

17 **As a young teenager:** McGilligan, *Alfred Hitchcock*, 54.

18 **picking up fleas:** Pat Hitchcock O'Connell and Laurent Bouzereau, *Alma Hitchcock: The Woman Behind the Man* (New York: Berkley Books, 2003), 14.

18 **case of St. Vitus' dance:** O'Connell and Bouzereau, *Alma Hitchcock*, 19.

CHAPTER 3: A PASSION FOR BLONDES

19 **placed the woman's head:** François Truffaut, *Hitchcock* (New York: Simon & Schuster, 1983), 44.

20 **had collapsed onstage:** *Daily Mirror*, January 11, 1926.

21 **"No dancing required . . .":** Henry K. Miller, *The First True Hitchcock: The Making of a Filmmaker* (Oakland: University of California Press, 2022), 8.

21 **"the first true . . .":** Truffaut, *Hitchcock*, 43.

22 **"Those were the great days . . .":** Donald Spoto, *The Dark Side of Genius: The Life of Alfred Hitchcock* (New York: Ballantine Books, 1984), 67.

22 **"a short, corpulent . . .":** June, *The Glass Ladder* (London: Heinemann, 1960), 156.

23 **discuss the golden wig:** "'The Lodger': A Murder Film in the Making," *Daily Mail*, March 22, 1926.

23 **Although in the novel:** Patrick McGilligan, email discussion with author.

24 **"Is the lodger really a vile murderer . . ."**: "'The Lodger,'" *Daily Mail*, March 22, 1926.

25 **standing on plate glass**: Truffaut, *Hitchcock*, 45–46.

25 **"All I had to do . . ."** Quoted in *Belfast Telegraph*, January 22, 2022.

27 **Mander was a man who took**: John Pascoe, *Madeleine Carroll: Actress and Humanitarian, from* The 39 Steps *to the Red Cross* (Jefferson, NC: McFarland, 2020), 15.

28 **"I think women are less . . ."**: Roger Burford, "A New 'Chair' Which a Woman Might Fill," *The Gateway* 1, no. 3 (July 1929): 100–103.

28 **"I found that although . . ."**: Burford, "A New 'Chair' Which a Woman Might Fill."

CHAPTER 4: GOODBYE TO ALL THAT

30 **receive her bachelor of arts degree (Honors French)**: John Pascoe, *Madeleine Carroll: Actress and Humanitarian, from* The 39 Steps *to the Red Cross* (Jefferson, NC: McFarland, 2020), 7.

30 **"Makeup is a serious . . ."**: Pascoe, *Madeleine Carroll*, 13.

31 **English star Gertrude Lawrence**: Pascoe, *Madeleine Carroll*, 37.

31 **before the altar**: "British Movie Star Weds," *The Leader-Post*, October 24, 1931.

31 **"The truth is that . . ."**: Pascoe, *Madeleine Carroll*, 59.

32 **"a kind of mesmeric trance"**: Spoto, *The Dark Side of Genius*, 146.

32 **"the Birmingham tart"**: Mike Lockley, "The Ice Maiden," *Birmingham Evening Mail*, February 25, 2017.

32 **"We deliberately wrote . . ."**: McGilligan, *Alfred Hitchcock*, 168.

33 **"relates more to sex . . ."**: McGilligan, *Alfred Hitchcock*, 167.

33 **He once bet a friend**: McGilligan, *Alfred Hitchcock*, 99.

34 **"Mr. Hitchcock, I've got to go to the bathroom"**: Pascoe, *Madeleine Carroll*, 200–201.

35 **Hitchcock appeared imperturbable**: *Sunderland Daily Echo and Shipping Gazette*, February 16, 1935.

36 **"It would be hard to . . ."**: Pascoe, *Madeleine Carroll*, 67.

37 **corner feeding his morphine habit**: Pascoe, *Madeleine Carroll*, 71.

37 **"He was a very coarse . . ."**: Pascoe, *Madeleine Carroll*, 71.

37 **"Nothing gives me more . . ."**: Spoto, *The Dark Side of Genius*, 153.

38 **"Oh, yes, I've had experience . . ."**: Spoto, *The Dark Side of Genius*, 180.

39 **The other woman, Dorothy Everard**: "Madeleine Carroll Freed," *Lincoln Journal Star*, December 12, 1939.

40 **"She wears no . . ."**: Sterling Hayden, *Wanderer* (Golden Springs Publishing, 2015), loc. 5307, Kindle.

40 **"a place to be used . . .":** Hayden, *Wanderer,* loc. 5323.

41 **One of the bombs fell:** Pascoe, *Madeleine Carroll,* 117.

CHAPTER 5: A GOLDEN GLOW

43 **manifest listed her as "Joan Hitchcock":** Lane, *Phantom Lady,* 71.

44 **only about fifteen:** Lane, *Phantom Lady,* 23.

44 **arrived in shocking red:** Lane, *Phantom Lady,* 29.

45 **Hitchcock had dinner:** McGilligan, *Alfred Hitchcock,* 197.

45 **was "rather disconcerted":** McGilligan, *Alfred Hitchcock,* 197.

46 **Selznick shot Harrison down:** Lane, *Phantom Lady,* 94.

46 **the last 10 percent:** Lane, *Phantom Lady,* 96.

47 **"a triumvirate, always conferring":** Lane, *Phantom Lady,* 106.

47 **"Hitch had this monumental immobility . . .":** John Russell Taylor interview for BBC, PMP.

48 **"I love it. She has . . .":** United Press, "Girls, Don't Let Femininity Slip," *Los Angeles Times,* July 5, 1957.

48 **"Carol could have easily . . .":** Lane, *Phantom Lady,* 145.

50 **"Hitch told me what . . .":** Spoto, *The Dark Side of Genius,* 248.

51 **"When I came to America . . .":** Donald Spoto, *Notorious: The Life of Ingrid Bergman* (New York, HarperCollins, 1997), 83.

51 *herrgårdsflicka,* **the manor house girl:** Laurence Leamer, *As Time Goes By: The Life of Ingrid Bergman* (New York: Harper & Row, 1986), 33.

52 **"I almost took the life . . ."** Ingrid Bergman to Petter Lindstrom, undated letter. Given to author by Petter Lindstrom.

52 **"Adolphson put his two . . .":** Off-the-record interview.

52 **"Ingrid was upset because Edvin . . .":** Elsa Holm interview.

54 **There he took:** Petter Lindstrom interview.

55 **"The man Frau Adler . . .":** Lindstrom interview.

55 **"Daughter of Germany":** Spoto, *Notorious,* 142.

56 **"I was banned from . . .":** Åke Sandler interview.

59 **There was fifty-two-year-old Victor Fleming:** Spoto, *Notorious,* 154.

59 **"the day after the picture . . .":** James Bacon, *Made in Hollywood* (New York: Warner Books, 1977), 60.

60 **"Ingrid was like . . .":** Alf Kjellin interview.

61 **"I won't do this . . .":** Spoto, *Notorious,* 210.

62 **"a woman's cameraman . . .":** McGilligan, *Alfred Hitchcock,* 342.

63 **such words as "lecherous":** Joseph I. Breen to David O. Selznick, letter, May 19, 1944, Spellbound Production files, MHL.

63 **"mating":** Joseph I. Breen to David O. Selznick, letter, June 19, 1944, MHL.

63 **The book title:** Joseph I. Breen to David O. Selznick, letter, June 30, 1944, MHL.

63 **Bergman knew how:** McGilligan, *Alfred Hitchcock*, 343.

63 **"Ingrid, fake it":** Spoto, *Notorious*, 211.

63 **"Well, all my fun . . .":** Spoto, *The Dark Side of Genius*, 276.

64 **One evening at a dinner:** Spoto, *The Dark Side of Genius*, 292.

64 **"That's not the kind . . .":** Gregory Peck interview.

64 **"I had a real love . . .":** Brad Darrach, "Gregory Peck," *People*, June 15, 1987.

65 **"I felt I needed . . .":** Lynn Haney, *Gregory Peck: A Charmed Life* (New York: Carroll and Graf, 2004), 24–25.

65 **"One wears brown . . .":** McGilligan, *Alfred Hitchcock*, 341.

65 **each bottle a note:** McGilligan, *Alfred Hitchcock*, 342.

66 **"I had the feeling . . .":** Spoto, *The Dark Side of Genius*, 276.

67 **"You felt she'd never read . . .":** Larry Adler interview.

69 **"a grossly immoral woman . . .":** Joseph I. Breen to David O. Selznick, letter, May 25, 1945, MHL.

69 **"I think you know that . . .":** Joseph I. Breen to David O. Selznick, letter, May 25, 1945, MHL.

70 **"a zebra-skin print blouse . . .":** McGilligan, *Alfred Hitchcock*, 330.

71 **"a happy child":** Scott Eyman, *Cary Grant: A Brilliant Disguise* (New York: Simon & Schuster, 2020), 18.

71 **hang out again with Scott:** Spoto, *Notorious*, 245.

71 **"was at best bisexual":** Eyman, *Cary Grant*, 224.

71 **"Gays have been eager . . .":** Eyman, *Cary Grant*, 9.

72 **"Hitch never said anything . . .":** McGilligan, *Alfred Hitchcock*, 363.

72 **Hitchcock hosted a banquet:** Spoto, *Notorious*, 251.

73 **"Why aren't you . . .":** Norman Lloyd interview.

73 **"All I care about . . .":** Adler interview.

73 **an assignment from** *Life*: Steve Cohen, *"Rear Window:* The Untold Story," *Columbia Film View* 8, no. 1 (Winter/Spring 1990): 2–7.

74 **met up with Capa:** Spoto, *Notorious*, 206.

74 **"When they were in the hotel . . .":** Patrick McGilligan interview with David Freeman, PMP.

76 **"All that has to be done . . .":** Leonard J. Leff, "Ingrid in the Lions' Den: Cutting *Notorious,*" *Film Comment* 35, no. 2 (March/April 1999): 26–29.

76 **"goddamn jigsaw method of cutting":** McGilligan, *Alfred Hitchcock*, 241.

76 **"the one Hitch threw to Ingrid":** Eyman, *Cary Grant*, 225.

77 **"The boy that made . . .":** Leamer, *As Time Goes By*, 143.

78 **"If you need a Swedish actress . . .":** Ingrid Bergman and Alan Burgess, *Ingrid Bergman: My Story* (New York: Delacorte Press, 1972), 152.

78 **"just like a ship-wrecked person . . .":** Roberto Rossellini to Ingrid Bergman in Bergman and Burgess, *Ingrid Bergman*, 7–10.

79 **"Hitch, like a little rock . . .":** Ingrid Bergman to Petter Lindstrom, letter, July 19, 1948. Mr. Lindstrom gave the author this letter.

80 **"It's just a movie":** Spoto, *Notorious*, 294.

80 **"I was looking at those dark . . .":** Bergman and Burgess, *Ingrid Bergman*, 194.

81 **Roswita Schmidt, a German:** Spoto, *Notorious*, 297.

81 **"I'm going to . . .":** Quoted in Joseph Henry Steele, *Ingrid Bergman: An Intimate Portrait* (New York: Delacorte Press, 1959), 168; also Lindstrom interview.

81 **"Miss Bergman, while handsome to look on . . .":** Bosley Crowther, "Ingrid Bergman Plays Title Role in 'Joan of Arc,'" *New York Times*, November 12, 1948.

82 **Hollywood in January 1949:** Louella O. Parsons, "Mack Sennett, Originator of Slapstick Movies," *Fresno Bee*, January 24, 1949.

82 **When Lindstrom returned:** Lindstrom interview.

83 **"I was so fat I had . . .":** McGilligan, *Alfred Hitchcock*, 171.

83 **"the most promising juvenile . . .":** Marjory Adams, "Pat Hitchcock Does 'Violet' to Escape Family Dishes," *Boston Globe*, October 16, 1944.

84 **"Alma to my room for breakfast":** Whitfield Cook Diaries, Boston University Library.

84 **"I've been very lonely . . .":** Whitfield Cook Papers, Boston University Library.

CHAPTER 6: SWAN SONG

86 **"the vile and unspeakable . . .":** Ingrid Bergman and Alan Burgess, *Ingrid Bergman: My Story* (New York: Delacorte Press, 1972), 273–74.

86 **"In a horrible way . . .":** Robert Lacey, *Grace* (New York: G. P. Putnam's Sons, 1994), 69.

87 **"I was very nervous . . .":** Donald Spoto, *High Society: The Life of Grace Kelly* (New York: Harmony, 2009), 109.

88 **"the most perfectly formed . . .":** Lacey, *Grace*, 20.

89 **heavyweight boxing champion:** Lacey, *Grace*, 14.

89 **giant cement-mixing container:** Lacey, *Grace*, 23.

89 **"We were always competing . . .":** Lacey, *Grace*, 26.

90 **He met Margaret Majer:** Mrs. John B. Kelly, "Kelly Wealth Built on Bricks," *Miami Herald*, January 16, 1956.

90 **"I was always on my mother's knee . . .":** Lacey, *Grace*, 26.

90 **second Black woman physician:** "Woman's Medical College of Penn-sylvania," Wikipedia, https://en.wikipedia.org/wiki/Woman%27s_Medical_College_of_Pennsylvania, accessed February 2, 2023.

91 **"The good fortune of the entire . . .":** Mrs. John B. Kelly, "She Played Cin-derella and the Slipper Fit," *Miami Herald*, January 15, 1956.

91 **he ordered twenty-seven:** Lacey, *Grace*, 28.

92 **"a frail little girl":** *Kelly, "Kelly Wealth Built on Bricks."*.

92 **"I was always picking . . .":** Mrs. John B. Kelly, "Her Teen-Age Ambition Was to Be an Actress," *Miami Herald*, January 18, 1956.

94 **"She always had a way . . .":** Robert Lacey, *Grace: Her Lives, Her Loves—The Definitive Biography of Grace Kelly, Princess of Monaco* (Apostrophe Books Ltd.), Kindle, 39.

95 **"I stayed, talking . . .":** James Spada, *Grace: The Secret Lives of a Princess* (New York: Doubleday, 1987), 24.

95 **"I rebelled against my family . . .":** Spoto, *High Society*, 32.

97 **"She jumped into my arms . . .":** Lacey, *Grace*, 59.

97 **"Anything could happen . . .":** Spada, *Grace*, 147.

98 **"compared to her wealth . . .":** Spada, *Grace*, 34.

98 **"I never saw anything more splendid . . .":** Lacey, *Grace*, 63.

99 **"a bit of a creep":** Lacey, *Grace*, 68.

99 **"Gracie, go to your room":** Lacey, *Grace*, 70.

101 **give her jewelry and talk:** Lacey, *Grace*, 81.

101 **employed a method he called:** Laurence Leamer, *Capote's Women: A True Story of Love, Betrayal, and a Swan Song for an Era* (New York, G. P. Putnam's Sons, 2021), 112–13.

101 **"Does the bracelet have anything to do with it?":** Lacey, *Grace*, 84.

102 **"I wanted somebody . . .":** Lacey, *Grace*, 94.

103 **"She was in awe of him . . .":** Spada, *Grace*, 55.

103 **she called him "Baba":** Lacey, *Grace*, 102.

104 **Sinden shave his chest:** Donald Sinden, *A Touch of the Memoirs* (London: Hodder & Stoughton, 1984), 174–75.

104 **"Rumors sweeping England . . .":** Pete Martin, "The Luckiest Girl in Hol-lywood," *Saturday Evening Post*, October 30, 1954.

105 **Hitchcock was not about:** Peter Bordonaro, "Dial M for Murder: A Play by Frederick Knott/A Film by Alfred Hitchcock," *Sight and Sound*, Summer 1976.

105 **"An actress like Grace . . .":** Martin, "The Luckiest Girl in Hollywood."

105 **"I have found that . . .":** Gottlieb, ed., *Hitchcock on Hitchcock*, 96.

107 **"He flattered me by . . .":** Spada, *Grace*, 70.

108 **"Are you shocked, Miss Kelly?":** Lacey, *Grace*, 119.

108   "That Grace! She fucked everyone!...": McGilligan, *Alfred Hitchcock*, 448.

109   "The whole town soon...": Lacey, *Grace*, 113.

110   "an off-screen jinx...": John Belton, ed., *Alfred Hitchcock's* Rear Window (Cambridge, UK: Cambridge University Press, 1999), 105.

110   "He was very enthusiastic...": McGilligan, *Alfred Hitchcock*, 447.

111   **photographer based in part on Robert Capa:** Alex Kershaw, *Blood and Champagne: The Life and Times of Robert Capa* (Cambridge, MA: Da Capo Press, 2004), loc. 3453, Kindle.

112   "She has a lot of charm...": McGilligan, *Alfred Hitchcock*, 455.

112   "I combined the best...": Steven DeRosa, *Writing with Hitchcock: The Collaboration of Alfred Hitchcock and John Michael Hayes* (New York: CineScribe Media, 2011), 18.

113   **gotten down to 189 pounds:** McGilligan, *Alfred Hitchcock*, 486.

113   **it rose five and six stories:** Belton, ed., *Alfred Hitchcock's* Rear Window, 30.

113   **Lighting the massive set:** Belton, ed., *Alfred Hitchcock's* Rear Window, 30.

114   "look like a piece of Dresden...": McGilligan, *Alfred Hitchcock*, 462.

114   "I told her I wouldn't wear them...": Spoto, *High Society*, 125–26.

115   "Well, see if somebody...": Gregory Solman interview with James Stewart in John Boorman and Walter Donohue, ed., *Projections 5: Film-Makers on Film-Making* (New York: Faber & Faber, 1996).

115   **took him aside:** John Russell Taylor, *Hitch: The Life and Times of Alfred Hitchcock* (New York: Pantheon, 1978), 224. Note: There is no shot of Stewart looking at a mother and baby in the final film.

117   "I look for a man...": Dan Auiler, *Vertigo: The Making of a Hitchcock Classic* (New York: Smashwords, 2011), loc. 488, Kindle.

117   "I could see why many...": Michael Munn, *Jimmy Stewart: The Truth Behind the Legend* (New York: Skyhorse: 2013), 220.

118   **The outfit celebrated:** Belton, ed., *Alfred Hitchcock's* Rear Window, 94.

120   **he said he did not think so:** McGilligan, *Alfred Hitchcock*, 489.

122   "it was as if though...": Lacey, *Grace*, 140.

122   **He fondly recalled the evening:** McGilligan, *Alfred Hitchcock*, 465.

123   "Danielle, my character, has...": Tifenn Brisset, "Two Interviews about *To Catch a Thief*," *Film International* 11, no. 6 (December 2013): 13–21.

123   "What I loved about his character...": Brisset, "Two Interviews about *To Catch a Thief*."

123   "I shied away immediately...": McGilligan, *Alfred Hitchcock*, 522.

125   "kissed continuously by Grant...": Sarah Bradford, *Princess Grace* (New York: Stein and Day, 1984), 142.

127   "I was enraptured...": Oleg Cassini, *In My Own Fashion: An Autobiography* (New York: Simon & Schuster, 1987), 251.

127 **"the most enchanting days . . .":** Oleg Cassini, "Grace Kelly: Hollywood Princess," A&E *Biography*, 1998.

128 **higher purpose in shooting:** Spoto, *The Dark Side of Genius*, 352.

130 **"Looking back, I'm not sure . . .":** Spoto, *High Society*, 141.

130 **"I have many acquaintances here . . .":** Martin, "The Luckiest Girl in Hollywood."

130 **"I so hope that we shall . . .":** Cassini, *In My Own Fashion*, 263.

133 **Thus began a six-month-long:** Cassini, *In My Own Fashion*, 209.

134 **went into one of the rooms:** Lacey, *Grace*, 180.

135 **"How and when did *this* develop?":** Cassini, *In My Own Fashion*, 266.

135 **covered by 1,600 journalists:** Cassini, *In My Own Fashion*, 243.

135 **the Kellys paid a $2:** *Grace Kelly: The Missing Millions*, British Channel 5 documentary, 2021, https://www.youtube.com/watch?v=UaY05KoVdkA.

136 **"The Prince Rainier thing was her parents' . . .":** Brigitte Auber interviews with Tifenn Brisset, 2011 and March 2013, *Film International* 11, no. 6, PMP.

CHAPTER 7: ALL IN LAVENDER

138 **inundated her with flowers:** Stephen Rebello, *Alfred Hitchcock and the Making of* Psycho (New York: Soft Skull Press, 2013), 63.

139 **operation to remove gallstones:** McGilligan, *Alfred Hitchcock*, 517.

139 **"Don't you know it's . . .":** Rebello, *Alfred Hitchcock and the Making of* Psycho, 64.

140 **1956, theater owners declared:** Helen Bower, "They Lead the Box Office," *Detroit Free Press*, December 9, 1956.

140 **"There is a fire . . .":** "Cinema: A Star Is Made," *Time*, July 29, 1957.

140 **"In ancient Hollywood practice . . .":** "Cinema: A Star Is Made."

141 **"If you wanna bring . . .":** "Cinema: A Star Is Made."

142 **"I often got knocked . . .":** Simon Hattenstone, "I Had to Leave Hollywood to Save Myself," *The Guardian*, February 15, 2021; Mary Myers, "For Kim Novak Acting Filled a Void," *Wall Street Journal*, May 5, 2020.

142 **resided among "the jerks":** "Cinema: A Star Is Made."

142 **Jane, swinging from tree:** Myers, "For Kim Novak Acting Filled a Void."

142 **"My parents made me feel . . .":** Myers, "For Kim Novak Acting Filled a Void."

142 **"It was in my early teens . . .":** Hattenstone, "I Had to Leave Hollywood to Save Myself"; *Telegraph*, October 12, 2012.

143 **she had been sick:** Ruthe Stein, "'Dreams' and Memories," *San Francisco Chronicle*, June 12, 2012.

144 **signed on at the Caroline Leonetti:** Peter Harry Brown, *Kim Novak: Reluctant Goddess* (New York: St. Martin's Press, 1986), 20.

146 **"This girl has probably . . .":** Brown, *Kim Novak*, 35.

146 **"She will never be able to act, Harry . . .":** Brown, *Kim Novak*, 36.

146 **sent the story out:** "Rides to Fame on a Bike," *Miami News*, January 23, 1954.

147 **big, bold lips like Crawford:** Kim Novak interview.

147 **"Send the dumb Polack in . . .":** Hattenstone, "I Had to Leave Hollywood to Save Myself."

147 **"You're nothing but a piece . . .":** Brown, *Kim Novak*, 43.

147 **"People that were under . . .":** Novak interview.

147 **Novak the "lavender blonde":** Brown, *Kim Novak*, 76.

147 **the car out in the driveway:** Joan Herrold, "Kim Novak Bares Truth," *Pittsburgh Press*, June 28, 1956.

147 **"The color was designed . . .":** Garven Hudgins, "Kim Novak Likes Lavender, Short Men, Foreign Accents," *Sioux City Journal*, August 19, 1956.

148 **home for single actresses:** Lois Berg, "Bye-Bye Bike," *Los Angeles Times*, May 22, 1955.

148 **"He'd have people watching what I'd . . .":** Novak interview.

148 **"I put Kim Novak at . . .":** Hedda Hopper, "Top Film Newcomers," *Los Angeles Times*, January 2, 1955.

149 **"Girls such as Kim Novak . . .":** Brown, *Kim Novak*, 90.

149 **"Nobody talks more about Kim's . . .":** "Cinema: A Star Is Made."

151 **bought one for him:** Hattenstone, "I Had to Leave Hollywood to Save Myself."

151 **"steady boy friend but I'm not sure . . .":** "Guys She's Got, But No Romance," *New York Daily News*, May 26, 1956.

151 **Bandini pursued her across:** Louella O. Parsons, "Italian Priest's Gift," *San Francisco Examiner*, May 26, 1956.

151 **"The count is extra special . . .":** Aline Mosby, "Kim Novak in Confused State," *Coshocton Democrat*, April 17, 1956.

151 **"It's a lousy script . . .":** Novak interview.

152 **"I did complain a bit . . .":** Novak interview.

152 **"Yes, my dear . . .":** Jan Stuart, "Hollywood Was Yesterday," *Newsday*, October 7, 1996.

152 **her words crossing back and forth:** Novak interview.

153 **"Did you know this . . .":** Brown, *Kim Novak*, 142.

154 **"He succeeded in making . . .":** McGilligan, *Alfred Hitchcock*, 524.

154 **$250,000 for her services:** Auiler, *Vertigo*, loc. 1477, Kindle.

154 **"She became docile, obedient, and . . .":** Brown, *Kim Novak*, 143.

155 **"Kim, this is only a movie . . .":** John Russell Taylor, *Hitch: The Life and Times of Alfred Hitchcock* (New York: Pantheon, 1978), 241.

155 **"I want you to love me for me":** Auiler, *Vertigo*, loc. 587.

156   **"Thank God I had Jimmy Stewart . . ."**: Munn, *Jimmy Stewart: The Truth Behind the Legend*, 237.

156   **twenty setups to get the shots:** Auiler, *Vertigo*, loc. 1502.

157   **"You might try lifting your feet":** Auiler, *Vertigo*, loc. 1509.

157   **"Kim was sort of aloof . . .":** An Oral History with C. O. Erickson, Interviewed by Douglas Bell, 2001–2002, MHL.

157   **"He got very upset . . .":** Novak interview.

158   **considered it "a phallic symbol":** Auiler, *Vertigo*, loc. 1840.

158   **unbutton an extra button:** "Cinema: A Star Is Made."

159   **"I didn't know what I was supposed to do . . .":** Novak interview.

159–160   **"He wanted the rhythm . . .":** Novak interview.

161   **"Judy surrendered herself . . .":** Novak interview.

161   **"It was so real to me, the coming out . . .":** Auiler, *Vertigo*, loc. 2085.

163   **to the Helpers Charity Ball:** Louella O. Parsons, "Movies Call Up Hugh O'Brian," *Indianapolis Star*, November 29, 1957.

164   **borrowed Madeleine's glorious green gown:** Novak interview.

164   **Judy's brown wig:** Stein, "'Dreams' and Memories."

164   **"I was in love with Richard . . .":** Novak interview.

164   **another man who had come:** Stein, "'Dreams' and Memories."

164   **"You know, I reached a point . . .":** Sam Kashner, "The Color of Love," *Vanity Fair*, September 3, 2013.

165   **on the *Vertigo* set to take pictures:** *Larry King Live*, CNN, January 5, 2004.

165   **"Did you ever think . . .":** Scott Feinberg, "Why Kim Novak Had to Leave Hollywood to Find Herself," *Hollywood Reporter*, March 10, 2021.

165   **"I remember waking up . . .":** Novak interview.

165   **"Where are you?":** Novak interview.

165   **cooking pork chops and collard greens:** Wil Haygood, *In Black and White: The Life of Sammy Davis, Jr.* (New York: Knopf, 2003), 352.

165   **"Sammy had an innocent . . .":** Novak interview.

166   **"Something inside of me . . .":** Roger Ebert, "Looking Back at 'Vertigo,'" *Chicago Sun-Times*, October 17, 1996.

166   **"Nobody in this section of the country . . .":** Ida B. Wells-Barnett, *On Lynchings* (Amherst, MA: Humanity Books, 2002), 29.

166   **"It was just a blatant, sexual . . .":** Haygood, *In Black and White*, 361.

167   **Chicago columnist Irv Kupcinet wrote:** Brown, *Kim Novak*, 159.

167   **had his Mob friends tell Davis:** Hattenstone, "I Had to Leave Hollywood to Save Myself."

167   **"She doesn't ruin the story . . .":** McGilligan, *Alfred Hitchcock*, 564.

167   **"Perhaps I should just say . . .":** Mel Heimer, "My New York," *The Kane Republican*, February 19, 1958.

167 **decked out in lavender, from the sheets:** Kashner, "The Color of Love."

169 **she collided with another car:** "Kim Novak Uninjured in Wreck," *Fort Worth Star-Telegram*, December 7, 1966.

169 **a great mudslide descended:** "Bad Luck for Kim," *Detroit Free Press*, December 9, 1966.

169 **"I got back on the highway . . .":** Stuart, "Hollywood Was Yesterday."

169 **They had horses, llamas, dogs:** Emma Brown and John Calendo, "New Again: Kim Novak," *Interview*, February 15, 2012.

170 **stoked on tokes of marijuana:** Hattenstone, "I Had to Leave Hollywood to Save Myself."

170 **"Life is what you make it . . .":** Novak interview.

CHAPTER 8: A DELICATE BALANCE

172 **Alma went ahead cooking:** Spoto, *The Dark Side of Genius*, 404.

173 **he stopped going to the restaurant:** Spoto, *The Dark Side of Genius*, 405.

174 **could not get Princess Grace:** McGilligan, *Alfred Hitchcock*, 566.

174 **Saint had just given birth:** Jon Krampner, *Ernest Lehman: The Sweet Smell of Success* (Lexington: University Press of Kentucky, 2022), 87.

175 **"Honey, I think you should find . . .":** Jordan Riefe, "Eva Marie Saint on Kissing Cary Grant," *Vanity Fair*, September 2, 2014.

175 **"Mom, I don't know what . . .":** Eva Marie Saint interview.

176 **same criticism he made of Kelly:** Spoto, *The Dark Side of Genius*, 405.

176 **"Everybody was very kind . . .":** Saint interview.

177 **"One of his greatest gifts . . .":** Spoto, *The Dark Side of Genius*, 567.

178 **too sweet and pure to play:** Joseph Kaye, "A New Star to Arrive," *Kansas City Star*, August 1, 1954.

180 **her "sweet characterization of a soldier's wife":** Brooks Atkinson, "First Night at the Theatre," *New York Times*, November 4, 1953.

180 **"as though being together was enough":** Kaye, "A New Star to Arrive."

181 **"I called him my sugar daddy . . .":** An Oral History with Eva Marie Saint, interviewed by Mae Woods, 2009–2010, MHL.

182 **"I acted just like a rich . . .":** Spoto, *The Dark Side of Genius*, 405.

182 **"You're a kept woman":** Sheilah Graham, "'Plain Jane' Eva Learns About Sex Appeal," San Antonio *Express and News*, December 13, 1959.

182 **"a heavy black silk cocktail . . .":** Graham, "'Plain Jane' Eva Learns About Sex Appeal."

182 **"He didn't want the wide-eyed . . .":** Graham, "'Plain Jane' Eva Learns About Sex Appeal."

183 **"How could you tell . . .":** Saint interview.

183 **"I've done a great deal for Miss Eva . . .":** McGilligan, *Alfred Hitchcock*, 567.

184 **a person who applied the coloring:** Saint interview.

184 **"He used to tease about that":** Saint interview; An Oral History with Eva Marie Saint, MHL.

184 **Saint said, "Hi, Cary":** Saint interview; An Oral History with Eva Marie Saint, MHL.

184 **Grant complained not only:** Nancy Nelson, *Evenings with Cary Grant: Recollections in His Own Words and by Those Who Knew Him Best* (New York: William Morrow, 1991), 215.

184 **supposedly naked in a barrel:** John Russell Taylor interview, BBC, PMP.

185 **"Ernie, do you realize . . .":** Spoto, *The Dark Side of Genius*, 406.

186 **"Everyone told me not to do . . .":** Krampner, *Ernest Lehman*, 88.

186 **"All right, all right. So now . . .":** An Oral History with Eva Marie Saint, MHL.

188 **"do three things: lower your . . .":** An Oral History with Eva Marie Saint, MHL.

188 **"I found, when I got . . .":** Graham, "'Plain Jane' Eva Learns About Sex Appeal."

190 **"We sat on the bed to go over . . .":** Krampner, *Ernest Lehman*, 92.

190 **"You think you've written . . .":** Nelson, *Evenings with Cary Grant*, 215.

191 **In Chicago, the cast and crew:** Eleanor Page, "Hitchcock to Turn Chicago Hotel into Set for Movie," *Chicago Tribune*, September 6, 1958.

191 **Garland's concert at Orchestra Hall:** Lucy Key Miller, "Glum into Garland," *Chicago Tribune*, September 2, 1958.

191 **"Everyone in the theater . . .":** Saint interview.

191 **"I just don't know how you . . .":** Scott Eyman, *Cary Grant: A Brilliant Disguise* (New York: Simon & Schuster, 2020), 326.

194 **"I prefer a nice drawing-room . . .":** Richard C. Wald, "Excitement at the Plaza," *Herald Tribune*, September 7, 1958.

194 **"Eva Marie, you don't get your coffee . . .":** McGilligan, *Alfred Hitchcock*, 567.

194 **"Excuse me, that light is . . .":** Saint interview.

194 **"Mommy, there's dirt . . .":** Graham, "'Plain Jane' Eva Learns About Sex Appeal."

196 **"Wasn't it marvelous?":** Krampner, *Ernest Lehman*, 95.

196 **"I took a lot of trouble . . .":** Edward White, *The Twelve Lives of Alfred Hitchcock: An Anatomy of the Master of Suspense* (New York: W. W. Norton, 2022), 95.

196 **"You go to work on . . .":** White, *The Twelve Lives of Alfred Hitchcock*, 96.

CHAPTER 9: THERE REALLY WAS A HOLLYWOOD

199 **Hitchcock and his minions foraged:** Rebello, *Alfred Hitchcock and the Making of* Psycho, 16.

200 **decimated breasts and skin:** Rebello, *Alfred Hitchcock and the Making of* Psycho, 13.

200 **"The narrative surprises . . .":** Anthony Boucher, "Criminals at Large," *New York Times*, April 19, 1959.

200 **"started to scream, and then . . .":** Robert Bloch, *Psycho* (New York: Simon & Schuster, 1959), 39.

200 **"I think that the thing . . .":** Rebello, *Alfred Hitchcock and the Making of* Psycho, 19.

201 **a crew from his television series:** Rebello, *Alfred Hitchcock and the Making of* Psycho, 28.

202 **"How would you feel if Norman . . .":** Rebello, *Alfred Hitchcock and the Making of* Psycho, 39.

202 **"stunted skyline of Stockton . . .":** Leonard Gardner, *Fat City* (New York: New York Review Books Classics, 1996), loc. 121, Kindle.

205 **"How could you do this . . .":** Janet Leigh, *There Really Was a Hollywood* (New York: Doubleday, 1984), 15.

206 **did not lead to the rapture:** Leigh, *There Really Was a Hollywood*, 24.

207 **the resort photographer took her picture:** Michelangelo Capua, *Janet Leigh: A Biography* (Jefferson, NC: McFarland & Company, 2013), 10.

207 **"that smile made it . . .":** Emery Wister, "Cinderella Girl's Smile," *Charlotte News*, August 23, 1947.

208 **"The town is showing . . .":** Morgan Hudgins, "Cinderella Herself," *New York Times*, August 10, 1947. When the *Times* ran its story, Leigh had just had her twentieth birthday.

209 **with "mental cruelty":** "Screen Star Divorces Ex-Orchestra Leader," *Hartford Morning Journal*, July 22, 1948.

211 **accompanied by the man:** Betty Lyou, "Whirl Around," *South Gate Daily Press-Tribune*, January 27, 1950.

211 **"devastatingly handsome young man—beautiful, really . . .":** Leigh, *There Really Was a Hollywood*, 113.

211 **"look[s] sweet and vulnerable":** Tony Curtis with Peter Golenbock, *American Prince: A Memoir* (New York: Harmony Books, 2008), loc. 1779, Kindle.

212 **shining their shoes in front:** Curtis with Golenbock, *American Prince*, loc. 46.

212 **Bernie and his brother Julius in an orphanage:** Curtis with Golenbock, *American Prince*, loc. 545.

212 **He had done some acting:** Curtis with Golenbock, *American Prince*, loc. 1430.

213 **made their first public appearance:** Sheilah Graham, "Mature to Be Six Months in Cast," *Los Angeles Evening Citizens News*, September 9, 1950.

213 **"Sounded to us like the fans . . .":** Bill Doudna, "Spotlight," *Wisconsin State Journal*, October 18, 1950.

215 **"KING AND QUEEN OF HEARTS":** Capua, *Janet Leigh*, 67.

215 **"publicity mad exhibitionists . . .":** Capua, *Janet Leigh*, 64.

215 **"I can unequivocally state . . .":** Leigh, *There Really Was a Hollywood*, 129.

215 **"a powerful drive for immaculate order . . .":** Jamie Lee Curtis, "Memories of Mother," *More*, May 2010, quoted in Capua, *Janet Leigh*, 50.

216 **When he grasped a wineglass:** Curtis with Golenbock, *American Prince*, loc. 2196.

216 **"After I married Janet . . .":** Curtis with Golenbock, *American Prince*, loc. 1990.

217 **"Don't worry, kid":** Curtis with Golenbock, *American Prince*, loc. 2213.

217 **"that an affair would have . . .":** Capua, *Janet Leigh*, 71.

217 **"After a week of debauchery . . .":** Curtis with Golenbock, *American Prince*, loc. 2340.

218 **Leigh the novel *Psycho* in October 1959:** Janet Leigh with Christopher Nickens, *Psycho: Behind the Scenes of the Classic Thriller* (New York: Harmony, 1995), 29.

219 **"I hired you because you are . . .":** Leigh, *There Really Was a Hollywood*, 255.

219 **Leigh invented an entire life:** Leigh with Nickens, *Psycho*, 61.

219 **leave the grotesque mannequin:** Rebello, *Alfred Hitchcock and the Making of Psycho*, 76.

220 **"What he liked to do most . . .":** Rebello, *Alfred Hitchcock and the Making of Psycho*, 89.

220 **place a toilet in her dressing room:** Leigh with Nickens, *Psycho*, 47–48.

220 **"Here's your piece of the pie . . .":** Rebello, *Alfred Hitchcock and the Making of Psycho*, 61. At this point, Hitchcock was still referring to the main female character as "Mary," the name in Robert Bloch's novel. To simplify things, the name is changed here to "Marion."

220 **"The very geography seems . . .":** *Psycho* screenplay by Joseph Stefano (1960). Based on the novel by Robert Bloch. Revised December 1, 1959, MHL.

221 **It is not a designer bra:** Rebello, *Alfred Hitchcock and the Making of Psycho*, 72.

221 **Hitchcock felt Leigh was self-conscious:** Rebello, *Alfred Hitchcock and the Making of Psycho*, 103.

224 **"All right, that's the way we'll do it":** Rebello, *Alfred Hitchcock and the Making of Psycho*, 88.

225 **The building was probably modeled:** Rebello, *Alfred Hitchcock and the Making of Psycho*, 68.

NOTES

227 **The studio paid Renfro $500:** Robert Graysmith, *The Girl in Alfred Hitchcock's Shower* (New York: Berkley Books, 2010), loc. 213, Kindle.

227 **heard her voice among the death screams:** Marli Renfro interview.

229 **actresses like Elizabeth Taylor:** Curtis with Golenbock, *American Prince*, loc. 3121.

229 **Leigh started drinking:** Curtis with Golenbock, *American Prince*, loc. 3022.

229 **The couple built a dance floor over:** Leigh, *There Really Was a Hollywood*, 272.

229 **The last guest did not leave:** Harrison Carroll, "Hollywood," *Wilkes-Barre Times Leader*, June 15, 1961.

230 **"It just went wrong right now . . .":** Leigh, *There Really Was a Hollywood*, 273–74.

230 **Tony had found her:** Curtis with Golenbock, *American Prince*, loc. 1033.

231 **"Helen, I also just wanted . . .":** "Bitter Suicide Note to Wife Left by Janet Leigh's Father," UPI, *Philadelphia Daily News*, August 14, 1961.

231 **It did not help in Argentina:** Curtis with Golenbock, *American Prince*, loc. 3154.

231 **downed a large number of red pills:** Curtis with Golenbock, *American Prince*, loc. 3208.

232 **Curtis speculated that:** Curtis with Golenbock, *American Prince*, loc. 3263.

CHAPTER 10: A PRIDE OF LIONS

233 **"jaunty assuredness, pertness . . .":** Moral, *The Making of Hitchcock's* The Birds, loc. 1038, Kindle.

234 **who desired trees and grass:** Tippi Hedren with Lindsay Harrison, *Tippi: A Memoir* (New York: William Morrow, 2016), 33.

234 **thinking of taking typing:** Hedren with Harrison, *Tippi*, 45.

234 **a "well-known director" had seen her:** Hedren with Harrison, *Tippi*, 34.

234 **an aide call her hotel room:** Hedren with Harrison, *Tippi*, 26.

235 **She simply signed the document:** Hedren with Harrison, *Tippi*, 36.

235 **"shorter and even rounder . . .":** Hedren with Harrison, *Tippi*, 37.

235 **was it turquoise blue or some other:** Moral, *The Making of Hitchcock's* The Birds, loc. 1050.

236 **paid her $500 a week:** Spoto, *The Dark Side of Genius*, 450.

236 **he would cast her in episodes:** McGilligan, *Alfred Hitchcock*, 580.

236 **shot over three days:** McGilligan, *Alfred Hitchcock*, 581.

237 **restaurant had begun:** McGilligan, *Alfred Hitchcock*, 560.

238 **"We want you to play . . .":** Hedren with Harrison, *Tippi*, 44.

238 **"Always a bridesmaid, never a bride":** "Jay Presson Allen and Evan Hunter, March 24, 1993, New York City," *On Writing*, undated, PMP.

308

239 **"Wasserman wouldn't hesitate . . .":** John Russell Taylor interview, BBC, PMP.

239 ***The Birds* was going to be his bid for respectability . . .":** Taylor interview.

239 **"an 'artistic' decision":** "Writing for Hitch: An Interview with Evan Hunter by Charles L. P. Silet," *Hitchcock Annual*, 1995.

239 **sent Hedren bushels of potatoes:** Hedren with Harrison, *Tippi*, 46.

240 **German-Norwegian mother taught school:** Tippi Hedren with Theodore Taylor, *The Cats of Shambala* (Acton, CA: Shambala Press, 1992), 22.

241 **earning $350 her first week:** Hedren with Harrison, *Tippi*, 18.

242 **"People assumed I sat there . . .":** Dr. Frank Vaccaro interview.

243 **seeking solace elsewhere:** Hedren with Harrison, *Tippi*, 29.

243 **brought her daughter's nanny, Josephine:** Hedren with Harrison, *Tippi*, 33.

244 **"A high comedy is played like drama . . .":** Alfred Hitchcock and Tippi Hendren discussing *The Birds*, Tape 1, February 24, 1962, 9, MHL.

244 **the sins of complacency:** Kyle B. Counts and Steve Rubin, "The Making of Alfred Hitchcock's *The Birds*: The Complete Story Behind the Precursor of Modern Horror Films," *Cinemafantastique* 10, no. 2 (Fall 1980): 15–35.

245 **"What would she go to all this trouble for?":** Hitchcock and Hedren, Tape 1, 14, MHL.

245 **Hitchcock flew up to Bodega Bay:** Moral, *The Making of Hitchcock's* The Birds, 109.

245 **schoolchildren stood holding up signs:** Evan Hunter, *Me and Hitch* (London: Faber & Faber, 1997), 58.

246 **"Something happened that was altogether . . .":** François Truffaut, *Hitchcock* (New York: Simon & Schuster, 1983), 290.

247 **"I had this insane sense of humor . . .":** Suzanne Pleshette interview, BBC, PMP.

248 **"He didn't have any experience . . .":** Moral, *The Making of Hitchcock's* The Birds, 120.

248 **"I really don't know much . . .":** Edward White, *The Twelve Lives of Alfred Hitchcock: An Anatomy of the Master of Suspense* (New York: W. W. Norton, 2022), 13.

249 **over $200,000 on mechanical:** Moral, *The Making of Hitchcock's* The Birds, 97.

250 **"Where shall I run, Alfred?":** "In the Picture," undated clipping, PMP.

250 **"I would bring Hitchcock tea . . .":** Veronica Cartwright interview.

250 **Berwick spread birdseed:** Moral, *The Making of Hitchcock's* The Birds, 115.

250 **"They had to stop shooting . . .":** Cartwright interview.

251 **The trainers placed 1,500 sparrows, finches:** Moral, *The Making of Hitchcock's* The Birds, 128.

251 **"Eventually, the birds settled on the floor . . .":** Cartwright interview.

251 **"Listen, Jessica, if one of them . . .":** Quoted from the diaries of Kenneth Williams, PMP.

251 **"Hitchcock had a little bit of a sadistic . . .":** Cartwright interview.

252 **"You could have spit it . . .":** Moral, *The Making of Hitchcock's* The Birds, 153.

252 **"It's like this girl Hedren . . ."** : Tony Lee Moral, *Hitchcock and the Making of* Marnie (Lanham, MD: Scarecrow Press, 2002), 245–46.

252 **"I saw him take a girl . . .":** Moral, *Hitchcock and the Making of* Marnie, 245–46.

253 **"The limo was just pulling . . .":** Hedren with Harrison, *Tippi*, 51.

253 **"He'd asked me to touch him . . .":** Hedren with Harrison, *Tippi*, 53.

253 **"He would say shocking things . . .":** Moral, *Hitchcock and the Making of* Marnie, 247.

254 **"a cage of misery":** Truffaut, *Hitchcock*, 288.

254 **plucked tiny bits of glass:** Moral, *The Making of Hitchcock's* The Birds, 149.

254 **"A part of me did wonder . . .":** Hedren with Harrison, *Tippi*, 52.

255 **wranglers had suffered twelve injuries:** Moral, *The Making of Hitchcock's* The Birds, 139.

255 **"It was very hard for Hitch . . .":** Quoted in Counts and Rubin, "The Making of Alfred Hitchcock's *The Birds*."

256 **Hunter had written several more pages:** Moral, *The Making of Hitchcock's* The Birds, 146.

256 **"wear hair in French roll":** Moral, *The Making of Hitchcock's* The Birds, 201.

256–57 **"Tippi always said . . .":** John Marshall interview.

257 **"We're going to lose all . . .":** "Jay Presson Allen and Evan Hunter, March 24, 1993, New York City," *On Writing*, undated, PMP.

257 **"Stanley Kowalski might rape her . . .":** Evan Hunter to Alfred J. Hitchcock, letter, April 2, 1963, MHL.

258 **"Well, you have to let them feel . . .":** Hunter to Hitchcock, letter.

258 **they spent two months together:** Hunter to Hitchcock, letter.

258 **"I've had a wonderful dream . . .":** Jay Presson Allen interview, BBC, PMP.

259 **"He liked to work with women . . .":** Allen interview.

259 **she said she never went back:** Tippi Hedren interview, BBC, PMP.

260 **"She doesn't have any feeling . . .":** Hedren and Hitchcock, *Marnie*, Tape 4, 7, MHL.

262 **"It was very difficult for Tippi . . .":** Allen interview.

262 **"both untalented and exploitive . . .":** Steven C. Smith, *A Heart at Fire's Center: The Life and Music of Bernard Herrmann* (Berkeley: University of California Press, 1991), 253.

262 **"aggressively romantic score":** Smith, *A Heart at Fire's Center*, 260.

262 **she did not love Marshall:** Hedren with Harrison, *Tippi*, 78.

263 **"When I say yes . . .":** Hedren with Harrison, *Tippi*, 78.

263 **"I was embarrassed for Tippi . . .":** McGilligan, *Alfred Hitchcock*, 610.

264 **the proper mindset to play Marnie:** John Russell Taylor, *Hitch: The Life and Times of Alfred Hitchcock* (New York: Pantheon, 1978), 272.

264 **"You're a fat pig," she said:** McGilligan, *Alfred Hitchcock*, 610.

265 **"It was quite likely that Tippi . . .":** John Russell Taylor interview.

265 **"I think he was having . . .":** Jay Presson Allen interview, BBC, PMP.

266 **"132 big cats, one elephant . . .":** Hedren with Harrison, *Tippi*, 179.

267 **might have been committing:** "Child Abuse and Neglect in California, Part 1," Legislative Analyst's Office, January 1996, https://lao.ca.gov/1996/010596 _child_abuse/cw11096a.html; "Exceptions to California's Statutory Rape Laws," Corrigan Welbourn Stokke, January 8, 2020, https://www.cwsdefense .com/blog/2020/june/exceptions-to-californias-statutory-rape-laws/.

267 **"I've thought a thousand times . . ."** Hedren with Harrison, *Tippi*, 128.

268 **slapped one of his sons:** Off-the-record interview.

268 **a lion bit Marshall's hand, creating:** Hedren with Harrison, *Tippi*, 184.

268 **"It's special to have . . .":** Marshall interview.

268 **Another day a lion bit:** Hedren with Harrison, *Tippi*, 163.

269 **"displaying great courage and responsibility . . .":** Hedren with Taylor, *The Cats of Shambala*, 198.

269 **called "The Noel Marshall Wing":** Rob Muraskin, dir., *Roar: The Most Dangerous Film Ever Made*, documentary, Filmways Pictures, 1981.

269 **"It [Roar] is probably the most . . .":** Muraskin, dir., *Roar: The Most Dangerous Film Ever Made.*

270 **"Hedren was a calculating narcissist . . .":** Dr. Heath King interview.

270 **"It wasn't a constant barrage of harassment . . .":** Alex Strachan, "Tippi-toeing around Hitchcock," *Calgary Herald*, October 19, 2012.

CHAPTER 11: THE TRIBUTE

272 **"awful" words on the cue cards:** Charles Champlin, "Ingrid Bergman: A Triumph over Time," *Los Angeles Times*, March 18, 1979.

272 **"I saw Hitch, who is quite lame . . .":** Champlin, "Ingrid Bergman."

273 **"the whole thing had a pathetic innocence about it":** David Freeman to Patrick McGilligan, letter, undated, PMP.

273 **"It is very tragic because . . .":** Alfred Hitchcock to Mrs. Gladys Hitching, letter, June 15, 1978, Alfred Hitchcock Collection, MHL.

274 **"When Hitchcock saw Alma . . .":** David Freeman interview, BBC, PMP.

274 **wheeled him out:** Alfred Hitchcock to Mrs. Nellie Ingram, letter, November 29, 1978, Alfred Hitchcock Collection, MHL.

275 **Hitchcock received a telegram:** David Freeman, *The Last Days of Alfred Hitchcock* (New York: Overlook Press, 1984), 62.

275 **"pleasure in this night's tribute . . .":** Champlin, *Los Angeles Times*, March 7, 1979.

275 **A knock at the door:** Freeman, *The Last Days of Alfred Hitchcock*, 63.

275–76 **"In America, you call . . .":** The 1979 AFI Tribute to Alfred Hitchcock, YouTube.

CHAPTER 12: THE LIVES

282 **"Just say I got out when . . .":** Mike Lockley, "The Ice Maiden," *Birmingham Evening Mail*, February 25, 2017.

283 **"I joke with him. 'You are a dog . . .'":** Laurence Leamer, *As Time Goes By: The Life of Ingrid Bergman* (New York: Harper & Row, 1986), 351.

283 **"I am not afraid to die . . .":** Greta Danielsson interview.

BIBLIOGRAPHY

Auiler, Dan. *Vertigo: The Making of a Hitchcock Classic.* New York: St. Martin's Griffin, 2000. Kindle.

Bacon, James. *Made in Hollywood.* New York: Warner Books, 1977.

Barr, Charles. *Vertigo.* London: British Film Institute, 2002.

Barzini, Luigi. *The Italians.* New York: Touchstone, 1996.

Basinger, Jeanine. *A Woman's View: How Hollywood Spoke to Women, 1930–1960.* Middletown, CT: Wesleyan University Press, 1993.

Bell, James, ed. *39 Steps to the Genius of Hitchcock.* London: British Film Institute, 2012.

Belton, John, ed. *Alfred Hitchcock's* Rear Window. Cambridge, UK: Cambridge University Press, 2000.

Bergman, Ingrid, and Alan Burgess. *Ingrid Bergman: My Story.* New York: Delacorte Press, 1972.

Bloch, Robert. *Psycho.* New York: Simon & Schuster, 1959.

Bradford, Sarah. *Princess Grace.* New York: Stein and Day, 1984.

Brown, Peter Harry. *Kim Novak: Reluctant Goddess.* New York: St. Martin's Press, 1986.

Callahan, Dan. *The Camera Lies: Acting for Hitchcock.* New York: Oxford University Press, 2020.

Capua, Michelangelo. *Janet Leigh: A Biography.* Jefferson, NC: McFarland & Company, 2013.

Carnes, Patrick. *Out of the Shadows: Understanding Sexual Addiction.* Center City, MN: Hazelden, 2001.

Cassini, Oleg. *In My Own Fashion: An Autobiography.* New York: Simon & Schuster, 1987.

Charles River Editors. *American Legends: The Life of Kim Novak.* CreateSpace Independent Publishing Platform, 2015.

Curtis, Jamie. *Janet Leigh & Tony Curtis: Psycho.* Morrisville, NC: Lulu Press, 2021.

Curtis, Tony, with Peter Golenbock. *American Prince: A Memoir.* New York: Harmony Books, 2008. Kindle.

DeRosa, Steven. *Writing with Hitchcock: The Collaboration of Alfred Hitchcock and John Michael Hayes.* New York: CineScribe Media, 2011.

Eyman, Scott. *Cary Grant: A Brilliant Disguise.* New York: Simon & Schuster, 2020.

Freeman, David. *The Last Days of Alfred Hitchcock.* New York: Overlook Press, 1984.

Gardner, Leonard. *Fat City.* New York: New York Review Books Classics, 1996. Kindle.

Gilmore, David D. *Misogyny: The Male Malady.* Philadelphia: University of Pennsylvania Press, 2001.

Gottlieb, Sidney, ed. *Hitchcock on Hitchcock: Selected Writings and Interviews.* Berkeley: University of California Press, 1995.

Graysmith, Robert. *The Girl in Alfred Hitchcock's Shower.* New York: Berkley Books, 2016. Kindle.

Haney, Lynn. *Gregory Peck: A Charmed Life.* New York: Carroll and Graf, 2004.

Haygood, Wil. *In Black and White: The Life of Sammy Davis, Jr.* New York: Knopf, 2003.

Hedren, Tippi, with Lindsay Harrison. *Tippi: A Memoir.* New York: William Morrow, 2016.

Hunter, Evan. *Me and Hitch.* London: Faber & Faber, 1997.

Kapsis, Robert E. *Hitchcock: The Making of a Reputation.* Chicago: University of Chicago Press, 1992.

Kershaw, Alex. *Blood and Champagne: The Life and Times of Robert Capa.* Cambridge, MA: Da Capo Press, 2004. Kindle.

Krampner, Jon. *Ernest Lehman: The Sweet Smell of Success.* Lexington: University Press of Kentucky, 2022.

Kunzle, David. *Fashion & Fetishism: Corsets, Tight-Lacing & Other Forms of Body Sculpture.* Stroud, UK: Sutton, 2004.

Lacey, Robert. *Grace.* New York: G. P. Putnam's Sons, 1994.

Lane, Christina. *Phantom Lady: Hollywood Producer Joan Harrison, the Forgotten Woman Behind Hitchcock.* Chicago: Chicago Review Press, 2020.

Leamer, Laurence. *As Time Goes By: The Life of Ingrid Bergman.* New York: Harper & Row, 1986.

———. *Capote's Women: A True Story of Love, Betrayal, and a Swan Song for an Era.* New York: G. P. Putnam's Sons, 2021.

Leigh, Janet. *There Really Was a Hollywood.* New York: Doubleday, 1984.

Leigh, Janet, with Christopher Nickens. *Psycho: Behind the Scenes of the Classic Thriller.* New York: Harmony, 1995.

Lister, Kate. *A Curious History of Sex.* London: Unbound, 2020.

McGilligan, Patrick. *Alfred Hitchcock: A Life in Darkness and Light.* New York: It Books, 2004.

Miller, Henry K. *The First True Hitchcock: The Making of a Filmmaker.* Oakland: University of California Press, 2022.

Moral, Tony Lee. *Hitchcock and the Making of Marnie.* Lanham, MD: Scarecrow Press, 2002.

———. *The Making of Hitchcock's* The Birds. New York: Open Road, 2010.

Munn, Michael. *Jimmy Stewart: The Truth Behind the Legend.* New York: Skyhorse, 2013.

Nelson, Nancy. *Evenings with Cary Grant: Recollections in His Own Words and by Those Who Knew Him Best.* New York: William Morrow, 1991.

Paglia, Camille. *Birds.* London: British Film Institute, 2020.

Pascoe, John. *Madeleine Carroll: Actress and Humanitarian, from* The 39 Steps *to the Red Cross.* Jefferson, NC: McFarland, 2020.

Rebello, Stephen. *Alfred Hitchcock and the Making of* Psycho. New York: Soft Skull Press, 2013.

Sinden, Donald. *A Touch of the Memoirs.* London: Hodder & Stoughton, 1984.

Smit, David. *Ingrid Bergman: The Life, Career and Public Image.* Jefferson, NC: McFarland, 2012.

Smith, Steven C. *A Heart at Fire's Center: The Life and Music of Bernard Herrmann.* Berkeley: University of California Press, 1991.

Spada, James. *Grace: The Secret Lives of a Princess.* New York: Doubleday, 1987.

Spoto, Donald. *The Dark Side of Genius: The Life of Alfred Hitchcock.* New York: Ballantine Books, 1984.

———. *High Society: The Life of Grace Kelly.* New York: Harmony, 2009.

———. *Notorious: The Life of Ingrid Bergman.* New York: HarperCollins, 1997.

Steele, Joseph Henry. *Ingrid Bergman: An Intimate Portrait.* New York: Delacorte Press, 1959.

Taylor, John Russell. *Hitch: The Life and Times of Alfred Hitchcock.* New York: Pantheon, 1978.

Thomas, Bob. *King Cohn: The Life and Times of Harry Cohn.* New York: McGraw Hill, 1990.

Truffaut, François. *Hitchcock.* New York: Simon & Schuster, 1983.

White, Edward. *The Twelve Lives of Alfred Hitchcock: An Anatomy of the Master of Suspense.* New York: W. W. Norton, 2022.

Wood, Robin. *Hitchcock's Films Revisited.* New York: Columbia University Press, 2004.

Young, Caroline. *Hitchcock's Heroines.* San Rafael, CA: Insight Editions, 2018.

PHOTO CREDITS

INDEX